Canadian Television

Film and Media Studies Series

Film studies is the critical exploration of cinematic texts as art and entertainment, as well as the industries that produce them and the audiences that consume them. Although a medium barely one hundred years old, film is already transformed through the emergence of new media forms. Media studies is an interdisciplinary field that considers the nature and effects of mass media upon individuals and society and analyzes media content and representations. Despite changing modes of consumption—especially the proliferation of individuated viewing technologies—film has retained its cultural dominance into the 21st century, and it is this transformative moment that the WLU Press Film and Media Studies series addresses.

Our Film and Media Studies series includes topics such as identity, gender, sexuality, class, race, visuality, space, music, new media, aesthetics, genre, youth culture, popular culture, consumer culture, regional/national cinemas, film policy, film theory, and film history.

Wilfrid Laurier University Press invites submissions. For further information, please contact the Series editors, all of whom are in the Department of English and Film Studies at Wilfrid Laurier University:

Dr. Philippa Gates, Email: pgates@wlu.ca
Dr. Russell Kilbourn, Email: rkilbourn@wlu.ca
Dr. Ute Lischke, Email: ulischke@wlu.ca

75 University Avenue West
Waterloo, ON N2L 3C5
Canada
Phone: 519-884-0710
Fax: 519-884-8307

Canadian Television
Text and Content

Marian Bredin, Scott Henderson, and
Sarah A. Matheson, editors

WILFRID LAURIER
UNIVERSITY PRESS

This book has been published with the help of a grant from the Canadian Federation for the Humanities and Social Sciences, through the Aid to Scholarly Publications Programme, using funds provided by the Social Sciences and Humanities Research Council of Canada. We acknowledge the support of the Canada Council for the Arts for our publishing program. We acknowledge the financial support of the Government of Canada through the Canada Book Fund for our publishing activities.

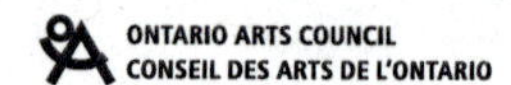

Library and Archives Canada Cataloguing in Publication

Canadian television : text and context / Marian Bredin, Scott Henderson, and Sarah A. Matheson, editors.

(Film and media studies series)
Includes bibliographical references and index.
Issued also in electronic format.
ISBN 978-1-55458-361-4

1. Television broadcasting—Canada. 2. Television broadcasting—Social aspects—Canada. 3. National characteristics, Canadian. I. Bredin, Marian II. Henderson, Scott, 1965– III. Matheson, Sarah A., 1968– IV. Series: Film and media studies series

PN1992.3.C3C38 2012 302.23'450971 C2011-904866-3

(Film and media studies series)
Includes bibliographical references and index.
Type of computer file: Electronic monograph.
Issued also in print format.
ISBN 978-1-55458-388-1 (PDF).

1. Television broadcasting—Canada. 2. Television broadcasting—Social aspects—Canada. 3. National characteristics, Canadian. I. Bredin, Marian II. Henderson, Scott, 1965– III. Matheson, Sarah A., 1968– IV. Series: Film and media studies series (Online)

PN1992.3.C3C38 2012a 302.23'450971 C2011-904867-1

Cover design by David Drummond. Text design by Catharine Bonas-Taylor.

Waterloo, Ontario, Canada
www.wlupress.wlu.ca

This book is printed on FSC recycled paper and is certified Ecologo. It is made from 100% post-consumer fibre, processed chlorine free, and manufactured using biogas energy.

Printed in Canada

Contents

Foreword

One Thing about Television and Ten Things about Canadian TV

JOHN DOYLE

One Thing about Television

Simply put, I believe in the benign influence of the medium. I've been a TV viewer since the age of four and a TV critic for more than a decade. When I began writing about television there was still a widespread belief among educated, well-intentioned readers of *The Globe and Mail* that TV was an instrument to engineer conformity. It is nothing of the kind. As television has expanded from a handful of commercial-supported, over-the-air networks into a multitude of niche channels, and technology has changed every aspect of it, television has become an instrument of subversion and change. Raw, live news footage beggars language in its power to influence opinion and attitude. Dramas and comedies aimed at a discerning audience, and made for broadcasters that don't rely primarily on advertising support, have the freedom to tell stories that challenge rather than comfort an audience.

The hostility toward television among an educated audience in Canada has always seemed peculiar, if not outlandish, to me. It was, after all, a Canadian academic, Marshall McLuhan, who pioneered the serious study of television and the manner in which the consumer participates in all that television achieves. McLuhan's legacy often seems thin in Canada while it prospers elsewhere. One can speculate that as Canada asserted a national identity and culture for itself, primacy was given to literature and art while the study of popular culture of all types was ignored or downgraded. And yet as a country so vast that, pre-Internet, one could justifiably claim that television and radio linked distant communities and created uncommon instances of shared experience, it seems obvious that scholars should extrapolate meaning from television. Just as they extrapolate meaning from novels. They do so now with greater emphasis than before. In fact the study of television is a rare arena in which journalism and scholarship meet with ease—the impact of television compels the journalist to seek out greater understanding that must be conveyed to the reader who feels that profound impact. And that greater understanding is supplied by those academics who are unconstrained by daily or weekly deadlines. The medium is utterly compelling as a subject for both journalism and scholarly research, and its influence should never be underestimated.

Television can kick open the shutters in a closed society. I wrote a book about this very subject. My memoir, *A Great Feast of Light: Growing Up Irish in the Television Age*, is about the impact of television on Ireland in the 1960s and 70s. An extraordinary thing happened when I was around four years old. It was then, in rural Ireland, that electricity finally became available to everyone. People had light in their homes. Shortly afterwards, television arrived, and that meant people had light from other places. In conventional US network TV programs they saw sunny California, the bright lights and ideas of the world outside. Small-town Ireland was then fairly isolated from the rest of the world, ruled by priests, traditions, and steeped in anti-British politics. Divorce and contraception were outlawed, many books and films were banned, and new ideas of any kind were viewed with a suspicious eye. Ireland was a conservative Catholic society. There were rules about this, that, and the other. And much of the establishment was vaguely terrified by television because of all of these foreign things on it and what was being discussed, even in innocuous programs.

A famously conservative member of the Irish Parliament, Oliver J. Flanagan, was outraged and appalled by television. He stood up in Parliament and fomented against it, and described all of the things that people talked about that hadn't been talked about before, like sexuality and adultery. And he declared, in a confusion of rage and hysteria, "There was no sex in Ireland before television!" What he meant, of course, is that people were talking about sex because it was sometimes talked about on TV. Oliver J. Flanagan was afraid of what today we call "the water-cooler moment" created by TV—that moment when people talk about their shared interests at work. And what everyone shares, mainly, is the experience of watching television.

Ten Things about Canadian TV

1. The Two Strands

There are two genres of Canadian TV drama. One is best described as generic. Recently I was in Ireland and noticed that the CanWest Global teen drama *Falcon Beach* and the CTV teens-on-skis drama *Whistler* were airing there. As far as the local audience is concerned, these shows are vaguely if not emphatically American, with their emphasis on good-looking characters, love triangles, individuals overcoming some minor obstacle to achieve success. These shows follow a pattern that can be found in hour-long drama anywhere in the world.

The viewer watches passively. There is no social realism to jolt the viewer into thoughtful response. The series are essentially set in fantasy locations—whether the beach in summer or the ski slopes in winter. The characters are going through typical, age-old coming-of-age developments. There is an honest but troubled leading young man. There is a female bitch figure. There is a wealthy family or rich character; there is a poor family or figure. A lesson is learned about adult responsibility, even as most of the drama concerns the avoidance of adult responsibility by young people. It's always the same. These Canadian shows are created from a template, which is why they are sold and watched around the world. At the same time there is a second genre of Canadian TV, one that instinctively includes elements that distinguish it from American TV and, indeed, from most TV around the world.

While I was in Ireland I noticed that another Canadian series was airing there: *Trailer Park Boys*. This brings me to the second, more interesting genre of Canadian TV drama, one focused on what can be summarized as "hosers, whores, boozers, and losers."

At the core of *Trailer Park Boys* is habitual criminality. There is acceptance of growing marijuana as a legitimate occupation, much cigarette smoking, regular fistfights, and occasional gunplay. A couple of characters are homosexual, but nobody takes any notice. All of this is delivered to viewers with dialogue that is highly profane. Content like this undermines everything thought appropriate for American audiences. Mike Clattenburg once remarked that when he conceived the *Trailer Park Boys* concept he thought of it as *COPS* from the criminals' point of view,[1] and there is a remarkable cultural self-assurance to Clattenburg's vision—it's simply the opposite of what is thought of as the template for US network content.

Now, there is a parallel stream of Canadian TV drama that fits into the "hosers, whores, boozers, and losers" category. It just lacks the loquacious profanity of Ricky, Julian, and Bubbles. I mean the dramas created by Chris Haddock. *Intelligence*, his latest, follows in a direct line from his previous dramas, *Da Vinci's City Hall* and *Da Vinci's Inquest*. What have these shows been about? Mainly the need to create an acceptance of illegal drugs and prostitution in the culture. Throughout *Da Vinci's Inquest* and *Da Vinci's City Hall*, the hero, Dominic Da Vinci, had several aims—creating a red-light district in Vancouver, establishing a needle-exchange program, and moving the problem of grow ops out of police jurisdiction to make it a civic rather than a criminal matter. *Intelligence* offers a drug dealer as a hero. It tells viewers that illegal drugs are part of the commercial culture, just hidden from official view. Again, all of this goes against everything thought appropriate for American audiences and counters the view of the world presented in most mainstream American TV. *Intelligence* is another example of cultural self-assurance. It and the two Da Vinci shows, all from Chris Haddock, assert that we're different here. If they are not read as anti-American, at least they are obviously anti-American TV.

2. No Playwrights, Please

A few years ago the acclaimed playwright George F. Walker was unleashed on the Canadian TV world. He created for CBC the legal drama *This Is Wonderland*. Walker once said in an interview with my colleague Kate Taylor of *The Globe*, "First and foremost, an audience wants to be connected.... They connect emotionally."[2] Asked why he directed his own plays, he said, "I want to make sure they have a pulse. I don't want the intellectual approach to my work that I think is a big deal in Canadian theatre." With *This Is Wonderland*, Walker brought his emphatic theatrical style—that pulse—to Canadian TV. And it was a disaster. Every episode was filled with shouting, braying characters. Everything was written and acted in broad emotional terms to force viewers to connect emotionally.

I believe Walker fundamentally misunderstood television. He would have done well to remember Marshall McLuhan, who said in the early 1960s that "TV is a medium that rejects the sharp personality" and that "the success of any TV performer depends on his achieving a low-pressure style of presentation."[3] Put simply, and outside the area of theory, George Walker's *This Is Wonderland* was hard work to watch. It felt like an assault. Perhaps we go to the theatre to be assaulted and gain that cathartic release, coming out exhausted. But we don't want that on our couch at home.

In sharp contrast, Chris Haddock has, I think, a much more instinctive and truer understanding of the power of television. All the emotional melodrama—so adored by Walker—is drained out of *Da Vinci's Inquest*, *Da Vinci's City Hall*, and *Intelligence*. The result is often powerful television. Haddock's style is elliptical and quiet and his shows have the sort of skeptical intelligence that connects with viewers in the private emotional state in which they watch TV. The next time a distinguished playwright is commissioned to write for Canadian TV, I hope they watch a little TV before they impose their theatrical style on it. Anything else is an arrogant assumption about how television works.

3. *Canadians Like Victims*

Back to George Walker first. *Wonderland* was less about lawyers than it was about the victims of the legal system. In Chris Haddock's case *Da Vinci's Inquest* was really about the victims. Apart from its being a coroner's job to investigate what happened to a victim, the show focused on the victim's story. The fact is, Canadian viewers are drawn to stories about victims. TV movies and miniseries about Canadian victims always do remarkably well with viewers.

A few years ago, there was considerable surprise in the TV business when a CTV TV movie called *Tagged: The Jonathan Wamback Story* was a huge ratings success. Nobody should have been surprised. Canadians like to see the story of victims of violence and injustice. Because Canadians like to sympathize. In *Tagged*, fifteen-year-old Jonathan Wamback, a victim of bullying, limps back to school with brain damage after being brutally attacked by a gang of teenage thugs. But that scene, as dramatized, is clearly not intended to be a triumph over the enemy. It's simply about surviving. Here's this kid—who fought to regain his dignity and the use of his body after months of physical therapy—going back to show his enemies they haven't beaten him. As they watch the story unfold, what the audience feels is shame. It's not the superficial, feel-good sentiment that has always been at the core of prime-time TV and Hollywood movie entertainment. There's no victory for the main character. As the broken teenager limps painfully up the steps of his high school, what the audience feels is heartbreak.

Other Canadian TV movies or miniseries about victims have also done surprisingly well with Canadian viewers. And it's not just a TV phenomenon. Canadian pop music has a surprisingly large number of songs about victims.

4. From Satirist to Softie: The Morphing of Rick Mercer

As part of the comedy group that was featured in *This Hour Has 22 Minutes*, and located in the show's production base in Halifax, Rick Mercer was a merciless satirist. In recent years, with his own show, located in Toronto, and relying on the participation of politicians to get ratings, Mercer has become a kind of tame, in-house gagster for Canadian culture. An aside here. CBC TV is, I think, responsible for putting the marginalized Newfoundland culture of satire into the mainstream of Canadian culture. Thanks to national exposure on TV for such distinctly Newfoundland comedies as *CODCO* and *This Hour Has 22 Minutes*, the accepted style of comedy—especially political comedy—in Canada is the Newfoundland style. This is an aberration in a country where the English culture is anchored in Toronto and Vancouver.

The Newfoundland style is, obviously, based on its distance from the centre of Canada and on its Irish heritage. It is a style that cherishes sarcasm, savage wit, and the pricking of pomposity. Mercer is a notable example of this Newfoundland style, one that works particularly well on TV. But what has become clear is that the style is literally strengthened by closeness to Newfoundland. Take Mercer away from what nourishes that savagery, and its power is diluted. He's been absorbed into the mainstream.

5. The CBC Is Okay

Although I attack CBC TV management often in my columns, I believe that the CBC needs to exist. It's a matter of cultural literacy. A country without a healthy diet of continuing homegrown drama is lacking in the fibre of contemporary storytelling. And CBC TV is our best hope for that diet of homegrown drama. In every country that has even the vaguest notion of a culture and identity, there is a distinct link between the idea of itself and the fictive imagination. A country is simply inauthentic if its stories are not reflected back to itself.

That's why Canadian publishing is subsidized and Canadian television is regulated. At the root of the original, decades-old decision to support homegrown storytelling in print and on TV, there was a profound consensus about the need to keep storytelling alive. Besides, the money needed to keep Canadian stories on TV would be well spent in keeping an industry afloat and would amount to a mere fraction of what is needed to keep a factory or a mine open in some impoverished province. Even if the story on TV isn't a hit, at least the actors and crew can make a decent living and contribute back to the economy. In any case, sustaining the living thread of storytelling is a necessary endeavour, like ensuring health care and safe drinking water. Storytelling should be perceived as another aspect of literacy, and the CBC as its main tool for furthering it.

6. The CBC Is Screwed

Right now, I think CBC management is suffering from a bout of the narcissism of leadership. The CBC is a curious hybrid, simultaneously a public broadcaster and reliant on commercial revenue. As a public broadcaster it can afford to ignore ratings, and as a partly commercial broadcaster it can't. However, what's happened has been surreal—executives have set an audience target for many CBC shows, even documentaries, of one million viewers. The strength of any public broadcaster—even one that airs commercials—is that it can afford to be unpopular, sometimes. It can afford to be obscure, to be different. By setting audience targets that match commercial broadcast standards, CBC is asserting itself as another part of the commercial TV realm. My suspicion is that CBC executives want to be showbiz, not public broadcasting. And that's suicidal for any public broadcaster, because sometimes the show isn't going to be showbiz but only a show that matters on a smaller, more meaningful level to fewer people.

7. Why Does Corner Gas *Work?*

There are only eight characters. Nothing happens. That's why. *Corner Gas* is terrifically sweet, not sugary. And nothing really juicy ever happens. Often the show's appeal has been described as "coffee shop humour," but that doesn't really cover it. I think the appeal is, literally, the nothingness of it. There's no fighting, no gung-ho stuff about heroes and guns and mayhem and similar themes. There's no sex. A bunch of people in a tiny town swap low-key jokes and get excited about what's on the menu at the local diner. The cops are a bit incompetent and crime is non-existent. The harshest word heard is a coot hissing "Jackass!" Yet Canadian viewers love it. They lap it up. And I think that's partly because it's how we see ourselves. But it's also because *Corner Gas* is, in its nothingness, the opposite of almost everything else on TV. Part of the appeal is watching the half-hour being filled by what is meaningless, mundane, and too slight to ever seem worthy of television's attention.

8. Canadian TV Needs to Be Different, Tough, and Challenging

What we've seen in recent years in Canadian TV drama—*The Associates, Blue Murder, Whistler, Falcon Beach*, right up to CBC's *The Border* and Global's *The Guard*—has been too generic, too mild-mannered, too ordinary. In a country where *The Sopranos* can be shown on over-the-air TV, uncensored, we can tolerate something smarter and more sophisticated than what's been made recently. There have been exceptions, of course. But overall we can afford to spurn the antique American, mild-mannered storytelling model of continuing network dramas and look to American cable dramas and British series as inspiration. We can be more realistic, satiric, complex, and truthful. We can't afford to be ordinary any more.

9. Why I Hate George Stroumboulopoulos

This Stroumboulopoulos guy is huge. He was on CBC Newsworld hosting *The Hour* four nights a week, now he's on the main network with *George Stroumboulopoulos Tonight* and on CBC Radio too. Sometimes he's on again in the middle of the night. That's a lot of airtime. Compared with George, Peter Mansbridge is a mere mite, a flea hovering around the CBC schedule. Stroumboulopoulos is heavily marketed by CBC. I've seen *The Hour* many times now and discovered that not only is Stroumboulopoulos huge but he uses the word "huge" all the time. Once, he used it four times in eight minutes. I counted. Every darn thing he talks about is "a huge story." Otherwise it's "cool." Putting together the clues, I'd speculate that an important news item for Stroumboulopoulos is both huge and cool.

Of course, I don't actually hate George Stroumboulopoulos. What I find maddening are the claims that CBC makes for *The Hour*. CBC's position is this: "*The Hour* brings viewers a different take on the news. It's not a newscast. It's not a magazine show. This time, it's personal." Now that's BS, and often *The Hour* is total BS—glib, fast, flippant, half-assed, and full of itself. Of course, CBC is entitled to try to attract younger viewers hungry for a breezy, opinionated take on the news. But *The Hour* is just silly. It looks cheap and toxic, but it's just simple-minded piffle. Worst, it trivializes the news.

It's nothing personal. I'm sure George is a nice enough guy. But I think George Stroumboulopoulos is to CBC TV News programming what George F. Walker was to Canadian TV drama—an assault on the senses. Too much bluster, not enough quiet. Too much heat, not enough cool. Saying the word "cool" a lot, as Stroumboulopoulos does, fails to make anybody cool.

10. Why The Trailer Park Boys Rule

Trailer Park Boys is a weird and wonderful series and a uniquely Canadian phenomenon. Why? Because it's an anti-bourgeois soap opera, a cheerful and loving celebration of life at the bottom. In Canada we feel that as a society with government-supported universal health care and a host of other social benefits, we embrace those at the bottom of the social ladder. It's what makes us who we are. And *Trailer Park Boys* epitomizes that embrace. The core theme of the show is the need for friends, family, and community. As asinine as the main characters might be at times, they are forgiven by the community in the trailer park and loved by their pals and family. They form a supportive commonality. The characters might be losers, but they are loved. Best of all, this aspect of the show is recognized even by viewers who might be less than enamoured of the show's foul language and the unending criminality of Ricky, Julian, and Bubbles. Once, when the show was dismissed as merely vulgar by a writer for *The Globe and Mail*, a reader responded with a rejoinder in a letter to the editor. He wrote, "The Park is us. We are the Park." That's why the Boys rule.

Notes

1 Cavu Pictures, *Trailer Park Boys: A Visitor's Guide to The Sunnyvale Trailer Park.*
2 Taylor, "Playwright Shoots from the Gut."
3 McLuhan, *Understanding Media*, 141.

Part I

Television Studies in the Canadian Context

Challenges and New Directions

Introduction

MARIAN BREDIN, SCOTT HENDERSON,
AND SARAH A. MATHESON

Television Studies in the Canadian Context

In 1987, Mary Jane Miller introduced her groundbreaking study of Canadian television drama production with the obligatory review of existing literature in the field. Finding this literature somewhat wanting, she pointed out that

> no one has been taking a systematic look at whether the television drama we make in Canada is distinctive or imitative or innovative; whether it is informative or simply reconfirms our social norms; whether it is censored on a systematic basis or full of grave omissions, whether it is developing in insight, breadth, and sophistication. No one has really looked at how changing technology, the mandate contained in the Broadcasting Act, the cultural and political content, trends in broadcasting and changes in taste and, most important of all, the individuals who actually make the programmes have influenced the tales we tell each other about ourselves.[1]

Miller's own three monographs in Canadian television studies[2] have clearly done much to address these gaps in the research. Just as importantly, her work has paved the way for a second generation of television scholars at universities in Canada and elsewhere, many of whom have taken up one or more of the topics in Miller's list as major research projects. The same central issues identified by Miller remain resonant today, even amid a dramatic transformation in the media landscape. Of these issues, it is changing technology that perhaps is most central. Technological changes, and the excitement and anxiety they create, are prompting reconsiderations of policy mandates, leading to wholesale changes in Canadian media ownership, changing how programs are accessed and viewed, and, as a result of these upheavals, are altering the cultural role of television. The digital age is transforming all media, while globalization erodes the national boundaries that constrain media dissemination and access. Television, however, remains the most domestically rooted of all media. The nature of television regulation in Canada means that, by and large, access to foreign programming and networks is still controlled. Debates over licensing cable and satellite networks such as Fox News from the United States, or Al-Jazeera, headquartered in Qatar, demonstrate that television is still perceived as serving some form of national interest. Developments such as popular websites like YouTube and the proliferation of DVD box sets create the potential for expanded access to global television texts. At the same time, limitations based on IP-address identification (which can block Canadians' access to television sites such as the US-based Hulu.com) and the region coding of video and DVD products, reaffirm the control of television within national boundaries. In many ways television is still determined by domestic contexts that shape its texts and practices.

The complexities of recent change have had significant impact on the nature of television in Canada (and elsewhere). This book provides analysis of English-Canadian television texts within this moment of global change, and our specific critical focus on television content faces uniquely Canadian challenges. TV series come and go, and in this country the future survival of many individual programs is particularly uncertain. The series examined in this collection are not necessarily examples of the longest-running, most innovative, or even best television in Canada (although many of the texts referenced may indeed deserve such classification) but were chosen to help illuminate important arguments about Canadian television and the issues shaping it. Thus these case studies offer important insights and employ modes of analysis that have a wider relevance to the development of television studies in Canada.

This collection is driven by a desire to focus on specific television texts while considering these programs and genres within a wider understanding of their cultural, political, social, historical, and economic contexts. In his key contributions to television studies, John Ellis argues that television plays a central role in making sense of these everyday contexts and realities. Through all of its varied and shifting genres, television engages us in the processing of the "raw data" of reality as it "attempts to define, tries out explanations, creates narrative, talks over, makes intelligible, tries to marginalize, harnesses speculation, tries to make fit, and very occasionally, anathematizes."[3] This process of televisual "working through" that Ellis describes is directly relevant to the organizing principle of this book. Canadian television is, as Ellis might argue, one of the primary ways of generating explanations for and coming to terms with what we know about being Canadian. The contributors to this collection explore televisual forms and practices, including drama, documentary, reality TV, Aboriginal, and youth programs, in their permeation of domestic space and popular consciousness. While television cannot provide uniform or conclusive explanations for the contexts of Canadian experience, by giving narrative coherence to the uncertain present it "acts as a forum for our interpretations."[4] At the same time, television's technological development, economic structure, and cultural significance are determined by our uncertain geopolitical and social-historical situation at the margins of the world's largest creator and exporter of entertainment and popular culture. Television's narratives about being Canadian reflect our ambivalent place as not American, while themselves existing as unsteady and indistinct images of national realties in a surrounding deluge of imported television content. Canadian television's task of "working through" is further displaced and decentred by the domination of American programming on Canadian networks and the widespread availability of US networks throughout Canada. This model may not apply in the same way to the distinct entity that is French-language Canadian television. While francophone production in Canada shares some political and economic attributes of the English-Canadian industry, other quite distinct cultural and social conditions drive much of its history and relationship with its audience. This book is focused primarily on English-Canadian television and its particular process of "working through." The contexts explored here have relevance to the broader fabric of Canadian television, but the unique issues for French-Canadian television are best served by other scholarly endeavours exploring those particularities.

The contributors to this book present ideas, arguments, and evidence about the social, cultural, political, and economic nature of English-Canadian television that were difficult to find in 1987. In this respect, the contributions to this book are the ultimate outcome of Miller's hope that Canadian television would be part of the curricula offered in departments of drama, communications, Canadian studies, and cultural studies.[5] Scholars who entered the field of television studies in the late 1980s, 1990s, and early 2000s could look to the pioneering work of Mary Jane Miller, Paul Rutherford, Paul Audley, Marc Raboy, and Richard Collins for the gradually emerging map of the discipline in Canada.

The breadth and scope of research represented in this collection reinforces our collective sense that Canadian television studies has entered its maturity. The collection analyzes the varied dimensions of Canadian television content, industry, policy, and technology through timely discussions of children's and youth programming, changing television technologies, reality TV, non-profit networks, television archives, music television, and a range of other topics. John Doyle's Foreword, in keeping with his regular writing on Canadian television, represents all that is engaging and perceptive in popular television criticism. The collection surveys the ideas of academics from several disciplines and methodological approaches and includes the perspectives of producers and practitioners in the industry. We hope that the examination of Canadian television content in its contemporary industrial and socio-political formation helps readers navigate some of the current uncertainty in the industry and stimulates further debate on the challenges facing television in Canada.

Within the theoretical framework of television as a collective working through, this book explores three key thematic paradigms. First, it is concerned with the materiality of Canadian television texts. At this level, contributors to the volume explore the history of Canadian television, preservation of the production data and archival artifacts of the domestic industry, and the degree of access to this material by television researchers. Second, the book engages a wide range of tools and methods in the textual analysis of English-Canadian television programming and the theorization of television content. As a field, research in television studies draws upon previous work in film studies, dramatic arts, media studies, popular culture, genre theory, and narrative analysis. Contributors to this collection likewise represent a variety of disciplinary backgrounds and approaches. Finally, the essays in this book deploy a number of strategies of contextual analysis that situate television within Canadian society. These interdisciplinary approaches are drawn from communication history, sociology, political economy, policy studies, production studies, audience studies, and Canadian studies. These various research approaches to English-Canadian television have their antecedents in the existing literature in the field. This literature can be productively reviewed in order to situate the current work presented in *Canadian Television: Text and Context.*

Prior to 1990, Canadian television studies was marked by its relative isolation from the growing body of research on popular television in the US and Europe. The emergence of what is now commonly referred to as British cultural studies took as one of its primary objects of study the circulation of representations on both commercial and public television in the UK. Similarly in the US, the emergence of popular culture studies was based on the close reading of popular television programs (among other forms) and their everyday use and interpretation by viewers. In the Canadian case, however, the study of television narratives and genres focused more directly on their relation to national identities and conflicts over American cultural influence in Canada. One of these studies was Morris Wolfe's 1985 book on Canadian television programming, *Jolts: The TV Wasteland and the Canadian Oasis*. As former TV critic for *Saturday Night* and teacher of film history at the Ontario College of Art, Wolfe considered the influence of Canada's public broadcasting culture on the development of television content, structure, mood, tone, and pace. As the title clearly indicates, he saw Canadian television as offering important space for the creation of culturally unique stories and narrative structures and in particular pointed to CBC television as a "countervailing force against the homogeneity of American commercial television and its Canadian imitators."[6] With detailed comparative discussion of several examples from genres including drama, comedy, documentary, TV movies, and children's programming, Wolfe came to the memorable conclusion that "much of American television (and film) is about the American dream—the world as we wish it could be, a place in which goodness and reason prevail and things work out for the best. Much of Canadian television (and film), on the other hand is about reality—the grey world as we actually find it."[7]

It was Mary Jane Miller's comprehensive study of CBC television drama from 1952 to 1987 in *Turn Up the Contrast* that fleshed out many of the distinctive attributes of Canadian public television programming in the postwar era. Her emphasis on the contrast presented by Canadian television drama perhaps demonstrates less concern with moral judgment than Wolfe's, but she also points to the role of the CBC in providing the space for innovation, experimentation, and the possibility of creating non-commercial television about contentious events and controversial topics. And like Wolfe, she concludes that "our television also shows us, far more unsparingly and consistently than American television does, our sins of commission and even of omission."[8] Miller supports her close reading of thirty-five years of programming with discussion of audience attitudes, critical response, and the politics of production and regulation in Canada. Her overview of Canada's "national television" of the era is unparalleled in any recent research, and her 1996 study *Rewind and Search: Conversations with the Makers and Decision-makers of CBC Television Drama* likewise remains one of the most thorough ethnographic studies of television production in Canada and elsewhere. Miller's focus on institutional analysis and the constraints that operate at the level of television production was complemented by other histories of television networks, including Sandy Stewart's 1986 history of the CBC and more recently Susan Gittins's comprehensive history of CTV and Chris Wood's study of the western origins of the Craig television network.[9]

While the initial study of television content in Canada revolved around its distinct national attributes and its contrast to American television, television scholars were also influenced by a uniquely Canadian approach to communication history and technological change. Originating in Harold Innis's concept of "the bias of communication,"[10] a strand of Canadian television research was focused on the impact of media technologies themselves on social, cultural, and psychological processes. Though Innis's work predated the widespread adoption of television, his notion of contrasting time and space biases of different communications media was clearly applicable to radio, and later to television. Broadcasting, as a space-biased medium, used high-speed technologies, generating rapid communication of messages from cosmopolitan imperial centres to the social, cultural, and geographical margins. Innis was interested in the link between communication and social change. He would have placed television among those technologies that supported centralized social structures and the administrative and commercial domination of space. Marshall McLuhan's subsequent focus on technological imperatives was more explicit about the impact of the television era. For McLuhan, media technologies were most significant for their effect on cognition and perception. As a "cool medium," television's low-definition image and "all involving sensory mandate" require a high degree of audience participation.[11] The perceptual shift triggered by television technology fosters changing social attitudes, the attention to depth and process in comparison to the fragmentation generated by the hot medium of print. This particular Canadian fascination with what is often inaccurately referred to as technological determinism is most thoughtfully analysed in Arthur Kroker's *Technology and the Canadian Mind* (1984). The concern with social and psychological functions of technology in Canadian television studies endures, with examples to be found in Joyce Nelson's *The Perfect Machine* (1987) and Derrick De Kerckhove's *The Skin of Culture* (1995).

Television studies in Canada has also been shaped by research into political economy and media ownership. In his neo-Marxist analyses of the commercialization of media and reliance on advertising revenue in television, Dallas Smythe formulated the concept of the "audience commodity": the audience as "product" being sold by networks to advertisers, but equally important, the work of the audience in learning to identify and consume the products advertised and promoted by television.[12] Smythe also saw the increasing integration of Canada into the American television and entertainment market as part of Canada's historical dependency on the US. Studies of the political economy of television led to arguments about the impact of "market failure" in the Canadian television industry. This argument suggests that, because it is always less costly for Canadian networks to import American programs than to invest in similar programming made in Canada, governments must intervene to protect, regulate, and subsidize the production of domestic television. The debate about market failure and the nature of government intervention is taken up in a variety of ways by Canadian political economists of media like Robert Babe, Vincent Mosco, and Marc Raboy.[13]

These scholars also focus on the tension between public ownership and private interests in the evolution of Canadian television. Raboy's comprehensive history of broadcasting policy as it relates to television covered territory first surveyed by Frank Peers in *The Public Eye* (1979) and later by Paul Audley in *Canada's Cultural Industries* (1983). Raboy suggests that while the public interest is supposed to prevail in conflicts between the public- and private-sector objectives of the Canadian broadcasting system, this is not always the case. In 1995 he argued that the television industry in Canada was fully hybridized. After 1980 it was characterized by a shift toward the privatization of conventional public broadcasting, but also by increasing public involvement in the private sector through mechanisms such as Telefilm subsidies, CRTC regulations, and the protection of cultural industries under free trade agreements.[14] While the literature on the political economy of Canadian television and its domestic policy environment does not devote much attention to the actual content of programming produced, it provides essential economic and social context for understanding why we have the kind of television we do.

Prior to 1990, much of the existing literature on Canadian television analyzed and celebrated the distinctiveness of domestic productions with sometimes uncritical assumptions about the link between television content and cultural nationalism. But new research at the beginning of that decade began to shift the terrain of the debate. Marc Raboy, for example, challenged the assumption that the CBC should alone represent the "public interest" in television and broadcasting. He pointed to the increasing tension between "dominant and alternative visions of the state, over the relationship of broadcasting to the politics of Canadian nationhood."[15] But the clearest challenge to the dominant thesis that Canadian television production was central to the articulation of Canadian identity and to the enactment of Canadian sovereignty was mounted by a British scholar and relative outsider to research in the field, Richard Collins.

Collins's provocative book *Culture, Communication and National Identity* (1990) represented an important turning point in Canadian television studies. In his analysis of television broadcasting in Canada, Collins dared to question the long-articulated, rarely challenged linking of cultural and political sovereignty. He argued that in spite of Canada's weak "symbolic culture" and Canadians' consistent preferences for American television, Canada has continued to have a strong political culture. Collins thus attempted to challenge some long-held nationalist beliefs about dependency and media imperialism and their impact on citizenship and national sovereignty. He questioned some of the key assumptions that had historically informed broadcasting policies and which tended to view Canadian television as something in need of protection, something that is beneficial to Canadians (whether they watch or not), and something upon which the survival of the nation and citizens' sense of national identity may in some way depend.

Predictably, Collins's book provoked controversy among Canadian scholars. Some appreciated the audacity of his inquiries, while others criticized what they perceived to be ill-conceived conclusions based on faulty logic or outdated evidence.[16] Regardless of how one felt about the arguments Collins presented in his book, the questions that he posed and the discussion they stirred had immense value in exposing unspoken assumptions that, until this time, were commonly accepted and perhaps even naturalized. Moreover, the attention he gave to content, to the programs themselves, highlighted the importance of providing concrete evidence from what was actually on television within policy debates that had previously overlooked programming altogether or dealt with it in quite abstract ways.

Culture, Communication and National Identity represented a new direction for discussions of television in Canada and opened the door to new approaches to the relationship between television and nation. David H. Flaherty and Frank E. Manning's 1993 anthology *The Beaver Bites Back? American Popular Culture in Canada* is a good example of a new approach that followed in the 1990s. The essays featured in the collection contemplated the impact of American popular culture on different forms of popular culture in Canada, television included. In taking up the question of the presence and popularity of American culture here, the editors sought to complicate "one-dimensional models of domination and dependency."[17] The collection moves away from simple (and by this time inadequate) media imperialism approaches to a more complex consideration of how Canadians engage with American popular culture.

The essays resist positing American culture as a monolithic force of Americanization acting upon passive and unwitting Canadian viewers, instead offering an important acknowledgement of the pleasures of American popular culture for Canadian audiences. Flaherty and Manning's anthology displays the influence of developments in audience studies that challenged traditional media effects research and the passive viewer model. The contributing authors highlighted possibilities of active engagement with media forms and explored a number of critical, resistant, and creative responses to popular culture through their focus on specific texts and case studies.[18] With so little work available on Canadian popular culture at the time, *The Beaver Bites Back?* was a refreshing and exciting work that began to move Canadian scholarship in new directions.

The year 1990 also saw the publication of Paul Rutherford's impressive tome, *When Television Was Young: Primetime Canada 1952–1967*. In some ways Rutherford's book reflected a traditional historical overview of Canadian television broadcasting, detailing its development and central policy questions, and discussing issues surrounding television production and delivery in those early years. However, his inclusion of what he referred to as a "viewer history" alongside economic and institutional histories added an important innovative component. Rutherford was interested in what people were watching on television, and therefore, in addition to a consideration of audience viewing patterns and effects research, he also introduced a discussion of content, examining popular genres and ideas about television as "art."[19] Rutherford's close reading of television content as an essential part of a complex and comprehensive history of Canadian television was a significant development. The case studies in *The Beaver Bites Back?* likewise spoke to the importance of anchoring broad ideas about the production and consumption of popular culture with evidence from analysis of popular texts themselves.

The Beaver Bites Back? placed Canadian television alongside other popular forms, and this has become a common way of approaching television as part of a broader study of the Canadian "popular." Geoff Pevere and Greig Dymond's *Mondo Canuck*, published in 1996, provided a historical overview of Canadian popular culture that included film, television, music, leisure activities, and even food. While not a particularly academic or scholarly look at Canadian pop culture, *Mondo Canuck* addressed a mainstream national audience and offered a nostalgic narrative that took the reader through a kind of walk down memory lane, complete with glossy photos that spoke to the styles and trends of decades past. *Mondo Canuck* was interesting in that it encouraged a revisiting of the past through popular texts and figures and suggested that Canadians share these cultural memories and experiences. While the authors present some interesting insights into different moments in our pop culture past, its most salient aspect is the view of the Canadian "popular" upon which the premise of the book rests. While *Mondo Canuck* often pokes fun at the hokeyness of much of Canadian pop culture and sometimes takes pleasure in identifying some of its memorable failures, the book reaffirms the popular resonance of these artifacts and recognizes a shared popular culture in which all Canadians may conceivably participate.

A number of scholarly publications have similarly approached Canadian television under the larger umbrella of popular culture. *PopCan* (1999), *Virtual Sovereignty* (2004), and *Canadian Cultural Poesis* (2006) are a few examples of collections that consider Canadian television alongside other popular forms. However, the question of the Canadian "popular" is, in these academic approaches, a much more complicated and at times contested concept than it is in *Mondo Canuck*. This is certainly the case in Joan Nicks and Jeannette Sloniowski's anthology *Slippery Pastimes* (2002), in which Canadian television is analyzed alongside a variety of other forms and practices including tourism, music, and sports, as many of the authors approach popular culture "as a site of negotiation and contestation."[20] In their introduction, the editors note that studies of the Canadian "popular" must also wrestle with the questionable degree of "popularity" of Canadian popular culture itself. The notion of the "popular" in Canadian contexts takes on varied meanings, since many Canadians' familiarity with their own popular forms may be limited or overshadowed by their enjoyment and consumption of foreign (predominantly American) culture. The thorny question of the dubious "popularity" of Canadian television (in English Canada in particular) is important for scholars struggling to make sense of how audiences are imagined and addressed (as, for example, national citizens, "viewing publics," or consumers), how television's relationship to national, regional, or local cultures can be conceptualized, and how texts that engage with popular formulas and modes of representation (most often appropriated from elsewhere) can be examined and evaluated.

Since 1990, studies of Canadian television as part of a larger popular terrain have been influenced by scholarship in popular culture and cultural studies from Britain and the United States. This influence shaped a view of television not only as a technology, an industry, or a collection of mass-mediated texts, but as a cultural practice that, as Graeme Burton notes, "is inevitably about the generation of meanings about culture and society."[21] Cultural studies perspectives thus highlight a view of culture that Raymond Williams defined as "the 'lived experience' of 'ordinary' men and women."[22] Cultural studies is also characterized by theoretical and methodological approaches that draw on a variety of different disciplines including sociology, political science, literary studies, film studies, communication studies, women's studies, and anthropology. The study of Canadian television is likewise marked by a multiplicity of critical methods such as ethnography, genre and textual analysis, gender studies, and political economy approaches. The diversity of scholarship represented in *Canadian Television: Text and Context* reflects this eclectic interdisciplinarity.

Studies of television have emerged within the context of popular culture studies, but this is by no means the only place where analyses of Canadian television can be found. The availability of recording technologies (first videotapes, and now digital formats) has made it much easier for scholars to apply the sort of close analysis that has been employed in film studies. As more interest in television programming develops (and as the relationship between film and television forms becomes more complex), scholars have begun to offer interesting analyses of Canadian series both past and present, contributing a valuable textual analysis that has been absent from many communications-oriented approaches. The 2006 "Special Issue on Intersections of Film and Television in Canada" of the *Canadian Journal of Film Studies* is indicative of these developments, presenting work that challenges the disciplinary separation of film and television and providing analyses that attest to the productive connections between the two media.[23] In their introduction to this *CJFS* issue, editors Peter Urquhart and Ira Wagman are optimistic that it will inspire further research and collaboration.

Several excellent books and anthologies on Canadian television have been published in recent years, including David Hogarth's *Documentary Television in Canada* (2002) and the Michele Byers edited collection examining the Degrassi phenomenon, *Growing Up Degrassi* (2006). Serra Tinic's persuasive analysis of television production in Canada, *On Location* (2005), provides a unique approach by highlighting the significance of place and region to discussions of policy and funding. Lorna Roth's *Something New in the Air* (2005) and Mary Jane Miller's *Outside Looking In* (2008) present very different, but equally important and compelling approaches to Aboriginal media and the representation of First Nations peoples on television. Other recent texts in the field serve to underscore the potential diversity that is emerging. Bart Beaty and Rebecca Sullivan have raised significant points of debate around policy issues in their 2006 book *Canadian Television Today.* Situating Canadian television within broader global contexts, Beaty and Sullivan "attempt to avoid the trap of nationalist navel gazing and extend the debate about television onto the global stage,"[24] underlining the fundamental ways in which Canadian television is no longer constrained by national boundaries. At the same time, the book seeks to address their frustrations at not being adequately heard while testifying during the House of Commons Standing Committee on Canadian Heritage hearings that resulted in the report *Our Cultural Sovereignty*.[25] While able to raise significant policy issues amid its contextualization of contemporary Canadian television, *Canadian Television Today* does not engage extensively with specific Canadian television texts.

The essays in Zoë Druick and Aspa Kotsopoulos's 2008 edited collection *Programming Reality* do focus directly on such texts. As their title suggests, the television texts under consideration are examined as part of Canadian media's tendencies towards realism. Druick and Kotsopoulos note: "The current proliferation of shows grouped under the category of reality-based programming provides an opportunity to reconsider the complex mediation of reality that television performs within the Canadian context."[26] While focusing on a familiar Canadian paradigm in realism, *Programming Reality* is able to demonstrate that diverse televisual responses to this paradigm can emerge in the current Canadian television climate. Both of these recent books demonstrate the growing diversity within the field and point to the range of issues available for further exploration. These examples of research published since 2002 indicate some of the innovative work currently being undertaken in the field.

Despite this recent scholarly focus on Canadian television, work in this area still tends to be marginalized within larger disciplinary fields such as media studies, film studies, popular culture, and Canadian studies. Many noteworthy essays on Canadian TV end up scattered in various anthologies and periodicals. Moreover, while studying Canadian television in the context of Canadian popular culture or within film studies may allow for a more comprehensive understanding of its operations within a larger cultural frame (and has undoubtedly led to some productive dialogues across disciplines), it may also inhibit the development of Canadian television studies as a separate discipline or field of study. While excellent research is undoubtedly under way, Canadian television studies is still in its youth, well behind the flourishing fields found in Britain and the United States and lacking the confidence and coherence found within those scholarly approaches. It is our hope that the essays collected in *Canadian Television: Text and Context*, representing innovative current research, will make a significant contribution to the growth of Canadian television studies and inspire continued dialogue and research.

This collection identifies what we perceive to be a new maturity in both Canadian television and in Canadian television studies. The chapters in this volume demonstrate the potential in moving beyond conventional discourses of cultural nationalism. Rather than entering into a debate over what Canadian television could or should do, the authors here address what it is doing. This book seeks to explore Canadian television within the realm of television studies, as opposed to being a book about Canadian national identity that happens to have television as its focus. The existing literature in Canadian television studies, as already outlined, has effectively established and explored central issues of national culture. Clearly any collection with a national focus must address questions of nation and identity, but here they appear among several thematic currents rather than as the primary issue. The parameters of nation are diffused through a range of other contexts that, in their combined analysis, permit a richer exploration of the varied terrain that is Canadian television.

It is certainly a step forward that Canadian television scholars no longer feel the need to agonize over issues of national identity or defend the role of television within the nation-state. Instead, greater focus can now be placed on the televisual texts and practices themselves, their structures and styles, their international currency, broader institutional structures, the nature of the media industry, relationships to new technologies, and a variety of other issues relevant to television studies. The essays here certainly benefit from and make use of earlier strands of research on television in Canada: the influence of the arguments introduced by Mary Jane Miller still resonate; the history addressed by Paul Rutherford still serves as a key reference point; and the attention to technologies considered by the likes of McLuhan and Innis continue to hold sway over television scholarship in Canada and more widely. Such foundational works have paved the way for the studies within this book. Because scholars have followed Miller's appeal to take "a systematic look at whether the television drama we make in Canada is distinctive or imitative or innovative,"[27] the possibility now exists to move beyond these foundational approaches. This is evident in the continued growth in the field of Canadian television studies.

The collection opens with a foreword by *Globe and Mail* television critic John Doyle. The witty and thought-provoking observations in his "Ten Things about Canadian TV" point not only to home truths for Canadian viewers but to issues that engage academic consideration as well. With journalistic precision, Doyle paints a familiar and accurate portrait of the Canadian television landscape. It is not only Canadian television that is put under the microscope, but also the histories and possibilities within Canadian television studies itself. The first section of this book, "Television Studies in the Canadian Context: Challenges and New Directions," which includes this introduction, addresses some of the broader developments in Canadian television, and Canadian television studies, as well as the more practical challenges that scholars have faced, and continue to face, in pursuing academic studies of Canadian television. Reflection is also central to Mary Jane Miller's chapter, a personal view of television studies in Canada. Hers is a reflection on, history of, and also challenge to Canadian television studies. The discussion of difficulties faced by early researchers and the author's unique insights into the origins of the field provide a welcome peek behind the curtains of academia. While her style is anecdotal and reflective, the issues that Miller identifies remain substantial. Jennifer VanderBurgh's examination of the problems faced by current Canadian television scholars demonstrates how concerns recognized by Miller still resonate. VanderBurgh considers the particular role played by archives and the lack of access to, or availability of, much of Canada's television heritage. While specifically discussing the Canadian context, she locates problems familiar to television scholars worldwide in the archiving, availability, and access to material so often neglected as "merely" pop culture and hence ephemeral. As VanderBurgh claims, "the record of Canadian-produced television content dating back to 1952 reflects the familiar story of any ephemeral media, much of it having been lost, unvalued, and/or inadequately cared for."

While texts can be archived, the processes of producing and viewing television are more difficult to catalogue. The collection's second section, "Contexts of Television Production in Canada," explores these processes of production and consumption—the contexts in which Canadian television performs its "working through." VanderBurgh extends McLuhan's ideas in pointing out that "television is not about watching programs, but about entering the televisual landscape ... a viewer's body integrates via electricity with the medium and with others, an experience similar to a shared central nervous system." Part of that televisual landscape includes the stars who appear on our screens. As Liz Czach suggests, any consideration of a Canadian star system must consider the relationship between our film screens and our television screens. While the sort of star system familiar in Hollywood has certainly not emerged in Canada, Czach makes key points about Canadian celebrity culture. She raises important questions for better understanding that culture and determining whether an English-Canadian star system is feasible or even desirable. As Czach suggests, a star system might emerge from more productive forms of multimedia cross-promotion in Canadian popular culture. Her recognition of the constraints imposed by market size and structure in Canada's television industry is echoed in the next two chapters. In her examination of the Aboriginal People's Television Network (APTN), Marian Bredin argues that producers of Aboriginal peoples' television face myriad challenges related to licensing restrictions and the complexities of financing. In his chapter on children's television broadcaster YTV, Kyle Asquith sees commercialism, or more precisely hypercommercialism, as the driving force in the production of children's programming. Both chapters explore the complexities of domestic television funding issues from very different perspectives. Bredin considers the difficulties faced by APTN in developing programming, while more optimistically noting the benefits, both economic and cultural, that this programming has provided, while Asquith explores the less positive ramifications of programming that is largely paid for by commercial interests who view children as consumers. In both cases it is not just television content, but the political economy of the national and global television industry, that is relevant to the arguments being made.

The last section of this collection, "Contexts of Criticism: Genre, Narrative and Form," explicitly analyzes representative texts from Canadian television. The authors of these chapters have selected texts that provoke broader debate about the workings of contemporary Canadian television. In her chapter, Michele Byers interrogates a number of TV series that produce narratives about Canadian youth. In her introduction, she posits that the way "these series highlight social differences among teens is significant within the broader lexicon of teen TV." Byers then demonstrates how specific Canadian youth television texts employ broader genre codes, creating "possibilities for disrupting myths about Canadianness by offering up narratives about youth who are Canadian and yet are often on the margins of Canadianness."

Questions about national narratives and identity are central to Derek S. Foster's consideration of the influence of American reality television in Canada. Focusing on the controversial CBC simulcast of a short-lived music reality series *The One*, Foster explores public debate about the show that circulated within the Canadian cultural scene and raises important questions about Canadians' relationship to what appears on their television screens. While the genre of reality television draws the ire of many critics, Foster acknowledges its popularity with viewers. He reminds us that audience engagement with the products of the genre help demonstrate "how all television provides opportunities for public fashioning and re-valuing of what Canadian culture is or ought to be."

Sarah A. Matheson's concern with genre revolves around responses to narratives of ethnicity and cultural difference in the situation comedy *Little Mosque on the Prairie*. The final chapters in the collection adapt established critical approaches to help make sense of the texts of Canadian television within the Canadian context. Matheson's chapter and Scott Henderson's essay on the television work of director Jerry Ciccoritti (particularly his 2005 Shania Twain biopic) take up two key concepts within media studies: genre and authorship respectively. Matheson provides a unique take on the *Little Mosque* phenomenon by demonstrating how its reliance on genre formulas may, in fact, be part of the larger aims of the series. As Matheson puts it, "reliance on convention [is] a central part of the way the program resists situating the Muslim community as 'other.'" Henderson uncovers themes and motifs in Ciccoritti's varied television work that illustrate how the director uses televisual styles and structures to reproduce, yet deconstruct, stereotypical forms of "Canadianness" in his stories.

While all of the chapters in this book emphasize the Canadianness of their subject matter, they do so by employing a range of disciplinary approaches drawn not only from television studies, but also from film studies, communication studies, history, sociology, and literary studies among others. This growth in the breadth and plurality of the field is perhaps the new "context" of Canadian television studies in its trajectory since the early struggles identified by Miller. Undoubtedly there is still much struggle and growth ahead amid challenging and changing times for the media industry and for television and media studies.

There is some irony that a book celebrating the maturity of Canadian television studies is appearing at a time when economic circumstances and the explosion of new mobile and digital technologies are threatening to recast the role of television in this country. Of course the problems found in Canadian broadcasting are not uniquely Canadian, but are being experienced by other national media industries as a result of global media consolidation and technological convergence, which transcend national borders. As national networks and media conglomerates reshape themselves in response to global forces, debates about the future of Canadian television will also be transformed. As the essays in this book demonstrate, the debate is no longer simply about the quality and diversity of Canadian television programs. Though we cannot offer any certain predictions about the changing contexts of Canadian television through the coming decades, the contributors to this volume have provided ample evidence that a vital and dynamic future for Canadian television studies is assured.

Acknowledgements

We would like to acknowledge those individuals and groups who have helped this book come to fruition. The Centre for Canadian Studies, the Department of Communication, Popular Culture and Film, and other units at Brock University supported the original Two Days of Canada conference, Television in Canada, at which some of the initial research for this book was presented. We would like to thank our colleagues at Brock and elsewhere for their interest in this project as it developed. We would especially like to thank Mary Jane Miller, whose role as senior scholar and mentor in the study of Canadian television has inspired us to make our own contributions to the field. Our research assistant, Heather Maguire, provided invaluable help with copy-editing, fact-checking, and compiling bibliographic entries. The book is much improved thanks to her professional approach and attention to detail. Lisa Quinn, our editor at Wilfrid Laurier University Press, has been a staunch advocate for the book throughout the editorial process. The readers of the manuscript offered generous and relevant commentary on the book, and we appreciate their willingness to bring their own expertise and critical reflection to bear on our work. Finally, we would like to thank our families, partners, and children for their love and patience when our scholarly pursuits inevitably overflow into our personal lives.

Notes

1 Miller, *Turn Up the Contrast*, 4.
2 Miller, *Turn Up the Contrast*; *Rewind and Search*; *Outside Looking In.*
3 Ellis, "Television as Working-Through," 55.
4 Ibid., 69.
5 Miller, *Turn Up the Contrast*, 4.
6 Wolfe, *Jolts*, 129.
7 Ibid., 78
8 Miller, *Turn Up the Contrast*, 378.
9 Stewart, *Here's Looking at Us*; Gittins, *CTV: The Television Wars*; Wood, *Live to Air.*
10 Innis, *The Bias of Communication.*
11 McLuhan, *Understanding Media*, 269.
12 Smythe, *Dependency Road*, 22.
13 Babe, "Regulation and Incentives"; Mosco, *Political Economy of Communication*; Raboy, *Missed Opportunities.*
14 Raboy, "Hybridization of Public Broadcasting," 105.
15 Ibid., 107.
16 For an overview of scholarly responses to Collins's book, see Attallah, "Richard Collins: The Debate on Culture and Polity."
17 Flaherty and Manning, "Introduction," *The Beaver Bites Back?*, 7.

18 John Fiske's book *Television Culture*, for example, offered an analysis of television that suggested that viewers are active and productive viewers. Another key work in this regard is Henry Jenkins's study of fan cultures in *Textual Poachers*. Jenkins demonstrated how viewers often engage with popular culture in resistant, creative, and active ways.
19 Rutherford, *When Television Was Young*, 5–6.
20 Nicks and Sloniowski, "Introduction," *Slippery Pastimes*, 4.
21 Burton, *Talking Television*, x.
22 Cited in Storey, *Cultural Theory and Popular Culture*, 47.
23 *Canadian Journal of Film Studies* 15, no. 1 (Spring 2006).
24 Beaty and Sullivan, *Canadian Television Today*, 3.
25 Ibid.
26 Druick and Kotsopoulos, "Introduction," *Programming Reality*, 1.
27 Miller, *Turn Up the Contrast*, 4.

1

From Kine to Hi-Def: A Personal View of Television Studies in Canada

MARY JANE MILLER

I AM ALWAYS AMAZED at the number of my university colleagues who don't watch television and are proud of it. I am surprised when a scholar writing about television makes clear that what gives it value must exclude what entertains. Television still connotes for many in our environment "mindless entertainment." The study of popular culture is considered suspect, and our work is thought to be fishing out of the mainstream—although just about everybody has an opinion about it. In my own field of Dramatic Literature, questions such as "why discuss television when you could be doing research on Shakespeare?" were common. As it happens, I taught Shakespeare for forty years, keeping up on the basic methodologies as they quite radically changed, and I will continue to reread his work for the rest of my life. However, there were hundreds of competent to excellent researchers in Shakespeare studies but very few in the unploughed field of television studies in this country, yet both the man for the last four hundred and the medium for the last sixty were, and are, popular entertainers.

That I managed to research and write about television drama as well as teach a more generally focused television and radio course is due to the unique access I had to the first twenty years of television drama available on kines[1] and videotapes. In this paper I offer a personal and therefore limited overview of television studies in Canada, particularly those that focus on the programs themselves, how they came to be preserved, how preservation changed with technology, how access has both improved and become much more difficult for today's generation of scholars, and how a group called the Association for the Study of Canadian Radio and Television / Association des études sur la radio-télévision canadienne (ASCRT/AERTC) took an interdisciplinary approach to television studies when such a way of looking at this material was quite rare.

Who Came to the Party?

Among those who have done excellent work in television studies are Marc Raboy, Lorna Roth, Valerie Alia, Martin Allor, Paul Attallah, Doris Baltruschat, Ross Eamon, Paul Rutherford, and Renee Legris. An annotated bibliography would include many others, some of whom did work on television and then left the field and others who stayed to make it their primary research focus. Most scholars working on anglophone Canadian television are published in journals of communication studies, sociology, ethnology, economics, political science, history, cultural studies, popular culture studies, and Canadian studies. However, in the early 1980s, when my first work on television drama took shape, no one but Paul Rutherford was looking at television drama, and he was working on the much broader field of Canadian prime-time television from 1952 to 1967. If an academic generation appears every twenty years, then there should have been two newer generations now working on television studies since I got down to work in 1980. Yet for years it was a bit lonely at the beginning, even though drama—sitcoms, soaps, cop shows, dramedy, drama specials, miniseries, docudramas, dramas for children and youth—is without dispute the most popular genre of television, just as it was of radio. In the 1990s English professor Linda Warley and film studies professor Christopher Gittings, who had two different points of view on a particular series in which I was also interested, *North of 60* (1992–97), made the work I was doing seem more like a conversation. The book in which the discussion appears, *Outside Looking In: The Representation of First Nations Television Drama,* contains five chapters on *North of 60*. Yet despite the fact that the series ran for six seasons and was followed by an unheard-of five made-for-television movies, an extensive literature search conducted in 2005, eight years after the series had ended turned up only one other article (by an American writer) that mentioned the series. However, in the last ten years, all kinds of Canadian television dramas are attracting more scholars who seem to be in it for the long haul.

Being the first to knock on the door has advantages and disadvantages. In thirteen years of applying for Social Sciences and Humanities Research Council of Canada (SSHRC) funding I never applied to the same committee twice. A publishing career begun in those early years also had to be eclectic. My articles appeared in *Canadian Drama, Theatre History in Canada, The American Journal of Canadian Studies, Journal of Popular Culture, The Canadian Journal of Law and Society, Canadian Theatre Review, Frequency/Fréquence* and *Canadart VIII Revista do nucleo de Estudos Canadenses* (Brazil)– and in books edited by historians, sociologists, archivists, and political scientists.[2] I knew we were making headway at home when the *Oxford Companion to Canadian Drama* (1990) included an article on television drama, as did *The Canadian Encyclopedia.* In 1997 and 2004, Horace Newcomb, one of the founders of television scholarship included dozens of articles and several overviews of aspects of Canadian television in the two editions of *The Encyclopedia of Television.* As one of the editors, I found it a pleasure to work with him.

Canada Goes Looking for Itself—Again

The first scholars to beat a path into this new territory were radio's children. The earliest were born before the Second World War; for example, political scientist Frank Peers got his B.A. in 1936. Many others were war babies or early boomers. There are advantages to being a war baby rather than a boomer—especially a boomer born after 1950. The boomers grew up with television as their constant companion. The early scholars who wrote about television reached voting age before they really saw much television. Instead, we learned to imagine (the oldest form of interactivity, surely) as radio told us stories using genres that would become familiar television staples: soaps, cop shows, kids' shows, sketch comedy, situation comedies, variety shows, and talent contests. Eventually American television poured across our borders, and Canadians living near these borders began to buy TV sets. Around 1953 or 1954 television appeared at a neighbour's or relative's house and the radio voices acquired faces: Sergeant Preston, Maggie Muggins, Jack Benny, Milton Berle, and even the CBLT[3] puppets Uncle Chichimus and Hollyhock.[4] Often these shows were glimpsed through interference called "snow." Even though we war babies were shaped by sound not vision, we are able to remember the excitement the new medium brought to our teenage years. Perhaps because of that early radio background and the fact that my first two degrees were in English and one of my grad courses was taught by Marshall McLuhan, my PhD dissertation was on BBC radio drama. Radio drama, I thought, was close to literature, yet "dramatic." I didn't know any better then. Having to travel to the UK to do it was another reason for a young Canadian aged 26 who had never been to Britain. Fortunately, the Canada Council (the SSHRC did not yet exist) agreed.

As far as formal education in English literature (my first degree) was concerned, honours English students in 1959–63 at the University of Toronto were given a production course called "Canadian and American Literature" to air. Every lecture of that first-year course except the last one was on American literature. In the last class the professor lectured on four poets, ten minutes per poet, ending with Bliss Carman, basically to the effect that it snows a lot in Canada. Irving Layton, PK Page, Margaret Avison, Leonard Cohen, all writing at that time, were not mentioned. As honours English students we discovered that we were not permitted to enrol in the pass course in Canadian literature and we were too busy to audit it. There were other gaps. Communications studies did not exist, nor did theatre and dramatic literature degrees. Popular culture? Ray Browne, one of the founders of popular culture studies on this side of the Atlantic did not launch *The Journal of Popular Culture* until 1967. It took a while for the concept to infiltrate north of the border, longer for it to be accepted.[5]

Later generations may find all of this a bit odd. They grew up under the maple leaf flag and take for granted our now-mature theatre and literature, our artists and opera performers, our hit bands and singers, etc. They have answered Northrop Frye's question about "where here is" and know who they are as diverse but recognizable Canadians. In the 1960s we were trying to find out who we were as Canadians and where "here" was. Many early theatre practitioners and novelists/poets took a chance on Canada in the 1960s and stayed home. Many others went abroad to the United States or Europe—and then came home. The first generation of television producers, such as Sydney Newman, who brought our realist drama to British television, left for the United States and Britain. But others, including Paul Almond, Eric Till, Philip Keatley, and Ron Weyman, remained to create the popular series *Wojeck*, *Cariboo Country*, and drama specials. All of us—makers, researchers, and teachers—had an unparalleled chance to shape the understanding of Canada right after Expo 67, although, inevitably, our nationalism was rooted in the generation of artists and scholars who preceded us.

Learning on the Fly

After five months' preparation at the University of Birmingham under a supervisor who was trying to start a drama and theatre program, I arrived at the door of London's Broadcasting House armed with an introduction to the Head of Radio Drama, Martin Esslin. Before 1966, no one had done a PhD on the BBC, and so I was given the red carpet treatment: access to the library resources, which included scrapbooks of reviews that were invaluable for trying to sift out what I wanted to hear, and scripts as broadcast recordings. They even gave me a thirty-day course in radio production, along with the new trainees, and let me sit in on several rehearsals, including one that was being recorded live. Each step was essential to understanding the process at that time. My BBC experience definitively shaped what I thought was necessary to know when I returned to research at home.

During those two years, I spent just six months in Birmingham. I commuted to London for periods of time, then moved there for my second year. Nevertheless, only a "red brick" (i.e., 'new' university) would take a chance on a dissertation subject as bizarre as radio drama or provide a supervisor like John Russell Brown, who was then a famous, youngish Shakespearean scholar who was also plugged into the contemporary theatre scene and who gave me a copy of Harold Pinter's original script for *The Dwarves*. At Birmingham for those first months, I attended early seminars on popular culture by Stuart Hall. More important to my project, I listened to a lot of BBC radio drama live, keeping notes off-air, since there was no useful way to make recordings from the radio, and tried to educate myself quickly in the nuances of accent—geographical location, education, and class being the essential clues to character that I had to discern as the dialogue flew by. During that period "swinging" London from 1966 to 1968 was an education in itself, with its riches of films, art galleries, theatre, and the other arts as well as the British Museum.

When I began teaching at Brock University in St. Catharines, Ontario, in 1968, my chairman in the English department thought I could teach theatre with this background. (I had been involved in a summer of theatre while teaching at the University of Western Ontario in 1964–66: that was my "practical" experience.) He also told me to get rid of my miniskirts, which were all I had. I bought two pairs of pants and turned all those skirts into tunics. St. Catharines, and probably most other small towns and cities, had not caught up with the changing zeitgeist. I taught theatre practice and directed plays for five years. What I learned made my radio dissertation much, much better. (I also directed four summer productions of Shakespeare in the 1970s.) My theatre experience has since convinced me that scholars planning to analyse television drama need to learn something about performance, gestural codes, subtext, costumes, props, and lighting—not just camera work. The camera work and editing and occasionally the performances get far too much attention. More problematic to me is that scholars from other disciplines, including film, very often ignore the dialogue, which is the spine of all good drama. My formal education in English literature and my informal "pick it up as you can" education in radio and theatre mean that I usually avoid that error.

Research in the 1970s

By watching and listening to television and radio in the early 1970s, I concluded that these media in Canada were in rather poor shape. After a valiant struggle in the later 1950s and 60s, radio drama almost disappeared in the 1970s as television completed its takeover of the airwaves and the audiences. Moreover, I discovered when starting my first sabbatical (1973–4) that, with all the permissions from CBC broadcasting executives I needed and all the goodwill in the world, the CBC could not give me access to enough radio and television drama scripts and, more importantly, enough recordings to allow me to begin substantial research in those fields. I had already determined as a basic rule of my work that in order to discuss radio, television, or theatre, I would have to see or hear it, preferably more than once. As I later learned, the CBC's holdings were in chaos at that time, but the apparently insoluble research problem of gaining access to radio and television materials in Canada was a shock after my unlimited access to scripts and recordings at the BBC. By 1973 things were so dire at the CBC that many well-known producer/directors and other cultural and academic figures formed a Committee on Television, which put together an intervention for the 1974 hearings of the CRTC. It called on the CRTC to scrap the CBC and then reinvent it. I became a minor researcher for them. Its substantial documentation of the CBC as well as its remarkably eloquent sections written by people such as Patrick Watson and Abe Rotstein and signed by many of the leading arts and letters figures of the day could be worth looking at for a historian today. I learned a lot by working on the Committee, listening to their impassioned discussions and then sitting in on the CRTC hearings.

Stay Tuned—It Gets Easier

By the mid-1970s I could see that the CBC TV drama department had started to make better television drama. After the legendary financial and artistic disaster of *Jalna,*[6] which consumed much of the already attenuated budget for television drama, the next two heads of drama turned the CBC drama department around: innovator and risk-taker John Hirsch and then steady and more subtle John Kennedy.[7]

In 1978, through ASCRT/AERTC (the founding of which I discuss later in this chapter), I met Sam Kula, then head of the Sound and Moving Images division of Library and Archives Canada (LAC).[8] Emboldened by a glass of wine, I asked him bluntly when it would be possible to look at the LAC holdings in television drama. His reply was to discuss a contract with me to help sort out and set priorities for acquisition and preservation of CBC kines from the earliest days, including the innovative anthologies. That addressed my primary research question about television drama at that time: had there been a golden age? In the summer of 1979 I spent my days in a tax warehouse where the kines were stored, viewing and describing them for LAC. Getting my hands on kines that I could play (very gently!) or videotapes that I could stop frame or rewind allowed me to view enough material that at summer's end I knew the CBC had made some excellent TV drama in the 1950s and 60s. With the help of the CBC library and unusual access to more recent drama videotapes over the next ten years given to me by John Kennedy, head of television drama, my knowledge grew. I made trips to Winnipeg and Vancouver to see more material, sat in on filmed location shoots. I sat in on sound edits and talked to everyone I met, from producers, directors, writers, actors, directors of photography, composers, and editors to cameramen (and a few women) and sound and lighting technicians. The interviews flowing from that time became *Rewind and Search: Conversations with Makers and Decision-makers in CBC Television Drama*.

Television scholars should engage in productive dialogue with creators and producers of television. In my view, postmodernism aside, challenging popular opinion about what is good and bad television, where warranted, is also very much a part of the job for scholars. There are still many myths, even among the makers of television drama, to be challenged. In 1982, I screened *The Paper People* (first broadcast December 12, 1967), a highly experimental drama directed by David Gardner from a script by Timothy Findley, while both were in the audience. Neither had seen it for many years. The program had had a hostile reception from nearly every television columnist at the time it was released. I was as nervous as the creators were when I rose to challenge those critical opinions in front of an academic audience who had just seen the film. When ASCRT/AERTC was honouring the achievements of director Donald Brittain in 1989, I presented a paper on his television work while he looked on.[9]

In the early 1980s producers Sam Levene and Maryke McEwen came with me to the University of Michigan for the first scholarly conference on television drama held in North America.[10] There they answered questions after the attendees had viewed their program and heard my paper about the CBC comedy-drama *Seeing Things* (1981–87) and (the next year) about the drama special *Blind Faith* (1982). It is a brave producer or director who, in front of a crowd of, in this case foreign academics, will listen to an analysis and discussion of their art. (Producers wince at the word "art," but quality television programming is an art—as well as a "black art.") The American academics accepted that their own drama on television evangelists *Pray TV* (1982) was blunted in comparison to *Blind Faith,*[11] a CBC-produced topical drama on televangelism, and they didn't quite get all the jokes in the episode of *Seeing Things*. These cultural differences were more starkly defined when an African-American scholar directly asked me why I referred to those who heard my paper as "you." Weren't we all the same on both sides of the border? I got nowhere in asserting our differences until I pointed out that during the summer of 1968 when their inner cities went up in flames, we closed our border crossings at Detroit and Buffalo. We had racial problems but we had no such riots. This particular discourse about differences is ongoing—and the readers of this collection will have to take it up in their turn. Persistence and patience are what we need to continue exploring these questions.

With all of these opportunities adding depth to my understanding of the process of getting television drama from page to TV screen, I continued to pursue what was basically a unique path in Canada at that time. As I mentioned above, Paul Rutherford was the only other person digging for programming material for his seminal study *When Television Was Young: Primetime Canada 1952–1967* (1990), but he was casting a much wider net at a narrower period. Even though our focus and methodology were different, each of us confessed that we hoped the other's book would come out first. We also agreed that our mutual choice of the same episode of *Wojeck* (1966–68) to discuss at some length would be a good thing, a rare occasion in Canada when two scholars published on the same material. In the end my *Turn Up the Contrast: CBC Television Drama 1952 to the Present* (1987) came out first.

Access for Contemporary Researchers

For a long time, analysts of dramatic programming remained scarce in the field. The limb was long and few were sitting on it. However, since the late 1990s, a new generation of PhD candidates in many fields have turned their attention to Canadian television programming. The serious problem for those researchers is that the access I had to the recordings of earlier television drama is gone. I discuss the limitations of Library and Archives Canada below. Moreover, almost none of the programming has been released on DVD, which can certainly limit the choice of what to discuss. The upside in later years is that the VCR, DVD, PVR, and digital formatting of programming mean that scholars can make their own off-air study recordings. I have nearly 600, most of them catalogued, all of them playable—but I started in the early 1980s. In fact I had to teach a summer course to afford an early VCR to record some of our many television gems. For example, on Sunday afternoons in 1982 the CBC broadcast *Rear View Mirror*, an eclectic mix of documentaries, quizzes, and pop music programs, including some of the treasures from the late 1950s and 60s, and introduced by people who made or performed in the programs. Younger scholars were in their cradles then. A few have now borrowed material from me for their dissertations or later research. A related note: in 1978 I was ASCRT/AERTC member of the Secretary of State's subcommittee on copyright for film and broadcast material. In 2011 "fair use" in classrooms is still not settled, even though every union involved as well as the CBC could profit from reasonable charges. Some key battles remain to be fought.

Actor, drama professor, television pioneer, and general polymath Mavor Moore did see that television drama scripts as well as all kinds of production records were deposited at York University. Unfortunately on a quick check the scripts were "clean" copies—not scripts as broadcast with their many pages of different colours denoting all the changes from script to shoot—and none were annotated by the director, composer, or sound editor. I am aware of one article on *The Paper People* that built an argument partly based on the ending in the clean copy of the script. The ending of the final version as rewritten, shot, and edited is completely different from the script the person had used. My paper on the same film was based on seeing it several times at the CBC. This reinforced one of my basic research axioms: I will not discuss any program I have not seen. The only exception is a chapter on *Radisson* (1957–58) in my most recent book *Outside Looking In: The Representation of First Nations Peoples in Television Drama Series*. The thirty-six half-hour films in English have disappeared, although the films in French (the series was filmed in both languages) may still exist at the SRC (which kept better records). *Radisson* was the exception to my rule because it sets the baseline for the analysis of the other later programming.

Enter ASCRT/AERTC

I was by no means the only person concerned with the fate of CBC materials. In the years when CBC access was impossible I found a congenial home in the Association for Canadian Theatre Research (ACTR), which was formed in 1976. There I met Howard Fink, an English professor, who would later establish the Centre for Broadcast Studies at Concordia. He was already giving shelter to a growing collection of orphaned radio programs and he was exploring a way of looking at radio drama using a crossover of disciplines with sociologist John

Jackson. Together with others we founded the Association for the Study of Canadian Radio and Television (ASCRT/AERTC). We managed to attract people from an eclectic mix of academic disciplines across the country: Renée Legris, Pierre Page, Robert Albota, Bob Hackett, Bill Hull, Liss Jeffrey, Peter Narvaez, Mary Vipond, Barb Freeman, Jacques Vermette, François Baby, Eleanor Beattie, and Paul Rutherford. From the beginning we also welcomed librarians and archivists to help the association lobby for the preservation of radio and television materials. Ernie Dick was essential in recruiting people. Rosemary Bergeron, Sylvie Robitaille, Michelle Cartier, Derek Reimer, Phil Savage, James Turner, and Brian Morrison were among the archivists and librarians who came on board. Regrettably, the Association included only a few "makers" of those programs: John Twomey and Damiano Pietropaulo, and one very helpful person in CBC middle management, A.H. Ross.[12] (Some of our members were well established; others were then grad students or on contract somewhere. Most are now flourishing.) The achievements of many francophone and anglophone makers of programming were honoured at our annual dinners, but few were active within the Association. We didn't really discover how to use those who were willing to participate. Finally, for a brief while, thanks to hard work by Howard Fink and others, we obtained a SSHRC subsidy for the journal *Frequency/Fréquence,* which did provide a place for some good papers but never really won a readership. However, Howard Fink and John Jackson founded the Concordia Centre for Broadcasting Studies (1981–present). With its huge collection of radio resources, it had an understandable emphasis on radio but I was honoured to be a research fellow, though not a very active one given the distances, until I retired in 2004.

One other important note: The members of ASCRT/AERTC remained together in the mid-to late 1970s when most of the other scholarly associations split along linguistic lines—incidentally leaving some francophone scholars from outside Quebec feeling orphaned; for example, distinguished scholars from the west and from Acadia University continued to work within ACTR after the association experienced a difficult split in the mid-1970s. In a way typical of our Montrealers' everyday experience, we simply spoke the language we knew better and our bilingual members translated when necessary. Despite the high-school "Diefenfrench" many of us learned in the 1950s, most of us had little acquaintance with the other official language but could understand the discussion even if we could not reply. I am close to monolingual. When I was president of the association for three years, and on the executive for many more, my francophone colleagues teased me gently and helped me enormously. My closest colleague in television studies for a long time was Renée Legris, whose knowledge of English verbs matched my knowledge of French nouns. We got along famously—and productively. Interestingly, ASCRT/AERTC did not split, even after the stresses of the 1995 referendum. Why? Because there were too few of us to function as two associations, because we had a lot of respect and affection for each other, and because our interactions had borne a lot of fruit. Why, then, did we end the association a few years later, folding it into the Canadian Communication Association, where our concerns were nominally a good fit? Because at that point in the 1990s there seemed to be no graduate students or young scholars interested in carrying on, and the rest of us were tired. A few considered joining the Film Studies Association but they were not then members of the Learneds,[13] and members seemed to be more preoccupied with the arcana of film studies. I note that many of the films in Canada are made with television partners, most Canadian films are seen on television, and films made for television are often sold to the Third World for showing in movie theatres.[14] Though Canadian film and television production overlap in these ways, nevertheless Spring 2006 was the first time in its sixteen-year history that the word "television" appeared in the title of an article or book review in *The Canadian Journal of Film Studies / Revue canadienne d'études cinématographiques*. That issue was concentrated on television.

Changing Perspectives on Preserving Programming

From the beginning ASCRT/AERTC was concerned with preserving the history of broadcasting including not only the CBC/SRC but also the private broadcasters. Ironically, earlier materials on kines were less vulnerable than tapes and films. In the early 1970s some tapes were wiped and reused. Some films were sold for the silver content. One of our unofficial missions was to preserve materials in private hands and to pressure the CBC/SRC into sending copies of all of their materials to the Sound and Moving Images division of Library and Archives Canada (LAC). By the mid-1980s the CBC started to establish an archive. It was also policy to send programs as well as paper records to LAC, but it was a struggle full of bottlenecks fuelled by indifference in the corporate culture at the CBC and legitimate anxieties about how long it took CBC personnel to access materials at LAC. Eventually the material did come through, although in the mid-1980s I found cans of irreplaceable kines of *Cariboo Country* (a remarkable anthology that appeared irregularly between 1960 and 1969) serving as a doorstop at the CBC's regional headquarters in Vancouver. Relations between what is now the LAC and the CBC and/or the regional archives have, I think, improved.

As an aside, the rise of provincial educational networks in the 1970s took some of the pressure off the CBC in fulfilling its mandate to educate as well as inform and entertain. However, too many good programs were not shared between networks, too many programs were underfunded, and too many of those provincial networks were threatened by the changing priorities of various political parties as they came and went in provincial elections. Moreover, not every province had its own educational network. There were many good creative children's programs, some independent documentaries for adults, a few offerings linked to college or university courses, and many talking heads—some very good talking heads—but little expensive drama. Latterly, educational networks have joined with other broadcasters to obtain second or third viewing rights. Although many academics have appeared on these networks over the years, I do not know of a series that examined the medium of television. In fact Moses Znaimer is the only person inside or outside the medium to actually look at television on a major network (a CHUMCITY co-production with the CBC) in a miniseries called *TVTV* (1995) that used television itself. His provocative series received an interesting response, and a complete issue in the *Canadian Journal of Communication*[15] was devoted to its discussion. The CBC has on occasion tried to link its programming with schools—for example, *Radisson* in the 1950s, and much more successfully with *Canada: A People's History* over two seasons in 2000 and 2001. But there are no coherent, consistent Canadian links that I am aware of on air, in print, or on the Web between academe and the other great teacher of our times—television.

Access to Broadcast Materials for Contemporary Scholars

Newer generations of scholars in Canada struggle to gain access to much of Canada's television heritage for several reasons. Not until the opportunities of reuse and reruns on multiple specialty channels made them more valuable did the materials have a better chance of survival. A few videotapes and then DVDs for some programs did appear, although there was scant CBC drama. For example, *Anne of Green Gables* is readily available, but Alliance Atlantis, the distributor, will not make the six seasons of *North of 60* or even any of its five made-for-TV movies available. Unfortunately, materials from the private sector have not been deposited in the LAC in any organized way. If you are looking for paper sources, people are very helpful with current access to programming deposited at the LAC. However, they cannot overcome the inherent limitation of too little money and too little space. They do not have the funds or personnel to copy a whole series or even a whole season of programming for viewing at LAC, nor do they have the facilities for successive days of viewing. Access to the paper files is much easier unless they are restricted for reasons such as details about contracts. It is also important that researchers preserve their own work in a similar fashion; a case in point are the audiotapes from the forty interviews I made in which people including upper-level executives discussed making CBC television drama, very frankly indeed, on the understanding that full access to the tapes and transcripts would be restricted until 2010. It would be helpful if other academic researchers got permissions and deposited tapes of their interviews at LAC. In fifty or a hundred years, what did not make it into the thesis or paper or book could be as useful as what did.

However, the contemporary researcher has a wealth of Internet resources that were unavailable in the 1970s, 80s, and early 90s. The most useful general source, and one which has remarkably few errors, is The Directory of CBC Television Series 1952–82,[16] which covers the full range of CBC programming in considerable detail and is quite easy to use. A newer addition is The Classic TV Archive hosted by Des Martin.[17] This website provides episode guides taken from *TV Guides* and is often checked with the Library of Congress and other sources. However, The Classic TV Archive only covers early Canadian television drama. Where I have checked it with my own research I have found it remarkably reliable.[18] This Web source welcomes additional information. Some, like Patty Winter's *North of 60* online guide,[19] are models of completeness and accuracy—and in her case fun. She gives the temperature at Fort Liard, which claimed to be the inspiration for the fictional town of Lynx River, includes pictures of the set on location as it is now, and also shares "list mama" duties on an active *North of 60* fan list. Her site has a section of short entries of episode numbers and titles only, a section with longer entries including writer and director credits, and a third section with a full description of each episode. There is also a section with complete cast lists for each episode and one that includes Gemini nominations and awards. Fan sites like this one are rare as of yet but have the potential to be a rich source of information and insight. However, user-generated content must be scrutinized carefully; many IMDb articles are incomplete and often error riddled. A new site, tvarchive.ca,[20] based in Canada, has sought my help on early material like *The Beachcombers*. That will be one of my next projects.

At 70, I can now see a new generation of scholars coming down the road to look at television's nearly sixty-year-old history in Canada, and it cheers my heart. For a while not many academics were actually interested in the programs themselves. But for a long while, no one seemed interested in television drama as a form that in my view influences audiences in ways sports, news, and documentaries cannot. My own work in recent years has been eclectic, using some of the methodologies of sociology, ethnography, historiography, and reception theory to cast light on the programming.

Facts are essential to our engagement with the world but fictions are often the most memorable, involving us at a personal level, taking us behind the closed doors, coaxing us to change our attitudes to AIDS or Residential Schools by getting us engaged with fictional characters who interest us, who may even make us develop some empathy with their situation. Drama works in quite a different way from news and documentaries, which is why the ever-vexing and essential hybrid genre of docudrama was born back in the days of radio—creating controversy ever since. Historians are invariably upset with television docudramas.

In 1980 I was invited to participate in a Learneds history panel, on the 1979 miniseries *Riel*, that was full of outrage. The context was the looming 1980 Quebec referendum, and the idea that the dramatic requirements of a television drama include compression of plot and provision of dialogue where no historical record exists did not impress them. Of course, there have been several controversies since, from the documentary with dramatized interludes, *The Valour and the Horror* (1992), to the more recent CBC refusal to rerun the docudrama *Prairie Giant: The Tommy Douglas Story* (2006) during elections. Consider the reception of the three CBC television versions of *Riel*: the intensely poetic version of the trial of Riel by John Coulter in the early 60s; the elaborate miniseries docudrama from 1979 that was ironically framed as a wild west show and featured a cast that was sympathetic to separatism; and the "chapter" on Riel in *Canada: A People's History*, a seventeen-episode, thirty-two-hour dramatized documentary series (2000–1) which had to reconcile the francophone and anglophone versions of our history. Historians may have been upset because viewers may remember the essence of the impassioned—and much shortened—speech of Riel to his fictional jury in those three dramas instead of the documented lengthy ramble of the real man on the real day. And historians like most of the rest of Canada will not have seen the hybrid mix of film and stage performances in *The Missing Bell of Batoche* (1996), the only version made by a Métis filmmaker, Bob Rock, and broadcast on SCN.

For several generations, drama has consistently trumped news, quiz shows, documentary, and even sports as the favourite genre for radio and then television audiences. New TV dramas have the highest casualty rate, but the major hits make the most money for the major networks, latterly through syndication and DVD sales. Even specialty channels are devoted to specific genres of

TV drama such as mysteries or cop shows. For the first time, with a careful search of listings and a DVD or PVR that records off-air for private-study copies, scholars can actually get their hands on (mostly American but some Canadian) materials from the previous few decades by searching the specialty channels. They can also borrow from the limited collections of study tapes made by older scholars, if they take good care of them. These study tapes, DVDs, and PVR recordings preserve the context of the broadcasts, as the copies sent to the LAC in recent years do not, because the study copies often contain commercials, stations breaks, and ads for other programs. As Ernie Dick, once at the LAC and then the CBC, told ASCRT/AERTC, what the archivists have is endless copies of speeches by Churchill. What they do not have is a typical day's radio programming from 1944. Archivists do not make that kind of record. Who will make it and send it to them? You, gentle reader? Think about it.

Notes

1 Kinescopes were filmed records of the image on the master monitor during live broadcasts. Before cross-country transmission was regularly available they were sent out to the regions. They are our only records of nearly a decade of drama. Some survived because according to labels on the cans it appears that someone at the end of the circuit had a broom closet and stuffed them into it.

2 It is hard to imagine now, but *Books in Canada* used to have me review the year in television drama in the 1980s, and, of course, columnists in newspapers and periodicals have been discussing television in Canada since its inception.

3 CBLT was the first local CBC television station in Toronto, launched on September 8, 1952. Prior to the local broadcasting of CBLT, Torontonians (and others in the Golden Horseshoe region of Ontario) were able to pick up signals only from Buffalo, New York, and surrounding area.

4 *Let's See* (1952–53), with its tongue-in-cheek introduction to the evening's programs, was produced by Norman Jewison among others. http://www.film.queensu.ca/CBC/L.html.

5 The American empire tried to recolonize us at the first conference of the Popular Culture Association to be held in Toronto in 1983. No Americans came to the Canadian panels (but they didn't come to them in New York City either. I organized Canadian pop culture panels for a couple of years). Ray Browne's well-intentioned effort to organize us into a branch of the association failed because we already belonged to associations that let all of us from all across the country meet once a year. We eclectic "pop cult" types habitually attended more than one association at its annual gathering. No analogy to the "Learneds" (now the Congress of the Humanities and Social Sciences) then existed. Also we were not impressed by the indifference in practice to Canadian popular culture. In fact even the cover of the program for the meeting got the War of 1812 wrong—the White House was burned in retaliation for the burning of York, not the other way

around. More than a decade later, the Popular Culture Association of Canada held its inaugural conference in May 2011, preceded by the Canadian Association of Cultural Studies (2005), both encouraging developments. Nevertheless, I learned a lot from attending national conferences of the Association for Popular Culture. As ever, I was picking up my education on the run through reading and through conversations at conferences.

6 See the many comments on the series in Miller, *Rewind and Search*.

7 As context: in the same period there was a year when CTV did only one half-hour of drama—not in a week but for the whole year. The CRTC had to intervene to compel them to take on this expensive area of television.

8 In this time period, the Sound and Moving Images division was housed in the National Archives. In 2003, the Standing Committee on Canadian Heritage was presented with Bill C-36, effectively amalgamating the National Archives and the National Library into Library and Archives Canada (LAC). For the sake of clarity, all references to the National Archives herein are under the title of Library and Archives Canada (LAC). For more information on the transformation of the National Archives, see http://www.collectionscanada.gc.ca/about-us/006/012006-219-e.html#h.

9 This was only three weeks before he died, as I later discovered. It showed the graciousness and the courage of the man. I think it also showed that honours from academe in any form are too rare for our television practitioners and that they are much appreciated.

10 Here is an instance of one person, an American professor at Michigan State, Lansing, trying to bring some idea to an American audience of academics of what Canadians were doing in television drama during the early 1980s. The rooms were full at the first and subsequent conferences on television drama in contrast to the empty rooms that greeted Canadian academics at the American Popular Culture Association. Over the years I presented the following papers: "Canadian Television Drama: The Defense of the Electronic Border," First International Conference on Television Drama, 1981; "*Blind Faith* and *Pray TV*," Second International Conference on Television Drama, 1982; "*Seeing Things* and *Wojeck*: CBC Variants on the Mystery/Copshow Genre," Midwestern Popular Culture Conference, Bowling Green, Ohio, 1983; "*Seeing Things*: American and Canadian Popular Culture Elements in the Series," National Popular Culture Conference, Toronto, 1983. "*Cariboo Country*: Canada's Response to the American Television Western," Third International Conference on TV Drama, University of Michigan, Lansing, 1983; "The Evolution of *The Beachcombers*-Thirteen Years of a Kidult Comedy," Fifth International Conference on TV Drama, University of Michigan, Lansing, 1985. All of these were turned into publications as one would expect (always think of conference papers as dress rehearsals), but in 1985, after organizing five conferences, the founder of the International Conference on Television Drama, Fred Kaplan, simply burnt out and ended the conferences. Even in America there were too few people to take on the organizational work involved. There was no regularly scheduled international conference on television drama as far as I know after that. On the other hand, e-journals have recently proliferated, providing new grist for the mills.

11 Miller, "Blind Faith and Pray TV."

12 I am probably not the only person who found the makers of programming completely focused on the next project until they hit later middle age, yet paradoxically they were willing to answer all kinds of questions. I do not recall that anyone ever refused to talk to me.

13 For a detailed history of the Learneds and Congress, see Fisher, *75 Years of Congress*.

14 See http://www.filmstudies.ca/ for an up-to-date version of the Film Studies Association's mission and http://www.filmstudies.ca/CJFS_backissuesINDEX.htm for back issues of their journal.

15 de la Garde and Nguyên-Duy, "TVTV: The Television Revolution."

16 Allan, "Directory of Television Series 1952–1982."

17 Martin, "The Classic TV Archive."

18 I note that one of my articles for *The Encyclopedia of Television* appears in almost unaltered form without permission on a "classic tv archive" fan site. When it's out there, it can be poached. It can also live forever, as I found out when someone emailed me to ask me plaintively to bring back *North of 60*—apparently because I had written a message about the program years before on a list now moribund but still archived—just one more learning curve for the radio generation.

19 Winter, "*North of 60*."

20 tvarchive.ca, "Home."

2

(Who Knows?) What Remains to Be Seen: Archives, Access, and Other Practical Problems for the Study of Canadian "National" Television

JENNIFER VANDERBURGH

CANADA HAS A TRADITION of archival and rhetorical support that enables the study of film, but the same is not true of television.[1] This chapter outlines why this is the case and makes the point that pragmatic conditions have prescriptive effects on how (or whether) so-called "national" television studies happen in this country.

In the last few years, the field of ephemeral media studies has expanded to include television archives in the context of digital and social media and, in particular, early attempts to theorize personal VHS collections as informal archives of ephemeral broadcast TV.[2] Two proposed amendments to the Copyright Act have (for the moment) aligned "fair dealing" with citizenship in Canadian public discourse. The Canadian Broadcasting Corporation (CBC) has begun web streaming a selection of programs from current seasons, making them available to download (presumably for a limited time) on iTunes. Michele Byers and I recently co-wrote two articles specifically related to trafficking in covert Canadian television archives (one in an special issue of *Critical Studies in Television* dedicated to TV archives), and a recent book by Marusya Bociurkiw includes a chapter entitled, "The Televisual Archive and the Nation."[3]

I include this context to suggest that this chapter sketches out conditions for Canadian television scholarship about which I (with others) are beginning to pay attention. While my perspective as a TV scholar presumably differs from archivists, industry stakeholders, and experts in copyright and licensing agreements, my research and teaching have been directly affected by the policies I mention that are outside my field. I am therefore invested to understand the complexities at work in these other fields and hope that others will be enticed to join the conversation.

Why the National Frame?

Ubiquitous as the medium of television is in Canada, archived Canadian television content is surprisingly difficult to find. Its idiosyncrasies specific to the medium and the concept(s) of "national industries" (including Canada's, Quebec's, First Nations', and the conflation of "industries" that produce content for television) have challenged attempts to archive, duplicate, and consolidate programs. Ironically, "Canadian-made" television content has been state funded in the hope that it will somehow elicit "cultural"—meaning federal—cohesion.[4] Pragmatic and conceptual factors are to blame for what Peter Urquhart and Ira Wagman in a special issue on television of the *Canadian Journal of Film Studies* call "the poor state of Canada's audiovisual archives."[5] And yet, the problem is not simply with the archival gesture. The problem is in creating *accessible* television archives that might be shared legally and communally in meaningful ways.

Jacques Derrida begins his meditation on "the archive" with the derivation of the term, which means both "commencement" and "commandment." This dialectic means that, while access to archived objects is necessary to begin scholarly work, the presence of an object in the archive is always/already mediated by framing discourses (e.g., by laws; by ideas of what has value; and by how it is catalogued/organized). In Derrida's theory of the archive, "men and gods" define and exercise social order and a sense of history and cultural memory. The archive is a "place from which order is given." It establishes, among other things, what work is possible for the scholar.[6] Taking Derrida's lead, in mapping the current landscape of issues relevant to television archives, I am also asking what this state—pun intended—implies for television scholarship in Canada. What, to follow Derrida's set up, do the gods have in store for the study of Canadian "national" TV?

While many of the same conditions apply for television content produced for or by other broadcasters in Canada (i.e., television that is not expressly "national" federalist), this chapter deals primarily with the concept of national television affiliated with the CBC. I do this not to hold an organization that is in no way mandated to be a public archive unfairly accountable for its lack of being one. Rather, my point is that if any television content should be made accessible to the public, it should be the CBC's. There are pragmatic reasons why.

The cultural pervasiveness of popular, informal digital archives such as YouTube, the content of which spans personal videos to broadcast television content, creates the impression, routinely expressed by my students, that any moving image exists and is accessible on the Web. In a time dominated by the global trafficking, and "television" content inflected by and watched on multiple platforms (e.g., DVD, the Web, and mobile devices), it is tempting to assume that "the national" is a naive frame for archiving television. There are, however, many pragmatic reasons particularly in Canada why "the nation" and national institutions continue to play key roles in determining archival initiatives and access to television content. For decades, there has been talk of television's potential to advance "global" citizenship—its ability to collapse space with the near-simultaneous transmission of images from one place to another, and lay the groundwork to create "global" connections—yet, the nation remains a central presence to television's production, distribution, and reproduction.[7] The television industry in Canada, as in other countries, is heavily subsidized by state-sponsored production funds and tax incentives. Television labour is mediated by national union agreements, which, paired with copyright law and licensing agreements, also decide the terms under which the reproduction and circulation of television programs can occur. Television transmission signals, although incapable of distinguishing national borders, are assigned national territory by state regulatory bodies, such as the Canadian Radio-television and Telecommunications Commission (CRTC). All of these factors dialectically inspire and reinforce a colloquial understanding that television happens in "the national interest."

This same rhetoric justifies support for national archives. One writer in *Archivaria*, the journal of the Association of Canadian Archivists, defines the archive as "society's memory bank." Neatly conflating "state," "nation," and "culture(s)" under the umbrella "society," this moniker captures the archive's precarious balance as a repository and a productive space that determines what and how "we" remember.[8] Strategic decisions about what objects should be preserved and what collections should be formed are exercises in how the archive defines the cultural "we" that it seeks to represent. The archive's ordered searchability is itself a meta-archive organized discursively, in a Foucauldian sense, around commonsensical understandings of historical narratives, themes, and meaning in the interest of "public" knowledge. These archival gestures, perhaps even more than the objects themselves, attempt to represent a sense of "home" in space and time. It is an attempt to unify something contested, what Erin Manning calls the country's "ephemeral territory."[9] Manning also turns to Derrida in "challeng[ing] the naturalization of the concept of home, drawing attention to the fact that 'home' is not a stable entity, but rather another of modernity's constructions."[10] For Manning, the "language of the nation" relies upon Derrida's "ontopology," "an implicit connection ... between ontology (being) and topos (territory, native soil, city, or body)."[11] Following Derrida and Manning, national archives can be read as attempts to provide evidence of this connection between being and placefulness so necessary for cultural nationalism. What follows bears this in mind and considers this rhetoric of the state useful insofar as it might be harnessed to improve the placement of and access to objects needed for television research.

Far from benign repositories or unproblematic iterations of "us," there is still something to be said for the enormous value of national archives. Their ideological association with national heritage maintains state funding and supports collections without obvious commercial potential. This becomes increasingly important as broadcasting institutions prioritize the digitization of their television archives based on the perceived value of images on the international "stock shot" market. Typically in high demand is news footage—indexical signs of "actual" events—that can be repurposed as essential content for documentaries. Less indexical dramatic programming has far less currency in this marketplace.

Canada's national archive, Library and Archives Canada, has considerable potential to serve as a warehouse for television content, yet the institution does not appear to prioritize either gathering or caring for television materials. While it remains the formal Canadian archive most accessible for dramatic television research, the collection is essentially an amalgam of donations, many of them deteriorating in their original formats. I have learned through personal experience that materials listed on their database are not guaranteed to be viewable. I have encountered a few one-inch tapes, pulled from their warehouse, that have completely lost their images. Although frustrating for any research trip, it is tragic for the life expectancy of the collection. In a climate of scarcity for records of Canadian-produced television content, each copy has value and presumably most copies of programs that deteriorate will not be replaced.

Obviously, this is a troubling proposition in many respects, not the least of which is that the state of and priority given to archiving television anywhere in Canada is out of step with the role of television media in Canadian cultural life. Considering that the average Canadian spends an average of twenty-two hours per week watching television, the status of television in any Canadian archive does not represent the importance of television to the lived experience of Canadians.[12] On one hand, the record of Canadian-produced television content dating back to 1952 reflects the familiar story of any ephemeral media, much of it having been lost, unvalued, and/or inadequately cared for, but on the other hand, there are also archival challenges that are specific to the medium of television.

Unwieldy TV

One of the challenges of archiving television lies in the ambiguous definition of a television "text." Broadcast television's ephemerality, theorized famously by Marshall McLuhan in *Understanding Media*, provides a counterpoint to print or even film—platforms which constitute different sensory experiences. For McLuhan, television is not about watching programs, but about entering a televisual landscape. In watching television, a viewer's body integrates, via electricity with the medium and with others, an experience analogous to a shared central nervous system.

Into the 1970s, imagining the phenomenon of broadcast television as continuous "flow" continued with Raymond Williams. For him, the indistinguishablity of programs from advertising, of one channel from another, and of the seamless transition from the end of one program to the beginning of a new one was a strategy that broadcast television used to keep viewers watching for extended periods.[13] Apparently lacking a clear beginning and end, television content provides unique challenges to identifying and archiving "the text." Questions about how to identify the "object" of television have plagued the medium since its inception, and are constantly at issue for archives.

Nam June Paik's 1974 installation *TV Garden*, remounted at the Guggenheim in 2000, embodied another particular challenge to archiving television: the growing volume of material. Evoking a television jungle, 150 working television screens were nestled amid 500 tropical plants. The artwork proposes to challenge viewers' initial impressions of technology by juxtaposing nature with video content played on television sets described as "glowing electronic flowers." As John G. Hanhardt reports, the video's narration "envisioned an expanded future for television ... when *TV Guide* would be as thick as the Manhattan telephone directory."[14] Imagining the proliferation of television content as organic growth in *TV Garden* offers a useful frame through which to engage the problem of archiving television. Television's content, ever changing and ephemeral, is also a physical expanding mass of video, DVD, or digital "objects."

A separate issue from how to intervene in television's flow is how to house it all. Particularly at issue is videotape, now perceived to be a cumbersome format for archives. In small numbers, videotape is not an issue, but I have heard anecdotal reports of large numbers of videotapes, such as large donations of long-running soap opera collections, being refused by archivists due to spatial considerations. Networks rely on the interest of archives as a way in which to offload video from their warehouses. What is not accepted will most likely be destroyed. Years ago, working on an anniversary documentary for a provincial broadcaster, my colleagues and I discovered that the pragmatic issue of reducing the cost of renting warehouse space had landed much of the broadcaster's early video collection curbside.

As a way to reconcile the volume of television content with the physical and financial limitations placed on holdings, many archives have adopted the practice of "representative sampling," collecting only a portion of a program's run. Archives working with this method will perhaps collect one season of a four-season series, or one year of a soap opera that aired for two decades. This time-capsule approach to archiving television is intended to give researchers a taste of a variety of programming without restricting intake to the archive around the notion of a television canon. Critics of this practice say that it endangers the viability of television research and pedagogy by inhibiting researchers from conducting comprehensive and detailed aesthetic analysis of television programs. It becomes difficult to write on patterns, tendencies, style, and discourse if only a fraction of a series can be used as evidence.

Access Denied

Volume and the ambiguous "object" of television are factors that have prescriptive effects on studies. Another factor is access. The spectrum of issues ranges from inadequate access to materials already sitting in archives to the inability of citizens (who are not broadcasters or media makers) to access or purchase duplicate copies of non-archived television. As established above, television scholarship necessitates multiple viewings of a television text, ideally with the option of procuring a duplicate copy so that the scholar's findings can be tested both with colleagues and in the classroom. This section will outline reasons why, barring the odd exception, "national" television is not accessible in this way.

The CBC has a long-standing relationship with Library and Archives Canada (LAC). LAC, unlike the CBC, is mandated to be a public archive for the citizens of Canada, though, like the CBC, its operation reflects federal budgetary allotments. In September 2007, archival access became a topic of public discourse when Library and Archives Canada reduced its hours of operation.

Around the same time, it was announced that the United Church of Canada/Victoria University Archives at the University of Toronto would close in 2008. These gestures consolidated debates about archives and conducting scholarly research in Canada, particularly within the Canadian graduate student research community where debate about access focused on the practical ramifications that reductions in the quantity of time spent with materials in the archive would have on students. Form letters addressed to Parliament expressed concern that the one-hour reduction of the national archive's operation would have a meaningful effect on the quality of graduate student research since the cost of extending out-of-town research trips would be prohibitively expensive.

Limiting access is an obvious way in which archives exercise authority, however inadvertently. Most often, of course, archives limit access without the intent to harm "public knowledge" or the research community. Normally, it is the inadvertent outcome of institutional archives of broadcasters and production companies who have not developed a culture of access. While limiting access in these cases happens for good reasons, it directly affects what is possible for scholarship. Certainly this has been the case with the CBC, presumably Canada's most complete and expertly cared for collection of historical television materials.

Marusya Bociurkiw contends that "the CBC archive is unique [in Canada] in that is offers selective scholarly access to its well-organized holdings"—the keyword being "selective." Considering that the CBC, as Bociurkiw eloquently puts it, "offers a discursive site rich with nationalist speech-acts and identity claims" and that it is also "a state-subsidized" corporation, it would seem its archive would be mandated to be accessible to the "national public," which it presumably serves. This, however, is not the case. As one CBC employee explained to me, the organization considers its archives "production archives," not "public archives." Archival material can be obtained, as stated on the Digital Archives frequently asked questions page, "for professional or commercial use." This is understandable, considering that the institution, plagued as it has been since the 1980s by budget cuts, cannot feasibly be all things to all people. At the moment, the governing institutional logic appears to be that the institution serves the public first by producing or purchasing television content on its behalf, and second, in making the ephemeral gesture of "broadcast," whether via television or the Web.

Both of these broadcast platforms make content accessible to the public for a limited time. Excluding the few shows available for purchase on DVD, or downloaded from iTunes, the only way outside the CBC to get a copy of a program that airs on the CBC (vintage or otherwise) is to purchase the show for commercial reasons (e.g., for broadcast) or to purchase a portion as "stock shot" in order to quote the material in another production, such as a news program or documentary. This is what the CBC means when it says that its archives are for "production" either for its own purposes or to comprise the "commercial" or "professional" content of industrial others. Understandably, therein lies the money.

To my knowledge, the CBC has had only one Corporate Archivist (from 1989 to 1996), a position held by Ernest J. Dick, who had worked previously at what is now Library and Archives Canada. Part of Dick's initial mandate was to canvas the CBC's archive holdings in forty CBC buildings across Canada. This resulted in the document presented to senior management titled, "The Future of CBC's Past: A Review of Archives" (1990). The report reflects what appears to be a long-standing perspective at the CBC that the institution's archives were perceived to benefit the institution for the purposes of, for example, "research for programs" (including content for Newsworld), "Canadianization," and "Retrospectives."[15] Into the 1990s, as the collection was digitized, stock shot revenue would presumably be an increasingly important activity of CBC archives and visual research. That the CBC did not see itself in the business of archives is articulated in the negative findings of the 1990 review that included "difficulty in finding material," disposal of "valuable material," "lack of credibility for CBC archives," and "lack of confidence in archives within CBC" resulting in a "tendency towards 'personal' collections."[16] Since this time, while digitization has presumably consolidated materials at the CBC, and its continued partnership with Library and Archives Canada makes certain materials available for the public, the principle that the CBC's archives are for production, not the public, remains.

The CBC's conceptualization of its archives as a source of visual research (i.e., stock shot) and programming available for professional purchase means that academic researchers are low on the CBC's list of priorities. Funding cuts appear to have prioritized a skeleton staff responsible for managing a mandate divided between caring for its holdings and facilitating visual research for the production of in-house news and current affairs programming. In this institutional climate, understandably, there is not the time, willingness, or physical space to support the research of non-paying citizen researchers from outside the institution. As much as we might gripe about this, one can see how television researchers, in this context, whose questions and practices translate to time spent supervising, locating objects, and monopolizing viewing machines, constitute a distraction to the "real work" happening there. In practical terms, the presence of researchers puts a strain on the department's existing priorities.

The trickle-down effect this is having on television research in Canada should not be underestimated. Since the CBC is a national broadcaster, in theory and policy accountable to "the public," the answer to an outside research request for the purposes of scholarly work is rarely an outright no, but colloquially it is highly discouraged. A colleague who, years ago, wanted to take her graduate students on a tour of the archive reported receiving a response that the CBC did not make a practice of allowing graduate students into the archive. While the academic community can certainly appreciate the reasons why, these informal policies restrict access to material and unwittingly stifle something that presumably is in the CBC's best interest: interest in Canadian "national" television content.

While McLuhan's insistence that "the medium is the message" is presumably partly responsible for de-emphasizing the analysis of television content in Canada, access to television content has undoubtedly been to blame. Except for a few researchers who have built long-standing relationships with the CBC, inadequate access to the archive informs the kind of work on television that can be done. Years ago when I asked the department whether I could make arrangements to watch six seasons of a major television series that was not available at LAC as research for my doctoral dissertation, I was asked whether I wanted to watch it in "real time," meaning, I suppose, whether I would speed up the process by watching the shows in fast-forward. Considering the conditions of the department, this was clearly a justifiable reaction to the amount of time it would take for me to watch the series, monopolizing their space and time. More than this, the comment reveals attendant perceptions of television research in Canada, the implication being that the show I was interested in was not worthy of careful attention and qualitative analysis. This is not an unusual reaction and has historical precedent.

Within the general framework of cultural capital, television is considered fairly lowbrow. Perhaps because of its historical associations in the 1970s and 80s as a scholarly discipline emerging from the technological and regulatory interests of the social sciences and communications, scholars have faced the challenge of relocating television content within other disciplinary frameworks such as film or cultural studies. Increasingly, television studies housed in film departments is becoming interested in textual analysis and aesthetics, which requires detailed attention to television content, the study of which requires multiple viewings. John Caughie, for one, made the landmark case that the analysis of television drama reveals iterations of national culture through aesthetics and discourse.[17] Others argue that television texts are symptomatic of post-national lived experiences.[18] In either context, close analysis of television content is considered worthwhile and necessary, but, in general, perceptions of television's value lag behind.

Returning to my experience at the CBC, I doubt that I would have been asked to "study" a Fellini movie in fast-forward. The precedent already exists to consider film a meaningful object. Television scholarship, likewise, needs its own "slow movement," an appreciation that aesthetic analysis takes time. In this particular instance, I was fortunate enough to bypass the CBC's archive, and benefited instead from the generous loan of informal, personal archives. A complete copy of the series I was interested in, a box of VHS tapes, was kept in the basement storage locker of a son of the series' lead actor. As a result of this serendipity, I was able to watch the series at home, in real time, with the benefit of taking notes based on multiple viewings.

It is no wonder, considering the current state of access to Canadian-produced television programs, that writing on the political economy, the policy, the history of television institutions, and the medium of television far outweighs writing on television content. At a time when television is migrating platforms, it is increasingly difficult to avoid television content as part of our lived experience. Television is perhaps ambient in everyday life, but not for study. It is customary for television to ride the elevator and otherwise comprise an ambient part of everyday life, yet it remains difficult to legally access television content for research purposes.[19] In Canada, this has ramifications not only for research, but also for teaching. Although it is legal to view television programs for research purposes at LAC and, at least in theory, at institutions like the CBC, these programs cannot legally be copied and shown in the classroom because of a historical tangle of issues involving licence agreements and creators who are understandably interested in maximizing financial return for their work. This means that research on most Canadian television cannot be shared with students in the classroom.

Rights to Television

Perhaps more than any other discipline in Canada, television studies is profoundly affected by rights issues. While LAC, for example, allows photocopies to be made of print material, and digital photographs to be taken of objects and art, no replica of a television record can be made or can leave the archive. Essentially, this is because licensing agreements forbid it. The reasons relate to three main concepts. First, the party who duplicates television content must legally hold the rights to the material. Second, showing television content in a public setting is considered a "broadcast" or at least an "additional use," subjecting the broadcaster to compensate the rights holder. While these two points appear straightforward, understanding the final point is to appreciate how fraught the issue of rights to television content has become in practice. This is to say that, in Canada, the production of television content and the negotiation of rights are facilitated by the competing interests of broadcasters, production companies, and a variety of creative and labour interests, where the friction between can muddy the waters. Each of these interested parties has lobby groups and substantial legal representation. At issue is who profits from duplicating and broadcasting Canadian television content. Further complicating the issue is that, at present, the amount of money available for DVD sales, in-class presentation, and Internet distribution may be prohibitively small for historical Canadian television content.

Theoretically, at least, ownership of a Canadian television program is shared jointly between a production company, writers, and performers. The terms of this joint ownership are negotiated in pre-production and held in agreement between the production company and unions, agents representing the interests of writers of text, writers of music, and performers. In Canada, some these unions are the Writers Guild of Canada; the performer's union for English-language recorded media, the Alliance of Canadian Cinema, Television and Radio Artists (ACTRA); and the American Federation of Musicians (AFM).[20] Joint ownership of television content happens only in theory, however, because a production company is required to obtain the rights to the material in order to negotiate its use with a broadcaster. In pre-production, the production company will negotiate agreements with all union members and other creative individuals, either "buying out" the right to their contribution entirely or negotiating rights for a period of time or a particular number of broadcasts in a particular context.

Canadian standard agreements for television have, historically, been based on the broadcast television model where each time a television program is aired it is considered a "performance." As the definition of broadcasting television content expands to include multi-platform outlets beyond "television," such as the Internet, DVDs, and mobile phones, for example, licensing agreements are becoming increasingly more complex. Still, the principle remains that, while a production company retains the rights to the program, it does not own the performances or the rights to the music or the written word used within the program unless these rights are "bought out" or otherwise negotiated at the outset of the production. As a result, broadcasters such as the CBC are required to construct agreements with production companies stating the number of times or length of time that the program will be aired, "performed," or otherwise distributed. The agreement will allow the program's circulation for a period of time, after which another agreement may need to be negotiated.

What this means is that broadcast rights for Canadian television shows expire. If following the letter of the law, in order to broadcast or duplicate a CBC show and license the non-theatrical educational rights for a university classroom, rights would need to be renegotiated with performers and writers of text and music, an enterprise that is prohibitively expensive and presumably complex. The CBC will not agree to sell an individual copy of an old program from their collection for educational use since it would not be worth their while to do so. Presumably this is because it is not financially feasible to procure the rights for the sale of one copy of a program. As a result, it is not possible to get a copy of a CBC program from the CBC that is not otherwise available for sale unless the purpose is for commercial or professional (read: not educational) use.

The CBC no longer itself negotiates what it calls (ironically) its "legacy" programming, which includes a catalogue of shows produced before the mid-1980s. The task of negotiating its back catalogue has been farmed out to Content Media Corporation (London/LA). Cultural nationalists in particular might be surprised to learn the extent to which Canadian television programs produced in the public interest, with public money, are not legally accessible to the public on account of rights and licensing circumstances. The CBC, Canada's public broadcaster, a major producer of in-house television content from 1952 until the 1980s who proclaimed until a recent slogan change, "Canada Lives Here," cannot automatically duplicate or broadcast the dramatic productions it aired during this period. When licensing agreements expire, the rights to the program revert to the production company. After the mid-1980s when CBC began co-producing most of its dramatic content, the concept of "ownership" became increasingly fraught. Whether or not programs like *Wojeck*, *The Beachcombers*, or *Street Legal* should be considered significant as artworks, texts, cultural documents, national iterations, or expressions of lived experience, rights issues are effectively holding culturally significant television programs hostage from academia and (if we want to take the cultural nationalist position) from citizens who paid for their production. These practices have a prescriptive effect on television studies in Canada, since they essentially determine which television programs can be studied and legally brought into the classroom and which shows will become a part of long-term collective cultural memory.

Dramatic programming is most affected by these conditions. In the interest of education and in the spirit of "fair dealing" under the Copyright Act, university instructors have traditionally circumvented lapsed formal licensing agreements for dramatic programming by showing personal copies of material recorded off of broadcast television, usually on deteriorating VHS tapes, which have been replaced by DVDs as the standard media platform at universities. Departments have tended to turn a blind eye to the practice of playing personal copies of shows recorded off-air, as have broadcasters and production companies. Increasingly, however, copyright and licensing agreements are becoming contentious issues at Canadian universities, many of which now have offices dedicated to ensuring that clearances have been obtained. Film and media instructors are often required to have their course syllabi vetted, and at least one department's collection of audio-visual materials was audited for illicit material (meaning non-licensed material).

The current culture of licensing poses a real and significant danger to the study of Canadian television. Fear of being held legally accountable for licence agreements means that instructors teach to what material is commercially available to the consumer—material that has been licensed for educational use. Even if instructors can procure a copy of an unlicensed program for her personal research, it cannot be legally shown in the classroom. This means that television considered significant will not be taught to students.

DVD releases tend to be determined by market forces or distribution deals negotiated at the start of a production, making available what is popular and recent—the former, considering Canada's consumer base, is a particular problem for Canadian television studies. While it is fortunate that *Little Mosque on the Prairie* (CBC/WestWind Pictures), *jPod* (CBC/I'm Feeling Lucky Productions), and *Being Erica* (CBC/Temple Street Productions) are available on DVD, their release is due to licensing agreements for distribution that were negotiated in pre-production, rather than merit or cultural importance. Their presence on DVD assures these series a place on course syllabi at the expense of more culturally significant shows that are not available on DVD. Examples affiliated with the CBC include the longest-running dramatic series produced in Canada, *The Beachcombers*, *Street Legal*, *Wojeck*, *Seeing Things*, *The Friendly Giant*, *Sidestreet*, *Quentin Durgens, M.P.*, *Cariboo Country*, and *Danger Bay*. While owning the right to reproduce a show in perpetuity on a variety of media platforms does not necessarily guarantee it a place within the canon of scholarly, cultural, or consumer memory, it does lay the groundwork. An early Canadian example of a show whose success is attributable to an initial buy-out of distribution rights is the *Degrassi* series (Playing With Time/CBC). Having the rights to the series enabled Playing With Time to engage in perpetual marketing and distribution (on VHS then DVD), which turned the series into a franchise that is recognized by multiple generations of viewers. *Degrassi*'s example demonstrates the potential that procurement of rights has for the long-term cultural success of a show in terms of both market value and cultural memory. If the CBC were to resurrect on DVD what it ironically calls its "legacy" programming—much of which did not achieve syndication or distribution beyond the initial broadcast and is therefore largely forgotten within cultural memory—there would not be, in most cases, the nostalgic appeal to make the case for a DVD release. The first season of the *King of Kensington* is one rare exception of a "legacy" series released on DVD. There are also idiosyncratic examples of licensed Canadian television programs that, although comparatively obscure, have been released on DVD because their rights agreements have been consolidated and procured (e.g., CBC's *The Forest Rangers*). Licensing agreements are effectively determining the canon of Canadian television at universities in a way that does not apply to syllabi related to film, literature, or art. This is particularly dangerous for a medium about which students already have a tendency to think of as disposable and ahistorical. For those who believe that television records patterns, discourses, and expressions of lived experience, it is cause for concern.

In 1996, the Audio-Visual Preservation Trust of Canada (AVPTC) was created as a partnership[21] with a mandate to protect the record of Canadians' "rich and distinctive heritage in moving images and sound."[22] The AVPTC's initiative of "conservation, preservation and public access" deals with the "protection of and access to" Canadian-produced audio-visual material that, in their words, is "fading away," both materially and in the sense of public memory.[23] Its founding document recommends improving access to materials by establishing "a voluntary central production registry system for film, video, radio, television and multimedia works ... linking the existing components such as the Registry of Copyright, Union Catalogue, Film/Video Canadiana and Canadian Heritage Information Network to provide producers, artists, broadcasters, distributors, custodians and users with information needed to facilitate access to the Canadian audio-visual heritage."[24] The notion of an accessible digital registry for television content made possible by Internet architecture is in keeping with a larger discourse, developing both nationally and globally, that relates to the value of sharing "knowledge." In Canada, the Social Sciences and Humanities Research Council of Canada is currently "investigating the challenges, benefits and risks associated with implementing an 'open access' policy that would make publicly funded research results freely available on the Internet to Canadians."[25] Underwriting this national movement to create a forum for accessible "knowledge" is the notion of transparency at the Council, being accountable for how taxpayers' money is spent.

In the transnational context, the International Federation of Television Archives (FIAT/IFTA) is an organization that, since 1977, has been seeking "cooperation amongst television archives" on issues of sharing and preserving materials. Its Television Studies Commission, which has representation from LAC, is addressing practical issues related to "the use of television archive material in scholarly studies and educational environments."[26] A number of developing transnational projects, such as the Internet Archive, BIRTH Television Archive, and LIVE, independent from FIAT, are exploring ways of collaborating and pooling technical support (PrestoSpace), resources, and materials to create digital and freely accessible online archives.[27] While the Internet facilitates the notion of national and international access to material in theory, there are practical reasons why it is not sufficient at this stage to address problems Canadian instructors have bringing television into the classroom. This is because Internet archives in Canada are still bound by licence agreements.

A few years ago, I spoke with an editorial board member and a rights analyst, both of whom worked on CBC's impressive, but now dormant, CBC Digital Archives Project that made over 10,000 video and radio clips from the CBC archives available to view through the Internet.[28] They explained that editorial decisions about what would be included in the online "archive" were based not only on a clip's perceived historical importance or popularity, but also on whether the rights to use it could be negotiated. The project, as a result, is heavy on news and current affairs programming, sports, and variety shows. Difficulties negotiating with one union in particular resulted in dramatic programs having minimal representation, with no more than five minutes of select programs available for use by permission.

While the CBC has a long-standing and often fractious relationship with unions, the case of the Digital Archives Project is instructive in that it foregrounds the complexity of facilitating a legitimate Internet archive. This was something of an obstacle for the AVPTC, who acknowledged that, for example, while "all artists, producers, broadcasters and distributors will be urged to participate" in an Internet registry, it could not mandate participation under current licensing and rights agreements. In 1996, while looking to the future, the AVPTC's founding document asked for the policy it required, stating that Departments of Canadian Heritage and Industry Canada "should take measures for the creation of mechanisms that would both ensure equitable and efficient management of rights (including compensation for the rights holders) and facilitate the use of Canada's audio-visual heritage held by public and private institutions."[29] Following a substantial funding cut in 2008, the trust and its activities were eliminated in 2009.

The CBC's Digital Archives Project does make legitimate access to its sample of television content available for classroom use with one important caveat: as long as the material is streamed live over the Internet from the CBC's website, the instructor has clearance to show the material for educational use. But here I will say something heretical in this time of Web saturation, which is that streamed video, while helpful in theory, is not reliable enough for use in the classroom. Personally, I have witnessed embarrassing moments for students and instructors where server malfunction or software issues have seriously railroaded a class. As an instructor, I want to come prepared for class with a televisual "object" in my possession, be it a DVD or a file saved on a file-sharing key or the hard drive of a computer. Downloading the CBC's digital files to these formats, while technically possible, would breach the licence agreement of their digital archives.

Circumstances for the use of televisual materials for teaching in Canada require teachers and scholars to breech licence agreements. Without legal recourse to obtain material, we (teachers) become our own archivists. Independently, we have developed ways of recording and translating broadcast television into useful formats for teaching and research.[30] There also exist long-standing informal exchange networks among television scholars, allowing material to be shared, bypassing formal archival institutions. Observing this country's history of informal archival practices can, I believe, provide pragmatic answers about what kinds of rights agreements and formal archival gestures we need.

These personal collections of recorded television content, dating back to the time of the VCR, are now invaluable resources. As mentioned, they are also illegal when shown in the classroom, and their deterioration is a source of considerable anxiety for scholars. At a conference I attended a few years ago, lunchtime conversations became a series of doomsday talks about what would happen if teaching tapes were lost or stolen. There would simply be no mechanism to replace them, since technically they were not supposed to exist in the first place. This highlights the tenuous position of the television scholar and television studies at Canadian universities. In a culture where research and teaching go hand in hand, presently television scholars cannot, for the most part, bring their research into the classroom or a conference without contravention of the law. It is not that teachers or university departments are opposed to compensating artists and production companies for the non-theatrical broadcast fees accrued by showing Canadian television content in the classroom—many of these scholars were once performers, writers, or media makers—my point in this chapter is that, at present, there is simply no mechanism to do so.

Conclusion

Returning to Derrida's theory of the archive, the case of Canadian television provides an example of how archives are productive. Whether objects are preserved and made available for teaching determines what scholarly work can be done. For those of us engaged in researching and teaching Canadian television, Canadian archival practices profoundly shape our methods and our work. The nation is an important frame in this circumstance. Following Arjun Appadurai's work on "mediascape" and "ideoscape"—terms he uses to describe a transnational flow of images and ideas that is changing perceptions of identity and nationhood—many scholars now agree that "the national" is becoming less relevant to the experience of media such as television.[31] While viewers might increasingly identify television as a global or transnational experience, in Canada, the nation is still very much on the scene as a regulatory presence whose geography is relevant to negotiating licensing and rights to television content. This is important to keep in mind amid the appearance of global, archival Internet initiatives for television—whether formally international arrangements such as FIAT or informal ones such as YouTube. As Darrell Varga writes of the relevance of analyzing film in the context of the national, "the nation is not simply imagined but lived materially. These material conditions include conditions of labour, social organization and exchange, and access to resources, but also systems of symbolic exchange—cultural interaction, education, and the mass media."[32]

My intention in this chapter has been to map current issues related to Canadian television archives as a way of understanding the role of the national in determining whether television content will be made accessible for learning. While I am skeptical that television archives provide evidence of a "national" memory, I am certain they provide evidence of television. Unfortunately, the rhetoric of cultural nationalism seems to be the discourse of choice required to justify the need for national archives. Whatever the convincing reasons are to preserve television records, clearly our current models in Canada are not adequate. The four features that scholars and teachers require are: skilful preservation of content; the ability to access content; the ability to duplicate content for research purposes; and the ability to legally share content with colleagues and with students in the classroom. One feature cannot be at the expense of others. Television material is accessible to view at LAC, yet it is not an exhaustive or prioritized collection. The CBC's archive is not accessible to researchers. Informal archival practices that obtain recorded television content are not legally admissible in the classroom.

Scholars remain divided about what television content remembers and records, but as the study of content is gaining currency, it is increasingly considered a legitimate discipline in departments at Canadian universities. If there is a central concern underwriting this chapter, it is that the new-found legitimacy for Canadian television studies is in danger if these issues are not resolved around access to television objects and the systemic rights issues that are inhibiting the ability to access and license material for classroom use. Consolidating television materials, as in the registry proposed by the now-defunct AVPTC would be helpful, but it is not essential. What is essential is that instructors and researchers have the ability to view and to share examples of Canadian television that represent the best and most important works, free from the market forces that determine what is released on DVD, and can, as a result, be licensed for classroom use. We can learn a great deal from existing informal archival practices in Canada, where scholars and teachers are devising their own best practices. We should formalize these practices and quickly, because, as an ephemeral medium with vast content, one thing we know about television is that there is so much to lose.

Notes

1 Important collections for film research in Canada include: the Film Reference Library, the National Film Board of Canada, Library and Archives Canada, and collections housed at universities.

2 See, for example, Hilderbrand, *Inherent Vice*; Byers, "The Empty Archive: Canadian Television and the Erasure of History"; and Acland, "The Last Days of Videotape."

3 Byers, "The Empty Archive: Canadian Television and the Erasure of History"; Byers and VanderBurgh, "Trafficking (in) the Archive: Canada, Copyright, and the Study of Television"; Marusya Bociurkiw, *Feeling Canadian*, 35–52.

4 For a general historical introduction to Canada's cultural nationalist approach to television see, for example, Peers, "Broadcasting and National Unity."

5 Urquhart and Wagman, "Considering Canadian Television," 4.

6 Derrida, *Archive Fever*, 1.

7 Marshall McLuhan's concept of the "global village" is an early precedent for thinking about television's capacity to enable transnational connections. For a more recent argument on the benefits of global citizenship or cosmopolitanism that has consolidated considerable debate see Appiah, *Cosmopolitanism*.

8 Dodds, "Provenance Must Remain the Archival Bottom Line," 4.
9 Manning, *Ephemeral Territories.*
10 Ibid., xvii.
11 Ibid., xvi.
12 Statistics Canada's interpretation of data collected between 1995 and 2004 is that the "average weekly hours of television viewing has been relatively stable," ranging from 21.4 to 23.2 hours per week. See Statistics Canada, "Television Viewing."
13 Williams, *Television, Technology and Cultural Form.*
14 Hanhardt, "Case Studies: Nam June Paik, *TV Garden,* 1974."
15 Dick, *The Future of CBC's Past,* 6.
16 Ibid., 6–7.
17 Caughie, *Television Drama.*
18 See, for example, Bociurkiw, who says that the book "attempts to question and denaturalize the workings of Canadian television as a surface for the emergence of nationalism." For Bociurkiw, the "post-national" (a reference to Appadurai) is "important, though not central" to the book (156).
19 McCarthy, *Ambient Television.*
20 See the following websites: http://www.writersguildofcanada.com/; http://www.actra.ca/actra/control/nat_home?menu_id=1; http://www.afm.org/about.
21 Partnership between the Department of Canadian Heritage, CBC/Radio-Canada, Library and Archives Canada, Telefilm Canada, Astral Media, Universal Studios Canada, and the National Film Board.
22 Audio-Visual Preservation Trust of Canada, "Conservation, Preservation and Access," and "Mandate."
23 Task Force on the Preservation and Enhanced Use of Canada's Audio-Visual Heritage, "Fading Away."
24 Ibid., 50.
25 Social Sciences and Humanities Research Council of Canada, "Policy Focus."
26 International Federation of Television Archives, "Television Studies Commission."
27 Internet Archive: www.archive.org/index.php; BIRTH Television Archive: www.birth-of-tv.org/birth/; Video Active: http://devel.videoactive.eu/VideoActive/Home.do;jsessionid=92EF4607ACE399F54C16EAFAAB4E8A8B; LIVE: http://www.ist-live.org/; Presto Space: http://prestospace.org.
28 Canadian Broadcasting Corporation, "Digital Archives Project."
29 Task Force on Preservation, "Fading Away," 50.
30 See Byers and VanderBurgh "Trafficking (in) the Archive."
31 Appadurai, "Disjuncture and Difference," 295–310.
32 Varga, "The Social Production of Place," 240.

Part II

Contexts of Television Production in Canada

3

Television, Film, and the Canadian Star System

LIZ CZACH

THE 2009 RELEASE OF *Trailer Park Boys: Countdown to Liquor Day* (Mike Clattenburg) is the most recent attempt to translate a successful English-Canadian television series into a big-screen triumph. *Countdown to Liquor Days,* like its predecessor, *Trailer Park Boys: The Movie,* follows in the tradition of films based on successful television series or characters, such as *Strange Brew* (Rick Moranis, Dave Thomas, 1983), *Brain Candy* (Kelly Makin, 1996), and *Duct Tape Forever* (Eric Till, 2002). The transfer of *Trailer Park Boys* from television's smaller screen to the bigger screen of the feature film suggests a belief on the part of producers and film financers that popular Canadian television can be channelled into the production of popular—that is, commercially successful—cinema. Central to the adaptation of television series to film is the assumption that the popularity and recognizability of well-known television personalities such as *Red Green*'s Steve Smith, the comedians of the *Kids in the Hall* troupe, or *Trailer Park Boys'* Bubbles, Ricky, and Julian can be relied upon to make the feature film more marketable. As these films illustrate, there is a significant intersection between English-Canadian television and feature film production that presupposes the easy transfer of television personalities to the cinema. Put more concretely, the television celebrity, it is hoped, might be easily translated into a movie star—a figure relied upon to raise the profile of the film and help sell tickets. Studies of Canadian media have not fully examined the intersections of television and film, and in this essay I will consider how television and film production might productively be brought together to better understand the development of a specifically

Canadian celebrity culture, or to put it more ambitiously, a Canadian star system.[1]

In his seminal study, *Stars*, Richard Dyer focuses principally on the Hollywood star system and American stars while acknowledging that his methodology and theorization may be applicable to other cinemas. He notes that the "specificities of these other places where stars are to be found would always have to be respected."[2] Recent studies of non-Hollywood star systems such as Ginette Vincendeau's *Stars and Stardom in French Cinema* (2000), Bruce Babington's *British Stars and Stardom* (2001), and Tytti Soila's *Stellar Encounters: Stardom in Popular European Cinema* (2009), among others, point to the manner in which attention to national and regional specificity in star formation can fruitfully expand our understanding of how stardom works beyond the hegemony of Hollywood. It is precisely this kind of attention to national specificity that I propose in this tentative first step towards outlining the parameters of a Canadian star system. In keeping with Dyer's caution to be respectful of the specificity of place, I will limit the scope of this inquiry to the English-Canadian context with the understanding that Quebec's linguistic and cultural differentiation from both English Canada and the United States has enabled it to foster an enviable homegrown star system.[3] Less apparent, however, may be the necessity of differentiating a domestic English-Canadian star system from the US star system since Canadians have a long history of celebrating the success of their compatriots in Hollywood. From Mary Pickford to Mike Myers and Michael Cera there is a long tradition of Canadians who have attained star status in the United States in what Charles Acland has termed a "star-system-in-exile."[4] Similarly, Thomas Doherty, writing on mockumentaries, has noted how "Canadian SCTV vets [Eugene] Levy and [Catherine] O'Hara [have been] long since annexed as American national treasures."[5] This annexation of Canadian talent into the American star system raises the question of whether a homegrown star system is either achievable or desirable. For example, Oscar-winning director Denys Arcand, discussing his English-language feature film *Stardom* (2000), has suggested that

> we have something against stars and against glamour. Here you have to go outside, become a star there (in Hollywood) and you come back and that's fine. But to grow ourselves a star, we don't like that. We're too puritanical. It's not in our culture. So ask yourself: Why don't we have Canadian stars? It's a question that is often put to me. Well, it's because we don't want any.[6]

Although Arcand's comments accurately characterize a widespread perception that Canada lacks its own star system, they fail to account for the zeal with which Canadians participate in celebrity culture via gossip magazines, celebrity news shows, and so forth. Thus, my guiding concern is not whether, but *how*, an English-Canadian star system might be understood.

Returning to the basic constituents of stardom will help us appreciate how stars are, or are not, produced in the contemporary Canadian context. In his influential work on the origins of the star system, Richard deCordova outlines a shift from the "picture personality" as a performer known to audiences only through his or her onscreen performances to the "star" who is both an onscreen performer but also an off-screen figure, that is, someone whose private life is of public interest. This onscreen/off-screen duality, and the attendant fascination it holds for the public, is formative of the film star phenomenon. Richard Dyer and John Ellis expand on deCordova's work to suggest that the star is fundamentally paradoxical in nature. Both contend that the star is presented as at once ordinary (a person just like you or me) and extraordinary (unlike you or me); as Ellis puts it, the "star image is an incoherent image. It shows the star both as an ordinary person and as an extraordinary person."[7] Furthermore, Ellis suggests that "the basic definition of a star is that of a performer in a particular medium whose figure enters into subsidiary forms of circulation, and then feeds back into future performances."[8] Dyer elaborates upon this system of circulation, outlining how stars are produced not only through films, but also through ancillary support mechanisms such as promotion, publicity, and criticism and commentary on the star's film roles across a range of media texts.[9] Promotion, for example, refers to texts, such as studio press releases or advertising materials that work toward the deliberate creation of a star image, whereas publicity is publicly disseminated material that does not appear to be directly promotional, including news stories, gossip columns, and so forth. Other avenues contributing to star formation include criticism and commentaries, which include film reviews, books or articles, as well as material that may present an interpretation and appreciation of the star as evident in, for example, an obituary. However, the privileged place for the manufacturing of a star's image is, of course, films. In short, these multiple media texts work together to create and disseminate a star image. Hollywood, with its prodigious film output, fan magazines, entertainment shows, and press junkets, illustrates how well the multiple avenues of exposure work to create a star system.

In English Canada, the conditions for generating and circulating a *cinematic* star image as outlined by deCordova, Ellis, and Dyer, has thus far failed to materialize. The low number of features produced yearly does not enable Canadian actors to build up a substantial body of work in feature films. Furthermore, disappointing box-office revenues of Canadian films suggest audiences are not seeing the films that are produced.[10] Promotional mechanisms such as fan magazines, talk shows, and highly anticipated awards shows have also been historically lacking in the Canadian media landscape, with the poor performance of the Genies being the most obvious indicator of meagre public interest. Very little publicity is generated in newspapers or magazines regarding Canadian film actors as there is seemingly little interest in their off-screen lives. And finally, critical commentary on Canadian feature films has been notoriously difficult to sustain, as witnessed by the lack of a single English-language magazine devoted to critical writing on Canadian films since the demise of *Cinema Canada* (defunct in 1989) and *Take One* (which ceased publication in 2006). The multiple mechanisms necessary for producing film stars in Canada have not developed. Considering the presumed absence of an English-Canadian star system, it is thus unsurprising to find little scholarly attention devoted to the phenomenon. When considered within the parameters set out by scholars such as deCordova, Dyer, and Ellis, Canada does indeed seem to lack a star system.[11]

Recent developments in the Canadian media landscape, however, suggest avenues that might help generate promotion and publicity for Canadian actors and films. In her work on the French star system, Ginette Vincendeau has pointed out how the Cannes film festival has helped domestic French cinema. In the Canadian context, events like the Toronto International Film Festival might similarly help to generate some "buzz" around Canadian films and actors. Perhaps more significant is the rise in Canadian-produced celebrity journalism in the form of television shows such as *Entertainment Tonight Canada*, *eTalk*, and *Inside Jam!* as well as a Canadian version of the celebrity-oriented magazine *Hello!* The flourishing of these media outlets ostensibly provides the opportunity to promote and celebrate homegrown productions and generate coverage that could foster the increased recognition of Canadian actors, films, and television programs. The question, however, is how Canadian-centred is Canadian-produced entertainment reporting? Does *Entertainment Tonight Canada* differ significantly from its American counterpart? To date, it seems these programs and magazines have been ineffective in providing significant publicity, promotion, or commentary on homegrown Canadian actors, television series, or films with Canadian content, and unsurprisingly they concentrate instead on Canadians in Hollywood (the aforementioned star-system-in-exile). For example, coverage of events such as the

Toronto International Film Festival focused on asking visiting (predominantly American) stars which designers they were wearing and whether they liked Toronto. While these programs have been ineffective in helping foster a domestic star system, they have been successful in generating new television personalities. For example, *eTalk* hosts Tanya Kim and Ben Mulroney are celebrities in their own right and often better known than many of the Canadian "stars" they report on. Thus, it is unsurprising that Ben Mulroney appears in a cameo on an episode of *Corner Gas* or in the film *The Trotsky* (Jacob Tierney, 2009) playing himself, or that both Mulroney and Kim show up on *The Globe and Mail* television columnist John Doyle's "Most Irritating Canadian" list, a tongue-in-cheek response to the CBC's *The Greatest Canadian* (2004). While showing up on a list of disliked Canadians is perhaps not the most flattering form of celebrity, it does nonetheless indicate their level of recognition. A lifestyle piece in the third issue of *Hello!* on *ET Canada* host Rick Campanelli further illustrates the celebrity of television hosts.[12]

If Canada does have the semblance of a star system, it is one that has been developed and sustained through television. Historically the most watched Canadian television has been public affairs and sports programming, and thus unsurprisingly some of our best-known celebrities are personalities from nonfiction programming. As Aniko Bodroghkozy has argued: "To the extent that the country has a star system, it is peopled with journalists, interviewers, and other public affairs/documentary personalities."[13] She goes on to note that Knowlton Nash, Barbara Frum, Lloyd Robertson, Sandy Rinaldo, Peter Mansbridge, David Suzuki, Pamela Wallin, Hana Gartner, and Moses Znaimer are our most recognizable "celebrities," truly indigenous celebrities as most of them would be unrecognized south of the border.[14] Bodroghkozy's list could be updated to include more current television personalities such as Rick Mercer, George Stroumboulopoulos, and Don Cherry. The type of celebrity that Canadian television has helped develop is clearly demonstrated in the cameo appearances on the popular CTV series *Corner Gas* (2004–9). Politicians, television hosts, and sports figures regularly appeared on the show, including former news anchor Pamela Wallin, handyman Mike Holmes, hockey player Darryl Sittler, and two prime ministers: Paul Martin and Stephen Harper. Given the absence of domestically produced movie stars, personalities produced through television (hosts, anchors) as well as regularly seen on television (politicians, sports figures) are the closest thing English Canada has to a star system.

The clearest attempt to account for the specific kind of televisual celebrity that Bodroghkozy describes is outlined in John Langer's 1981 article "Television's

'Personality System'" in which he differentiates between television's production of personalities and cinema's production of stars. All television genres, Langer argues, whether they are fictional or factual, are organized around a central persona, the television personality. In factual programming the central persona is usually the figure delivering the news or hosting a newsmagazine, and in a Canadian context personalities such as Peter Mansbridge, Hana Gartner, or Lloyd Robertson quickly come to mind. Langer contends that dramatic or comedic programming is similarly organized around a central character and points to Archie Bunker from the popular sitcom *All in the Family* as evidence of this. Furthermore, this focus on the central persona or television personality is apparent in the numerous shows named after principal leads: *McCloud*, *Columbo*, *Rhoda*, and so forth. This trend of naming programs after their central personalities is equally apparent in Canadian shows such as *Wayne and Shuster*, *The Red Green Show*, *Rick Mercer Report*, *Being Erica*, and *Republic of Doyle*. Even television commercials construct personalities to sell products, such as the long-running and well-known Maytag repairman. Canadian television personalities from commercials include "Joe" of Molson's wildly successful "I Am Canadian" advertising campaign and Ted the Canadian Tire Guy.[15] Langer's assertion that television produces personalities is well founded, but what is it about television's specificity as a medium that produces personalities and not stars?

For Langer, the television personality reaches the viewer in a fundamentally different way from the cinematic star. Television is a more intimate and immediate medium than cinema, since it is enjoyed in the privatized domestic space of the home, whereas cinema involves planning, going out, and viewing in public. Television personalities appear with regular predictability either daily (in the case of news and talk shows) or weekly (with dramatic programming or newsmagazines), and these routinized appearances further augment the sense of intimacy and familiarity that audiences feel towards television personalities. Television personalities seem accessible, whereas stars seem distant and remote since they appear on screen only once or twice a year. Langer summarizes these differences with a set of distinguishing terms that pertain to the star/personality systems: distance/intimacy, remoteness/immediacy, exceptionality/familiarity, and extraordinariness/ordinariness. The last of these, extraordinariness/ordinariness, is integral in distinguishing between television personalities and cinematic stars. As Langer notes:

> Whereas stars emanate as idealizations or archetypal expressions, to be contemplated, revered, desired and even blatantly imitated, stubbornly

> standing outside the realms of the familiar and the routinized, personalities are distinguished for their representativeness, their typicality, the 'will to ordinariness' to be accepted, normalized, experienced as *familiar*.[16]

Langer's characterization of the idealized cinematic star and its stark dichotomy with the ordinariness of the television personality is reminiscent of Edgar Morin's positioning of the star as an ethereal, otherworldly creature of adoration that, as Morin puts it, "live[s] at a distance, far beyond all mortals."[17] The ordinary television personality is distinct from the cinematic star who is both ordinary *and* extraordinary. Thus, television, Langer contends, is only capable of producing personalities and not stars.

In the decades since the publication of Langer's essay, the media landscape has dramatically altered. The rise of "quality television" and the post-network era, DVDs, the Internet, video on demand, and illegal downloads have irrevocably shifted the televisual landscape. Recent reconsiderations of Langer's seminal essay have argued that the "television personality" is too restrictive a category and has perhaps outlived its usefulness. Key to these criticisms is that Langer has cast his net too wide in covering all types of television appearances as well as all fictional and non-fictional characters within the broad category of the television personality. James Bennett differentiates the kinds of performances television produces, suggesting that there are categories within the television personality, such as the televisually skilled performer who is adept at presenting on television and the vocationally skilled performer who has a specific skill set such a cook, gardener, or handyman.[18] While these further distinctions in the types of television personalities are productive, more pertinent to my discussion here is Deborah Jermyn's examination of Sarah Jessica Parker's role as Carrie Bradshaw in the HBO television series *Sex and the City*. Jermyn convincingly argues that Parker's image has been articulated through the paradoxical construction of the extraordinary/ordinary paradigm usually reserved for cinematic stars. Like the cinematic star, Parker's private life gets reported on in the media and her star image is presented as both ordinary (wife and mother) as well as extraordinary (glamorous fashion icon). However, rather than argue that Parker is solely a television star, Jermyn is attentive to the way that SJP started on stage and then moved from television to film and back again. As Jermyn notes, "All of this points to a fluidity increasingly common in contemporary stardom where movement between the two media appears to be burgeoning and where *television*, rather than film, may operate as the primary mechanism in bestowing A-list status.[19] This insight speaks directly to the English-Canadian context, as it appears that television is the primary mechanism for generating possible stardom whereas film productions operate as a secondary support, or ancillary mechanism. Whereas the traditional cinematic star study approaches of both Ellis and Dyer consider television as a support to the main function of film stardom, Canada provides an ideal case study in how this hierarchy might be inverted to highlight the role television plays in the careers of actors who traverse both media.

A closer look at the career of Paul Gross illustrates how film and television roles intersect in the development of possible stardom in the English-Canadian context. One of Canada's most recognizable actors, Gross recently appeared in a small cameo as an actor playing a Mountie in the feature film *Barney's Version* (Richard J. Lewis, 2010). This appearance makes a tongue-in-cheek intertextual reference to Gross's best-known role as the earnest Mountie Benton Fraser on the television series *Due South* (1994–99). That *Barney's Version* would make an intertextual reference to a *television series,* alongside cameos by auteurs such as Atom Egoyan and David Cronenberg, indicates the degree to which Gross's constable is considered identifiable to audiences, while minimizing distinctions between Canadian television and film (*Barney's Version* after all is a film about a television producer). Although *Due South* had a somewhat complicated production history, it is significant as one of the first Canadian-produced television series to air on an American network, and although it never became a huge hit in the United States, it was popular in Canada and had a devoted fan base. *Due South* reruns continue to be shown on cable, all four season are available on DVD, and the series cemented Paul Gross's popularity. When producer Robert Lantos set out to make what he hoped would be the most commercially successful English-Canadian film ever made, *Men with Brooms* (Paul Gross, 2002), he counted upon Paul Gross to translate his television appeal to the big screen. Gross not only starred in *Men with Brooms,* but he also wrote and directed the film. Following this, Gross appeared in a number of film roles, made-for-television movies, followed by the television series *Slings and Arrows* (2003–6), before again tackling the roles of writer/director/actor in the 2008 period war piece *Passchendaele.* He then returned to television to play a lead role in the short-lived American series *Eastwick* (2009–10) and subsequently starred in the Canadian film *Gunless* (2010). In an interesting inversion of the phenomenon I described at the outset of this chapter in which television shows are translated to the big screen, the CBC recently aired the first season of the television series *Men with Brooms*—based on the film. The translation of the film to a television series again illustrates the interplay between television and film. In the *Men with*

Brooms TV series, Gross reprises his role as Chris Cutter but his appearance takes the form of a voice-over narrator rather than as a regular cast member. If stardom, as Ellis noted, relies on the star entering into subsidiary forms of circulation that feed back into future performances, these forms need not be media-specific. Why should television performances not feed back into future film performances and vice versa?[20] The career of Paul Gross illustrates how stardom may rely precisely on the feedback and crossover between television and film.

The career of actor Fred Ewanuick offers another example of how television and film performances are mutually interdependent in both formulating an actor's persona and contributing to his or her potential stardom. Ewanuick has produced a substantial body of work in both Canadian television and film productions in a relatively short time. Best known as the town idiot Hank Yarbo on the successful CTV comedy *Corner Gas* (2004–9), Ewaniuck also appeared as Nick Papathanasiou in another CTV comedy, *Robson Arms* (2005–8), and currently stars as Dan in *Dan for Mayor* (2010–).[21] In addition to these regular television characters, Ewanuick has performed in numerous films: *The Delicate Art of Parking* (Trent Carlson, 2003), *Young Triffie's Been Made Away With* (Mary Walsh, 2006), and *Black Eyed Dog* (Pierre Gang, 2006). In the last of these, Ewanuick plays a supporting role that further illustrates how performances in Canadian film and television feed into each other. The film is set in a small town on the Miramichi River and features a down-on-her-luck waitress struggling to deal with the myriad of problems that face her: a violent ex-boyfriend, a mother with mental illness, a distant father, and so forth. Ewanuick appears in the film as a small-town cop. Jason Anderson, reviewing the film in *The Globe and Mail*, was critical of the film's inability to construct any genre coherency. He notes, "The appearance of *Corner Gas*'s resident doofus, Fred Ewanuick, as a cop is equally incongruous, seeing as *Black Eyed Dog* has none of the sitcom's affection for small town existence."[22] This comment illustrates how Ewanuick's close association with his Hank character from *Corner Gas* is read back into his role in *Black Eyed Dog,* underscoring how television and film appearances work in tandem. Additionally, Ewanuick's role as Hank is reminiscent of his role in the 2003 mockumentary *The Delicate Art of Parking* (Trent Carlson, 2003). In that film Ewanuick plays a somewhat dim-witted parking cop who has trouble asserting his authority and is run over roughshod by his fellow traffic cops and disgruntled ticketed car owners. Ewaniuck is, to a degree, being typecast, but whereas typecasting has traditionally referred to the repeated casting of actors in similar roles across different films, he is being typecast in his roles in both television and film, the performances in each medium working to reinforce the characters in the other. The regularity of his screen characters across a range of television and film performances not only works to construct a consistency in his screen persona but also increases his recognizability, contributing to his potential stardom.

If audiences recognize Paul Gross in his cameo in *Barney's Version* and chuckle at the intertextual reference to his *Due South* character, or if reviewers note the similarities between Ewanuick's character in *Corner Gas* and his role in *Black Eyed Dog,* does this mean these actors are stars? In the interplay between television and film with an emphasis on television as the primary mechanism in bestowing stardom in Canada, is recognition of actors who moved back and forth between film and television sufficient for stardom? At present, English-Canadian "stars" like Paul Gross and Fred Ewaniuck might be best understood as having revitalized Richard deCordova's category of the "picture personality." To reiterate, Richard deCordova characterizes the "picture personality" as an actor who was primarily known to audiences through his or her performances in films. Extra-filmic discourse in magazines, newspapers, lobby materials, and so forth was limited to the onscreen performer, and any effort by fans and the audience to assert the personality's real-world identity was referred back to their performances in film by the producers, distributors, and press. Diane Negra has productively revisited the picture personality to suggest the manner in which it might be mobilized to understand the careers of contemporary actors.[23] In her analysis of the "indie queen" Parker Posey, Negra suggests a form of "niche stardom" that bears much in common with the picture personality of the 1910s in that there is little discourse on the actor's private life and the actor becomes indistinguishable from his or her roles. It is precisely this kind of contemporary version of the picture personality that is currently evident in Canada. However, unlike the picture personality of the 1910s that was recognized from film to film, the contemporary picture personality is *recognized across various media texts*: television series, theatrical films, movies of the week, and so forth, but little about the off-screen "real" life of the personality is known. Any off-screen information or appearances are used to feed back into the onscreen image. This symbiotic relationship between character and actor is most clearly evident in the case of the *Trailer Park Boys* films and television series in that the actors who play Ricky, Julian, and Bubbles never make promotional appearances out of character. As Negra points out, "just as in an earlier era of picture personalities, publicity and promotional coverage operate to heighten the power of onscreen characterization by endowing it with the status of reality rather than supplementing it through knowledge of the performer's offscreen identity."[24] In the case of the *Trailer Park Boys*, codes of realism are established in the film's mockumentary format and further heightened through the collapse of character and actor. A trailer for *Trailer Park Boys: The Movie* satirizes the notion that anyone other than Ricky, Julian, or Bubbles could portray them in the feature film. The promo depicts Ricky, Julian, and Bubbles auditioning a series of actors for the film and ends with Bubbles's realization that "We're gonna have to play ourselves, boys." Julian agrees, noting: "These people are just awful." The trailer makes clear that no one other than the original Trailer Park Boys could play the characters. Similarly, it is difficult to imagine anyone other than Rick Moranis and Dave Thomas playing the McKenzie brothers or another actor taking on Steve Smith's role of Red Green. These contemporary picture personalities collapse, to one degree or another, the distinction between actor and character.

Revitalizing deCordova's picture personality as a contemporary formation within a media landscape that includes television, film, and the Internet, among other media venues, holds suggestive possibilities for how screen personas and personalities emerge in the English-Canadian context without establishing a full-fledged star system. For the time being, in lieu of stars, contemporary picture personalities are produced with a degree of recognizability such that audiences may be able to identify "that guy from *Due South*" or "that doofus from *Corner Gas*" when either Gross or Ewanuick cross over from one medium to the other. In the interplay between film and television our most recognizable actors are contemporary picture personalities known to us through their various screen performances, while their names and the details of their off-screen private lives, the constituents of stardom, continue to remain elusive.

Notes

1 In a special issue of the *Canadian Journal of Film Studies* on the intersections of film and television, editors Urquhart and Wagman suggest that "rather than treating film and television as separate entities, never to be touched by each other's influence, much could be gained by bringing the two into conversation with each other, to examine the sites were film and television appear to cross paths." Urquhart and Wagman, "Considering Canadian Television," 4.

2 Dyer, *Stars*, 3.

3 As Patrick Huard, co-star of the popular film *Bon Cop, Bad Cop* (Erik Canuel, 2006), puts it: "We have this weird star system in Quebec—weird because it's a small market, but everyone does know the stars here. The actors, the comedians, and the directors are getting paid attention. It's because of our television shows and newspapers

and everything; it's always the local artists who get the big part of the coverage." Quoted in Marchand, "Quebec Fans' Loyalty." Also see Dickinson, "Being at Home with Roy Dupuis and Pascale Bussières."

4 Acland writes: "There is a *star-system-in-exile*, as Canadian spectators watch local heroes in U.S. film and television, which both links and differentiates Canadian spectatorship to and from U.S. cinema." Acland, *Screen Time,* 191.

5 Thomas Doherty, "The Sincerest Form of Flattery."

6 Kirkland, "Stardom Slips."

7 Ellis, "Stars as Cinematic Phenomenon," 304.

8 Ibid., 303.

9 Dyer, *Stars*, 60–63.

10 The poor performance of English-Canadian films is often discussed and well documented in Canadian media studies and policy. As Acland has succinctly pointed out: "Canadian film's absence has an unusual presence in the popular imaginary." Acland, "Screen Space," 2.

11 For example, André Loiselle's inquiry into the career of Canadian actor, director, and writer Don McKellar suggests that he is a cinematic persona rather than a cinematic star. See Loiselle, "The Radically Moderate Canadian."

12 "Rick Campanelli," 78.

13 Bodroghkozy, "As Canadian as Possible," 575.

14 Ibid., 587n38.

15 For further analysis of Molson's "I Am Canadian" campaign see Wagman, "Wheat, Barley, Hops, Citizenship," 77–89. Although well-known, Ted the Canadian Tire guy was not necessarily well liked. The personality was parodied on *The Rick Mercer Report* and tied for first place (with Ben Mulroney) on John Doyle's Most Irritating Canadian List. Canadian Tire retired Ted and the campaign in 2006.

16 Langer, "Television's 'Personality System,'" 185; original emphasis.

17 Morin, *Stars*, 9.

18 Bennett, "The Television Personality System," 34.

19 Jermyn, "Bringing Out," 81; emphasis in original.

20 Doty has addressed this question in relationship to the production of Lucille Ball's star image through television and film. See Doty, "The Cabinet of Lucy Ricardo," 3–20.

21 It is interesting to note that Ewanuick is not the only television actor to appear simultaneously in at least two series. Gabrielle Miller also appeared in both *Corner Gas* and *Robson Arms,* while John Cassini was a regular cast member in both *Robson Arms* and CBC's *Intelligence* (2006–7). This suggests that not only appearances across film and television but appearances in more than one television series may play a significant part in star production.

22 Anderson, "Black Eyed Dog."

23 Negra, "'Queen of the Indies,'" 71–75.

24 Ibid., 74.

4

Producing Aboriginal Television in Canada

Ostacles and Opportunities

MARIAN BREDIN

TELEVISION PRODUCED BY and for Aboriginal peoples is a new content stream within the rapidly diversifying Canadian industry. Aboriginal television is still at a formative stage but gaining strength and momentum with the creation of the Aboriginal Peoples Television Network (APTN). Launched in 1999, APTN has built a presence in the Canadian television landscape and generated the development of new Aboriginal programming from across the country. Moving into its second seven-year licence term, the network continues to establish cultural and economic roots within Aboriginal communities and cultivate a small but significant non-Aboriginal viewership.[1] Before the creation of APTN, there was no national outlet for Aboriginal television in Canada and relatively little incentive for mainstream networks to acquire or develop information or entertainment programming that reflected the nation's Indigenous peoples. Aboriginal television created before 1999 was linked closely to regional Native broadcasters in the north, much of it produced for remote communities in Aboriginal languages. The introduction of a new national network triggered an unprecedented need for new programming.

Managing this initial increase in demand for Aboriginal content and securing its supply from independent producers presents some challenges for APTN as it takes its place in the Canadian television industry. Focusing on the relationship between the network and Aboriginal producers, this chapter explores the political economy of Aboriginal television. It considers key obstacles and opportunities in Aboriginal television production arising from the structure of Canadian television financing and the complex nature of broadcast licence agreements. It analyzes features of APTN's mandate, membership, and non-profit structure that sometimes conflict with the needs of independent television content production. Emerging First Nations television involves the adaptation of existing genres and formats and the creation of new ones as Aboriginal production capacity grows. These processes are illustrated by discussing programming strategies from APTN's early seasons, surveying key new Aboriginal production companies and partnerships in the Canadian television industry, and considering potential future trends and directions for APTN and its production partners. This chapter focuses primarily on the emerging Aboriginal television production industry, touching tangentially upon those policy trends that first triggered and then shaped changing conditions for Aboriginal television producers in Canada.

Finally, this chapter traces developments in Aboriginal television drama with reference to specific series, including *Moccasin Flats,* broadcast on APTN and Showcase in three seasons (2003–6), and *Hank William's First Nation,* carried on APTN for its debut season in 2007. The production histories of these two programs follow a similar trajectory from their respective origins in an innovative television drama workshop and a feature film, which both garnered enough critical acclaim and audience interest to lay the groundwork for later creation of the two series and broadcast agreements with APTN. While these programs also share textual similarities in their exploration of the daily experience of life in Aboriginal communities, they are produced by two quite different companies, one Aboriginal-owned and the other not. A comparison of these programs and the conditions of their production raises key questions about the constitutive elements of Aboriginal content.

Development of APTN Programming since 1999

In August 2005, APTN had its licence renewed by the Canadian Radio-television and Telecommunications Commission (CRTC) for a second seven-year term, with the commitment to continue to bring Aboriginal perspectives to Canadian television viewers. In the nine years since its launch, APTN has shifted from a heavy reliance on programming acquired from national public, provincial educational, and federally funded regional Native television broadcasters, to its current role in generating a significant supply of new, independently produced Aboriginal programming. The existence of APTN has triggered an important cultural and economic diversification in the domestic television production industry in the form of emerging Aboriginal-owned film and television production companies. Rising demand for Aboriginal content in the first decade of APTN's operation has had the same impact on the Aboriginal production industry that CRTC regulations requiring domestic content on Canadian networks has had on the wider industry since these regulations were implemented in the 1970s. One important difference is that while the Canadian commercial networks manage to air only between 50 and 60 per cent Canadian content, APTN airs more than 80 per cent Canadian and Aboriginal content.[2] The regulatory tools that helped build a Canadian television production industry have had a similar and possibly even greater impact in the Aboriginal context. While commercial networks like CTV and Global rely on a financial model that collects Canadian advertising revenue from rebroadcasting US drama and entertainment programming, APTN functions as a hybrid non-profit public network with a specialty-television funding model. Less dependent on ad revenue and imported content, APTN uses its social and cultural mandate and public service objectives as an indirect economic trigger for Aboriginal cultural production.

The content screened on APTN today has some of its origins in Canadian Native broadcasting policy and Aboriginal cultural activism throughout the second half of the twentieth century. A brief history of APTN's origins in northern Native television and its evolution from its predecessor Television Northern Canada (TVNC) is essential to understanding the current conditions and contradictions in the Aboriginal production industry. More than thirty years of broadcasting history and video production in the north and in Native communities have been skilfully traced by Lorna Roth, Valerie Alia, and Michael Evans,[3] among others. In these accounts, APTN's origins are closely linked to regional Native broadcasters supported by a federal program called Northern Native Broadcast Access Program (NNBAP). The thirteen groups supported under NNBAP are variously referred to as Native communication societies and as northern Native broadcasters. Though not all of them actually hold or held broadcast licences, all have received federal funds to produce radio and/or television content since 1984. According to the Department of Canadian Heritage's 2003 evaluation of NNBAP, "thirteen NNBAP-funded societies broadcast in 20 or more languages, plus English and French. The Aboriginal audience north of the Hamelin Line is now estimated at 500,000 people in 423 target communities ... Nine groups produce television (although only seven are funded under NNBAP for this purpose). Total original production is 27 hours per week, or 1404 hours per year. This has nearly doubled since 1986. Of the seven organizations funded by NNBAP for television production, six produced 50% or more of their programming in Aboriginal languages."[4] Today most of the Aboriginal-language programming seen on APTN[5] is produced by one of these nine NNBAP groups. It is important to note that APTN receives little or no direct public funding for this content, but purchases the completed programming from the regional Aboriginal producers.

Originally, each of the Native communication societies made its own arrangements with regional, provincial, and national radio and television channels to carry programming to the communities they served. These individual arrangements were notoriously unstable and did not provide optimal scheduling for Aboriginal content. The NNBAP societies and their constituent communities were at the mercy of distributors like Cancom, CBC, and TVO, for whom Aboriginal programs were not always a priority. Northern television producers successfully lobbied for a dedicated satellite channel to carry these programs across the north, and TVNC was licensed in 1992 for this purpose. While TVNC did have a CRTC broadcasting licence, it was primarily a distributor of NNBAP programs. Unlike APTN, TVNC never had its own production funds and it could not use its licence to generate new or independent programming beyond that produced by the existing federally sponsored groups.[6] In effect, the NNBAP members of TVNC were caught in a system of finite and, in the 1990s, shrinking government resources. This was a "parallel" Aboriginal system, marginal to the new kind of broadcaster incentives and production funds being developed for the larger Canadian television industry.

During the 1990s, a number of forces contributed to the policy agenda for a truly national and genuinely independent Indigenous peoples' television network. In 1991, the new Broadcasting Act recognized the special place of Aboriginal people and the need for programming that reflects Aboriginal cultures in the Canadian broadcasting system "as resources became available." In 1993, TVNC argued that a third national public television service owned and operated by Aboriginal people would address this objective.[7] In 1996, the final report of the Royal Commission on Aboriginal People devoted considerable attention to the role of media in representation of and by Aboriginal people and recommended that the CRTC establish support mechanisms for Aboriginal broadcasting.[8] At the same time First Nations in southern Canada were calling for meaningful access to radio and television networks on a level comparable to that in the north. In 1998, the members of TVNC and an advisory group of southern Aboriginal media producers went forward with an application for a national network that would serve a core audience of Aboriginal people but that would address a non-Native audience as well.

In February 1999 the CRTC approved a licence for APTN with precedent-setting mandatory carriage on basic cable, while authorizing the collection of 15 cents a month per subscriber. APTN launched on September 1, 1999, from its headquarters in Winnipeg. It now has presentation centres in Yellowknife, Whitehorse, and Iqaluit and newsrooms in Ottawa, Yellowknife, Toronto, Halifax, and Vancouver.[9] The cable subscriber fee was raised to 25 cents upon licence renewal in 2005. This fee, collected from almost ten million households, gives APTN an essential financial independence. Cable fees generate more than $27 million in guaranteed annual income for the network, supplemented with $1.5 million in advertising revenue.[10] While there remains a general public misconception that APTN is largely supported by government grants, in fact the public indirectly supports the service through cable subscriptions.[11] Despite its reliance on the cable "specialty channel" financing model, most observers agree that APTN is firmly situated within the public broadcasting universe. The House of Commons Standing Committee on Canadian Heritage identified APTN as a national, speciality, not-for-profit, public broadcaster, along with two others (excluding the CBC and its channels): Vision TV and Cable Public Affairs Channel (CPAC). The common elements of these three public service broadcasters are national reach, speciality model funding, and their non-profit objectives.[12] These networks, along with the provincial educational broadcasters and community television, constitute the realm of not-for-profit "third-sector" television in Canada. APTN might be seen as an example of the diversification of this type of alternative public service television, with strong links to its audience and the communities it serves, yet independent of the vagaries of government funding and free of direct political control by either the Canadian state or Aboriginal political institutions.

In closing this condensed history of the origins of Aboriginal television, it must be reiterated that APTN has not replaced or displaced the northern Native broadcasters, although the relation between the NNBAP groups and APTN is evolving in new ways. As the NNBAP program evaluators argue: "The broadcast production and distribution supported by the [NNBAP] programs has been extremely successful. Aboriginal languages and cultures are being documented and transmitted through media, several hundred Aboriginal broadcasters and ex-broadcasters have developed the skills and knowledge to play leading roles in their communities, regions and nationally, and news and information are readily available to the Aboriginal public through their own media."[13] Today, NNBAP producers remain an essential part of the Aboriginal television industry, especially in their vital use of Native languages and their direct links to northern Native communities. Their goals are cultural and social rather than strictly commercial, but they provide important economic incentives for local Aboriginal communities to participate in television production. Many Aboriginal media producers, trained in the northern Native communications societies, now work as independent film or television producers; some have moved to APTN or have gone on to work at national media outlets like the NFB, CBC, or commercial networks. For APTN, the northern Native broadcasters produce current affairs programming, documentary series, and magazine-style programs on regional political, social, and cultural issues, but not higher-cost drama or comedy programming. Examples include *Nunavimmiut*, produced in Inuktitut by the Inuit Broadcasting Corporation, which covers current news and events as well as documenting traditional cultural practices. *Haa Shagoon*, in its ninth season on APTN, is produced by Northern Native Broadcasting Yukon in several Yukon Aboriginal languages with a more consistent focus on traditional topics and interviews with elders. These programs are popular in communities and regions where specific Aboriginal languages are spoken, but are not yet regularly broadcast with subtitles or in English or French versions. In an effort to broaden its production base for Aboriginal-language programming, ATPN has launched a new documentary series called *Voices of the Land*, commissioned from various independent producers or co-production partnerships. Produced in a variety of languages including Cree, Innu, Inuktitut, and Michif, these documentaries are subtitled in English.

In its first few years of operation, APTN relied heavily on NNBAP programming and existing "shelf product" from Canadian public, provincial, and commercial networks. This strategy allowed the network to provide interim Aboriginal content while new television series were developed and produced by independents. APTN built on this base with its own in-house current affairs programming, launching *InVision* in April 2000, a weekly phone-in program called *Contact* shortly after, and the biweekly broadcast of *APTN National News* in October 2002. Today APTN broadcasts two daily news shows and has news bureaus in ten regions of Canada. *Contact* is a live, weekly national phone-in program designed to "tackle the issues from a grassroots perspective and discuss what it means to be Aboriginal in the 21st century."[14] The program explores a variety of topical issues in Aboriginal politics and hosts discussions with Aboriginal experts and ordinary community members. *Contact* topics in the last five seasons have included residential schools, the role of the Internet in Aboriginal communities, a town hall on the proposed First Nations Governance Act, the role of non-Aboriginal people in Native spiritual ceremonies, and the Ipperwash Inquiry in Ontario. Weekly debates have covered everything from education to casinos, from federal funding formulas to crack and meth addictions among Aboriginal people. The broadcast discussion among the host, guests, and callers is complemented by an online forum based on a topical question and posted comments.[15] As an example of the current affairs genre, *Contact* is distinguished by the high degree of representation from Aboriginal people and extensive participation by callers and online posters from across the country in Aboriginal and non-Aboriginal communities.

Along with the launch of its ambitious news and current affairs programs, APTN began to acquire new content in several other genres. In its second season, the network received more that 1,000 proposals from independent Aboriginal producers and from these launched twenty new shows.[16] These included such long-term successes as *Long House Tales* and *Seventh Generation* for children and youth, *Venturing Forth*, *Cooking with the Wolfman*, and *First Music and Arts* to address a range of adult interests and tastes. In subsequent years APTN has made major commitments to develop and acquire programs from independent Aboriginal production companies. The process of generating programming proposals and providing broadcast fees to producers has triggered a significant growth in all areas of Aboriginal media production in Canada.

APTN's Impact on the Aboriginal Television Production Industry

By mid-2001 APTN was broadcasting 1,200 hours of original first-run Aboriginal programming annually. Broken down by sources these included 30 per cent from NNBAP contributors, 30 per cent from Aboriginal independents, 15 per cent from Indigenous television producers in other countries, and 25 per cent from other public and commercial Canadian television producers.[17] In its licence renewal application, APTN committed to raise the amount of programming (apart from news, current affairs, and sports) acquired from independent producers to 80 per cent. The network also committed to raise the fees paid to independents as a means of improving the quality of programming and to spend more money on program development. APTN's licence renewal application promised "the expenditure of more funds on the program development phase, which is critical to the maintenance and growth of the Aboriginal production community, and to the continuing refinement of programming concepts for national, Aboriginal television which is, after all, a new and largely unexplored medium."[18] The economic impact of the 30 per cent of APTN content currently acquired from non-NNBAP Aboriginal independents can be estimated from the almost $12 million value of APTN's 2006 film and television program rights.[19] If 30 per cent of this amount was spent on broadcast licence agreements for independently produced programs, APTN channelled about $3.6 million in licence fees to Aboriginal producers. If, on average, licence fees are assessed at about 30 per cent of production costs, these Aboriginal production companies raised the remaining 70 per cent of their budgets from other sources. By this relatively conservative estimate, APTN triggered another $12 million in independent Aboriginal television production in 2006, financed through a complex mix of public production funds and private investment.[20]

APTN also promised the CRTC that it would develop a variety of new program initiatives across a range of television genres, using the funds generated by its cable fee increase to invest in independent television production in several categories. Over the seven years of its second licence term APTN committed to spend $4.2 million on long-form documentary, $18.7 million on drama and comedy, $2.4 million on music and variety, and $2 million on regional "priority" programming including children's television and news and information.[21] When APTN issued its first clearly focused request for program proposals (RFP) for the 2004–5 season, the RFP identified a new youth focus: "The network's vision is to be the leader in providing high quality programming targeted to Aboriginal Youth."[22] Proposals were invited from Aboriginal individuals, Aboriginal production companies (51 per cent Aboriginal ownership and control), or joint ventures (Aboriginal production company and one other). The annual RFP process is now the sole means by which APTN acquires new programming. In 2007, the network identified its needs in specific priority programming categories, including six-to-seven-episode dramatic series such as *Rabbit Fall* and *Mixed Blessings*; music dance and variety such as *We Joggin'*; single long-form documentary or thirteen-episode documentary series like *Storytellers in Motion*; children and youth series such as *Wapos Bay*; lifestyle programs like *Fish Out of Water*; reality programs like *Rez Rides*; and talk shows such as *First Talk*.[23] APTN's "shopping list" reflects not only a strategic turn toward more youth-oriented programs from the independent producers, but also a clear preference for broadly appealing and entertaining content that reaches a diverse audience, including urban and rural, Aboriginal and non-Aboriginal, and speakers of English, French, and Aboriginal languages.

Though APTN has been highly successful in developing new Aboriginal television content in Canada, a number of obstacles to further growth in the industry can be identified. The first of these obstacles arises from the structure of Canadian television funding and broadcast agreements. One of these has already been alluded to, and that is the absolute decline in NNBAP funding levels. After a peak in 1988, a lengthy era of federal budget cuts led to a 50 percent decline in funding for these broadcasters over an 18-year period.[24]

There are few sources of other revenue available to Aboriginal television production groups in the north. Most of the Native communication societies report salary levels far below other Aboriginal organizations in their region, and they lose trained and experienced staff for this reason. A second major challenge for NNBAP broadcasters is their aging and inadequate equipment. Most have almost no budget to maintain or replace equipment, and this is compounded by the scarcity of skilled in-house technicians and lack of local repair service in the north.[25] Most NNBAP producers scrape up funds for equipment out of operating budgets, but the program was not designed to support capital equipment costs.[26] As APTN pointed out to the Commons Heritage Committee: "Ironically their equipment is failing just as their programming is beginning to reach a national audience through APTN ... The inability of these broadcasters to meet minimum industry technical standards has the regrettable impact of further marginalizing them from mainstream Canadian and international audiences."[27] In almost all cases, the NNBAP television producers cannot sell programs in other markets beyond APTN. Their audiences are restricted in part by the language of production and partly by production values, but also by the lack of channels similar to APTN that might carry Indigenous peoples' programming in other countries. Yet Aboriginal language content is a key part of APTN's mandate and television programming produced in Aboriginal languages is central to the cultural vitality of Aboriginal communities and the survival of some of the less widely spoken Native languages.

In the case of independent Aboriginal production companies not funded under NNBAP, the major barrier to growth has been their limited access to public funds set aside for Canadian television production. Having secured a broadcast agreement with APTN, or with other networks, the independents can apply for funding under the Canadian Television Fund (CTF), a joint federal government and cable/satellite industry fund, to make up most of their production costs. Within the CTF there is a specific envelope for Aboriginal-language Projects, which totalled $2.6 million in 2007.[28] Up to 70 per cent of production costs are eligible for CTF support, to $200,000 maximum. Projects must be in an Aboriginal language and be drama, children's or youth, documentary, performing arts, variety, or educational programming. The producer must have a broadcaster's commitment to air in an Aboriginal language, but versioning in French or English is also eligible for funding.[29] In 2007 the majority of this funding went to programs licensed on APTN, but two projects were funded for commercial networks; the Igloolik Isuma documentary *Exile* for History Television, and the Productions Taqramiut variety program *The New Canoe* for CTV.[30]

Apart from its relatively small size (in comparison the CTF Broadcaster Performance Envelope for English-language television was $157.2 million in 2007–8),[31] the CTF Aboriginal-language envelope does not always meet ATPN's needs. A production for a national audience will require an English or French version, while the Aboriginal-language envelope requires programming to be shot in Aboriginal languages. This forces producers to make multiple versions simply to be eligible for the funding, even though many Indigenous people in Canada no longer speak an Aboriginal language after decades of assimilation under social and educational policies.[32] Before 2004, Aboriginal producers who made programming not in a Native language also had to compete for funding from CTF English- and French-language envelopes. Alongside major players like Nelvana or Epitome Pictures, they were not often successful. One important exception was the Big Soul Productions drama series *Moccasin Flats* licensed for a second season on APTN in 2004 and successfully funded in the CTF English Drama category. Beyond APTN, Canadian broadcasters were not willing to take a risk on Aboriginal content in a highly competitive and restricted funding environment. When the "track record" of production companies was assessed on the basis of the number and amount of licence agreements made with broadcasters, Aboriginal independents were disadvantaged by having access to only one network. This classic Catch-22 made it difficult for Aboriginal content producers to move beyond the limited Aboriginal-language envelope for federal television funding, while preventing APTN from making licence agreements with a greater diversity of independent producers.

After 2004, the CTF moved to a new system called the Broadcaster Performance Envelope (BPE) that allocated specific funding amounts in each genre to individual broadcasters. Under the new system, "a producer presents a production idea to a broadcaster. The broadcaster then determines if the production would appeal to its viewers, and if the producer can realistically obtain further financing from other sources. Once the broadcaster agrees to support the production (i.e. through a licence fee and commitment to air), the production company may then apply to the CTF for financing from the broadcaster's envelope for an amount allocated by the broadcaster."[33] Broadcasters' CTF allocations in various funded genres are determined by four "performance factors": historic access, above-average licensing, regional production licensing, and audience success. Historic access refers to the broadcaster's previous track record in obtaining CTF funding. Above-average licensing is an incentive to reward networks who offer producers higher broadcast licence fees. The regional production licensing factor gives recognition to the number of programs that are produced outside of Toronto and Montreal. The audience success factor is the most heavily weighted for English-language television and is calculated based on the total hours tuned to CTF-funded or similar CTF-eligible programs generated by the broadcaster over the course of the previous year.[34] Under the BPE structure, APTN was allocated a total of $2.8 million in CTF funding for fourteen projects in 2007. The majority of this went to children and youth programs ($1.4 million) and the rest to documentary ($0.3 million), drama ($0.9 million) and variety programs ($0.2 million).[35] These amounts of CTF funding, in combination with the APTN licence fee, allow Aboriginal production companies to seek out other forms of public and private investment for their projects.

The shift to a more "market-driven" process, giving greater control over allocation of public production funds to the broadcasters themselves, along with the incentive system of rewarding broadcasters who acquire and promote quality Canadian television, has both positive and negative impacts for the Aboriginal television industry. APTN is rewarded for licensing most of its programming from the regions outside major urban centres, but clearly the network is disadvantaged somewhat under the other three performance factors. In competing for CTF allocations, higher points are awarded to broadcasters with the highest licence fees. The big commercial networks like CTV and Global can afford substantial fees, but as a not-for-profit broadcaster, APTN cannot offer its producers much advantage. Increasingly in Canada, large multimedia conglomerates have several channels "across which they can air a single series (thus spreading out the cost); APTN is one of the few stand alone, single service broadcasters."[36] APTN has countered this by entering into a number of co-production agreements with other public broadcasters, including CBC, Vision, and provincial educational networks like TVO and Saskatchewan Communications Network (SCN) to gain first- or second-window rights on programs it could not afford to develop on its own. In another instance, APTN entered into a "cultural alliance" with the Rogers-owned OMNI networks in 2004, with the goals of distributing programs to each other's audiences, guiding productions under development, and exchanging staff for professional development in areas such as sales, marketing, and news and current affairs.[37] More recently, in 2007 APTN partnered with Global, Knowledge Network, and Saskatchewan Community Network on *renegadepress.com* and with CBC on the documentary *The Experimental Eskimo*.[38] These strategies permit APTN to expand the audience for productions it has helped develop and to overcome some of its limited market power in the commercial television environment.

APTN also faces other obstacles to audience reach for its programming that are not shared by the mainstream broadcasters. In most urban areas

APTN is so high up on the channel selections that many viewers are not aware of the network, do not even realize that it is part of the basic cable package, and do not regularly surf through its shows with the chance of stopping to watch. APTN also faces challenges of measuring its audience, because the standard commercial ratings services (BBM and Nielsen) are not conducted in the northern territories or on reserves—precisely where many APTN viewers live. Under these conditions, arriving at a "total hours tuned" calculation for network programs must be less than exact. Despite these obstacles, APTN has shown impressive viewership increases in urban areas among all viewers since 1999.[39]

APTN's Cultural Mandate and Non-Profit Objectives for Television Production

In both private and public television sectors, independent production companies are used to dealing with broadcasters who have a relatively focused set of objectives and a clearly defined target audience. In the case of APTN, neither the commercial "specialty channel" nor the national "public service" broadcasting model is an entirely comfortable fit. APTN is mandated to provide Aboriginal-language programming, which in itself is complicated by regional linguistic differences and by the needs of many southern Aboriginal peoples who speak English or French. Within the general Aboriginal audience there are also significantly different needs among youth and elders, northern and southern, and urban and rural populations. Finally, APTN is mandated to reach a secondary, non-Aboriginal, audience who bring neither a language background nor extensive cultural knowledge to APTN programming. On top of this explicit recognition of the multitude of tastes and interests that APTN should reflect is an implicit conflict between perceptions of APTN as either an Aboriginal cultural organization in the business of broadcasting or, more narrowly, as a broadcaster in the business of providing Aboriginal content.[40] As APTN steers its way through these often competing and sometimes mutually exclusive mandates and objectives, some of these tensions are bound to be reflected in programming decisions and production opportunities.

Another challenge to a stable environment for television production at APTN lies in the nature of its organizational structure and board governance. APTN inherited its current "membership" structure from TVNC. The ten "member organizations" of APTN are the same as original members of TVNC. They include nine NNBAP organizations from each of Yukon, Nunavut, Labrador, the northern regions of Quebec, Ontario, Manitoba, and Saskatchewan, two from Northwest Territories, and the Kativik School Board in

Quebec. Each of these ten organizations elects or appoints a board member to APTN. The remaining eleven members of the twenty-one-person board are "members-at-large," including representatives from southern and urban First Nations communities. Such a large and diverse board could hardly be expected to immediately share a definitive long-term vision for APTN. In the tradition of TVNC, the board was initially more involved in management and programming, but its unwieldy structure led to some perceived conflicts of interest, questionable decisions, and a sense of exclusion by independent producers whose interests were not represented on the board.[41] Clear conflict-of-interest guidelines for APTN's board members were established in 2003 to address some of these issues. This does not mean that APTN cannot buy programs or services from board members' organizations, only that potential conflicts must be declared, the degree of benefit to members made public, and exemption taken from all related decisions. At the same time, APTN's Acquisitions and Licensing Policy makes it clear that acquisition decisions are made by APTN programming department staff, according to needs identified in the proposal process. This policy removes the board from immediate involvement in programming decisions.[42] These are movements toward greater arms-length governance at APTN and a more predictable environment for acquisition of independently produced Aboriginal programming.

The impossible task of meeting all Indigenous peoples' needs for education, information, and entertainment through one national television network means that APTN has faced criticism about its programming policies and strategies. This criticism has come not only from interests within the Canadian television industry who challenge the need for Aboriginal television in general, but also from First Nations groups and organizations who question the network's specific programming choices and directions. Most of this criticism has generated healthy debate about what types of programs the network should be developing and acquiring, but some of it has raised larger questions about APTN's relationship with independent Aboriginal production companies.[43] Key aspects of this tension were articulated during the 2005 CRTC licence renewal process in an intervention by the Independent Aboriginal Screen Producers Association (IASPA), a group of film and television producers, many of whom have worked in the industry in various capacities for several years. The IASPA intervention supported APTN's licence renewal with several conditions related to the network's governance and programming. These included recommendations for increased emphasis on first-language programming, a restructuring of the APTN board to open it up to new membership, social benefits packages that would divert APTN's increased cable revenue toward Aboriginal production funds and training programs, a third-party selection process for programming, creation of an independent news production outlet, and limits to in-house production at APTN.[44] IASPA's recommendations were intended to make APTN more open and accountable to Aboriginal producers, but also to involve APTN more directly in building capacity in the Aboriginal television industry.

APTN replied to the challenges presented by IASPA by arguing that many of the proposed recommendations were beyond the network's mandate as a broadcaster. In its response, APTN suggested that the tension between broadcasters and producers was characteristic of the domestic television industry and that it was not reasonable to expect that the network should relinquish its control over program development and acquisition to a third party. APTN went on to reiterate its support for Aboriginal-language programming and claimed that its board was representative of all regions and interests in First Nations communities and open to new independent members. Finally, while recognizing the need for additional funding for Aboriginal television and support for training Aboriginal people in production skills, the network argued that it was not appropriate to take revenue derived from cable subscriber fees and redirect it to purposes not directly related to the daily activities of the network: "APTN, obviously, supports initiatives that are intended to support the Aboriginal independent production sector.[45] We do not believe, however, that a transferred wholesale fee levy is an appropriate mechanism." In this exchange of views with IASPA, APTN recognizes some of its own constraints as a broadcaster and the limits to its ability to build capacity among Aboriginal production companies in a commercialized system with finite resources. While the network stated that it always gives preference to Aboriginal productions by Aboriginal producers, it does not preclude the participation of "non-Aboriginal individuals or companies as long as they have high Aboriginal content."[46] Partnerships and co-productions are the norm in the global television industry and fundamental to the successful financing of costly programming, especially in drama. As APTN increases the variety of programming types and genres, especially with its acquisition of new drama series in the last four years, the Aboriginal production industry is being challenged to meet this new demand. The rising cost of new content generates a tension between the need to tell Aboriginal stories according to appropriate cultural norms and interests, and the imperatives of television financing and production values. Non-Aboriginal producers can supply expertise and financial support in the creation of Aboriginal television, but what kind of compromises must be made in the process?

Increasing Aboriginal Production Capacity: New Formats and Genres

In its second licence term, APTN is clearly positioning itself as a broadcaster first and foremost. The network maintains a clear commitment to cultural, social, and public service goals while meeting these within the constraints of the competitive and commercialized Canadian television environment. As a fully fledged national broadcaster APTN has made a consistent effort to diversify its content, not only to attract a wider audience but also to develop beyond its early emphasis on documentary, information, and educational programming. Examples include the creation of "lifestyle programs" like *Cooking with the Wolfman*, a popular culinary program with award-winning chef David Wolfman and his Aboriginal guests from all walks of life. In 2002 APTN acquired *The Creative Native,* hosted by West Coast Aboriginal artist Tamara Bell. Over five seasons this program explored a wide range of artistic traditions, craft production, fashion, and design across North America. Several episodes were filmed on the Hopi Nation and in other Aboriginal communities in the US southwest. In November 2004 the series ventured into reality television with an episode called "Cree Eye for the White Guy." Non-Native contestants were judged on various "skills" by powwow participants. These types of programs inflect Aboriginal cultural knowledge within the formats and conventions of popular television genres.

As APTN continues to acquire more programming from independents, a number of key new companies have been established in the industry. Many of these companies were launched by producers who started their careers with the original Native communication societies. Mushkeg Media, for instance, was founded in 2001 by Paul Rickard, a former Wawatay Native Communications Society television producer. The company has co-produced several broadcast documentaries with the NFB, APTN, and SCN, including a series on Aboriginal languages called *Finding Our Talk.*[47] Rezolution Pictures was established in 2001 by Ernest Webb, who began his career at the James Bay Cree Communications Society in Mistassini and went on to work for CBC North.[48] Rezolution Pictures has made several award-winning documentaries broadcast on APTN and recently branched out into entertainment formats with *RezRides,* a series on "car culture" in Native communities. This company also produced *Moose TV,* the first Aboriginal comedy series for a broadcaster other than APTN. After a one-off episode carried on CBC in 2004, the concept was developed by Showcase into an eight-episode series for the fall of 2007. Experienced Native actors Gary Farmer, Adam Beach, and Jennifer Podemski play the main characters who start up a new television station in a small northern community. Directed by non-Native Tim Southam (*One Dead Indian*), and written by novelist/scriptwriter Paul Quarrington (*Due South*), the series represents a significant example of collaboration between Aboriginal and mainstream television producers and broadcasters.

APTN and Aboriginal production companies have encountered the most challenging combination of high costs and limited skills and technical resources in the creation of new television drama. *Moccasin Flats* was the first Aboriginal drama series in Canada, produced for the 2003–4 season by Big Soul Productions. Established in August 1999 by Laura J. Milliken and Jennifer Podemski as an Aboriginal-owned and -operated company, Big Soul started out with the youth information program *The Seventh Generation* for APTN and SCN. In 2000, Big Soul began a series of media empowerment workshops for Aboriginal youth called *repREZentin'*. The workshops trained participants in all areas of video production and culminated in half-hour drama episodes for television. The first instalment, *repREZentin' in Kettle and Stoney Point*, premiered on APTN in June 2001 and was followed by episodes from other Aboriginal communities across Canada.

RepREZentin' was the source for the first half-hour version of *Moccasin Flats* in 2002. Podemski and Milliken partnered with the Saskatchewan Institute of Science and Technology to train thirty Aboriginal youth from the North Central area of Regina, sometimes referred to by residents as Moccasin Flats. The youth combined on-location experience with classroom training to receive a diploma in film and television production.[49] This initial *RepREZentin'* episode was developed into a TV series for the 2003 season, also produced, written, and directed by an Aboriginal team. The series added well-known Aboriginal film and television actors Gordon Tootoosis (*North of 60, Legends of the Fall*), Tantoo Cardinal, and Andrea Menard in key adult roles. But much of the cast and the crew on *Moccasin Flats* were Aboriginal youth from North Central. The stories are derived from their experiences and deal with racism, low self-esteem, poverty, substance abuse, incarceration, gang violence, prostitution, suicide, and sexual abuse. The main characters include youth living with drug addiction, prostitution, and gang membership as well as young people who are parents, athletes, and university students. Through three seasons on APTN and Showcase, *Moccasin Flats* and Big Soul combined a social agenda for training and empowering young Indigenous people with a cultural mandate to tell the story of contemporary urban Aboriginal experience. The series' unique participatory model of television production underpinned what ultimately became a critically successful program. Big Soul has maintained its focus on youth television with its more recent productions including a TV movie,

Moccasin Flats: Redemption, and *By the Rapids*, an animated cartoon series following the story of an urban teenager relocated to the Native community where his successful lawyer parents grew up.

Hank William's First Nation, like *Moccasin Flats*, had its origins in a full-length film.[50] The 2005 film was created by non-Native Aaron James Sorensen and produced by his company, Peace Country Films. Sorensen's privately funded first feature was based on his experience working as a teacher, development officer, and entrepreneur in Wabasca, Alberta, and won several awards, including best director at the American Indian Film Festival in San Francisco.[51] The 2007 series is set in the fictitious rural Cree village of Wapahoo, and it trades the dark, gritty realism of *Moccasin Flats* for a more light-hearted look at Cree culture, values, and family and community dynamics. Sorensen explicitly set out to tell positive stories about First Nations communities that go unrepresented in the mainstream media.[52] Gordon Tootoosis plays the role of Cree grandfather and successful entrepreneur Adelard Fox. Writers Larry Mollin (*Beverly Hills 90210*) and Aboriginal author and screenwriter Jordan Wheeler joined Sorensen on the script. *Hank William's First Nation* follows the friends and family of Sarah and Jacob Fox and the season opens with Sarah's high school graduation. Voice-over commentary throughout the series is provided by Hank William Beauregard, unseen host at the local community radio station. Where *Moccasin Flats* immerses viewers in the conflict and violence of the urban 'hood, *Hank William's First Nation* is a more slowly paced family drama that tells the coming-of-age story of Sarah, her brother Jacob, and her friend Huey. While non-Native characters are secondary and somewhat marginal to both series, the two programs take quite different trajectories in their exploration of Aboriginal cultures. The youth in *Moccasin Flats* often seem to abandon, or be abandoned by, their families, elders, and communities, while the young people in *Hank William's First Nation* are clearly embedded in a web of community and familial ties. The series does not unduly romanticize the Cree village and it sometimes portrays absent or inadequate parents, limited standards of living, and lack of educational and employment opportunities. But *Hank William's First Nation* is consistently multi-generational and foregrounds the network of responsibilities between adults, youth, family, friends, and community members. In several episodes these responsibilities and relationships are explored through dialogue in Cree (with English subtitles) that give the show a sense of place and cultural location quite unique to Canadian television drama.

While both programs adapt the conventions of mainstream television drama to First Nations stories told from the Aboriginal perspective, they deal quite differently with experiences of racism and colonialism in their characters' lives. In *Moccasin Flats*, the residents of North Central live through the long-term social effects of residential schools, welfare dependency generated by the reserve system and transferred to the urban Aboriginal ghetto, violence, addiction, and abuse that can be traced directly back to colonial practices and attitudes in Canadian society. *Hank William's First Nation* deliberately brackets out these forces, not to ignore them or pretend they don't matter, but instead to highlight the sustaining role of culture and family in young people's lives. In one episode, the white school teacher Amanda spends some time explaining to her son how the complicated opposition between whites and Indians might be transcended if he is able to see their shared experience with the Cree residents of Wapahoo as "locals." Amanda, a new teacher and single mother who has moved to the remote northern town because she can't get a job anywhere else, suggests that there is shared space on the margins in which racial and cultural designations might sometimes, under some conditions, be superseded by social and geographical ones. *Hank William's First Nation* does not always represent white people in positions of authority in a very favourable light, but for the most part the history of colonialism and the racial tensions of the present occur offstage.

In the rather limited Canadian universe of Aboriginal television drama so far, these two programs approach the narratives of Aboriginal youth, cultural identity, family dynamics, and community relationships very differently. The simplest conclusion might be that the more accurate but less palatable version, *Moccasin Flats*, is created by Aboriginal producers and actors for an Aboriginal audience. But not all Aboriginal people recognize the stories and identities that emerge from North Central. For every young sex trade worker like Candy or drug dealer like Jonathon in *Moccasin Flats*, there is just as likely to be a motivated student like Sarah or aspiring writer like Jacob. The fact that Canadian television viewers have the possibility of choosing between or reflecting upon both sets of televisual representations is a sign of the diversity and growth of Aboriginal production capacity. APTN's 2010 season added to this diversity with the introduction of *Blackstone*, a compelling new drama that follows in the path established by *Hank William's First Nation* and *Moccasin Flats*. Produced by Prairie Dog Film + Television, the series explores the conflicts and tensions within a fictional reserve community, focusing on social breakdown and corruption within its political structures as they affect the lives of its residents. By examining local resistance to the corruption of the chief and council, the program locates the experience of neo-colonialism and decolonization not in the forces of non-Aboriginal society but directly within relations between members of the fictional community of Blackstone.

Beyond the superficial comparison of "positive" and "negative" images of Aboriginal people in the media, the emergence of Aboriginal television drama has engendered multiple expressions of the historical and social contradictions and local specificities of Aboriginal experience. The heterogeneity and multiplicity of Aboriginal narratives have found a channel within the Canadian public sphere and North American popular culture through APTN and other networks. The long-term impact of Aboriginal television production remains to be fully imagined, but may ultimately result in the gradual "indigenization" of Canadian media culture.[53]

Conclusion: Future Research Directions in the Aboriginal Television Industry

Analysis of Aboriginal television today adds exciting new dimensions to the study of the Canadian television industry and of global Indigenous peoples' media. The maturation of APTN as a broadcaster and the growth in production capacity at Aboriginal-owned companies represents an important cultural, social, and economic watershed. Some media critics might argue that the cultural space represented by APTN, Aboriginal-language television producers, and creators of Aboriginal entertainment television is hardly significant in the ongoing centralization and control of broadcast and digital media by transnational media corporations. But this chapter suggests that Canada's national Aboriginal television network creates ruptures and fissures in popular discourses about Aboriginal peoples and cultures, while contributing to the economic infrastructure and technical capacity for Aboriginal peoples to tell their own stories. Future studies of this emerging industry might look more carefully at the impact of Aboriginal content and Aboriginal production staff in non-Aboriginal companies or in multi-partner co-production projects. The place of digital distribution and webcasting in Aboriginal television must also be analyzed, as producers like Igloolik Isuma launch new global web portals such as Isuma TV for Indigenous peoples' film and video.[54] The question of culturally appropriate film and television training and education also needs to be considered as an increasing number of colleges and universities develop programs in Aboriginal media education. More research is needed into improving models of public funding to adequately support the growth of Aboriginal production capacity and to encourage broadcasters other than APTN to acquire Aboriginal content. In the area of Aboriginal-language television, scholars need to more fully understand the connection between television consumption and language use. As a practical issue, policy-makers need to address the diversification of NNBAP funding for Native broadcasters to increase their independence from governments while ensuring that Aboriginal-language television continues to evolve and reach its audience. Finally, much greater knowledge about the audience for Aboriginal television is required. Who watches Aboriginal television content, and in what social and cultural contexts? What is its cumulative impact on popular interpretations of Aboriginal culture and history? Further analysis of the political economy of Aboriginal television will be a key means of understanding the emergence of post-colonial Canadian popular culture.

Notes

1 Bredin, "APTN and Its Audience."
2 APTN Factsheet.
3 For detailed studies of Aboriginal broadcasting and video production in Canada see Alia, *Un/Covering the North*; Roth, *Something New in the Air*; and Evans, *Isuma: Inuit Video Art*.
4 Canada, Department of Canadian Heritage, *NNBAP Evaluation*, 24.
5 In 2007, 28 per cent of APTN's total programming was in an Aboriginal language. APTN Factsheet.
6 APTN, *Towards a Truer Mirror*, 8.
7 Ibid., 9.
8 Canada, RCAP, *Gathering Strength*, Recommendation 3.6.12.
9 Canada, Department of Canadian Heritage, *NNBAP Evaluation*, 27.
10 APTN, 2006 Annual Report, 7.
11 The proportion of monthly cable subscriber fees paid by cable companies to specialty channels varies widely. Cable companies have some discretion over the amount paid to commercial specialty networks, but fees paid to channels whose carriage on basic cable is mandated by the CRTC ranges from $0.11 for CPAC to $0.63 for CBC Newsworld. CRTC, *Broadcasting Decision, 2007-246*.
12 Canada, Commons Heritage Committee, *Our Cultural Sovereignty*, 225.
13 Canada, Department of Canadian Heritage, *NNBAP Evaluation*, 6.
14 APTN, *APTN National News: Contact*.
15 In 2007 the web forum hosted by APTN was relaunched as an independently hosted forum called Digital Drum.
16 APTN, *APTN Milestones*.
17 APTN, *Towards a Truer Mirror*, 17.
18 APTN, Supplementary Brief, 2–3.
19 APTN, 2006 Annual Report, 6.
20 These calculations are based on average budgets of CTF-funded productions. Participants in Canadian television financing include broadcasters, the Canadian Television Fund, federal and provincial governments, domestic production companies, foreign production partners, and distributors. See Canadian Television Fund (CTF), 2006–7

Annual Report, 41, 102. The CTF was restructured and renamed the Canada Media Fund in 2010, but these funding formulas remain relatively unchanged.

21 APTN, Supplementary Brief, 30.
22 APTN, *Request for Proposals*, 1.
23 APTN, Producing for APTN, 2.
24 APTN, *Towards a Truer Mirror*, 15.
25 Canada, Department of Canadian Heritage, *NNBAP Evaluation*, 3.
26 APTN, *Towards a Truer Mirror*, 16.
27 APTN, *Towards a Truer Mirror*, 16.
28 CTF, Aboriginal-Language Projects Results, 1.
29 CTF, Aboriginal-Language Projects Guidelines, 5.
30 CTF, Aboriginal-Language Projects Results, 1.
31 CTF, Approved BPE English-Language Applications, 10.
32 Canada, Commons Heritage Committee, *Our Cultural Sovereignty*, 226.
33 CTF, Broadcaster Performance Envelope Stream.
34 CTF, BPE Factor Weights—General Overview, 2.
35 CTF, Approved BPE English-Language Applications.
36 APTN, *Towards a Truer Mirror*, 17.
37 APTN, What's New, 2.
38 CTF, Approved BPE English-Language Applications.
39 APTN, Our Audience.
40 Strategic Inc., *APTN: Brand Equity Measure*, 9.
41 Ibid.
42 APTN, Reply to Intervention of IASPA, 13.
43 See especially the discussion in Jeff Bear's 2004 report for Telefilm Canada, "At the Crossroads," for some of this debate.
44 IASPA, Intervention in APTN Licence Renewal, 1–3.
45 APTN, Reply to Intervention of IASPA, 9.
46 Ibid., 12.
47 Mushkeg Media, About Mushkeg Media Inc.
48 Rezolution Pictures, Company Profile.
49 Showcase, *Sometimes Culture Is All You Have*, 2.
50 The title of the original film is *Hank Williams First Nation*, but in the series title *William's* is apostrophized to reflect the narrative voice of Hank William Beauregard.
51 APTN, *Hank William's First Nation—The Series*, 1; Chicken-Wing Pictures, *Press Kit, Hank William's First Nation—The Series*; 2.
52 *Hank William's First Nation*, *Press Kit*, 2.
53 For a fascinating comparative account of the Indigenization of public media and popular culture in the Latin American context, see Himpele, *Circuits of Culture*.
54 www.isuma.tv is a highly sophisticated global web portal for digital film and video that includes content from indigenous producers all over the world.

5

Hypercommercialism and Canadian Children's Television
The Case of YTV

KYLE ASQUITH

THIS CHAPTER EXPLORES the strategies that Canada's YTV uses to integrate advertising and content across its broadcast and non-broadcast platforms. Although YTV was born out of a boom in children's marketing in the late 1980s, it has recently climbed to a new plateau of commercialism. As I will delineate throughout this chapter, YTV can be described as a "hypercommercial" television environment. I begin by reviewing the history of children's television advertising and outlining the problem of hypercommercialism. Consistent with a "critical media industry studies" approach,[1] I then highlight YTV's on-air, online, and event marketing advertising opportunities through an analysis of YTV's programming, website, sales materials, press releases, as well as Canadian media industry news websites.[2] I conclude by situating hypercommercialism within Canadian English children's television in a larger neoliberal political economic climate.

Advertising on Children's Television: A Contentious History

Advertising directly to children is a relatively recent phenomenon in the larger history of consumer culture. While there is evidence of candy and cereal advertising prior to the 1950s, toy manufacturers such as Mattel did not market directly to children until the postwar years. As David Buckingham argues, children were not considered a "valuable" audience for many companies in the earliest days of commercial broadcasting.[3] The history of advertising to children parallels the history of television in North America; children's marketing efforts and commercial television emerged in the same era and have historically developed hand-in-hand. Starting in the 1950s, US programs like *Howdy Doody* and the original *Mickey Mouse Club* offered a unique platform where children could watch television with their parents. Canadian television was not immune to the discovery of children as an advertising target in the postwar years. When the Canadian Broadcasting Corporation (CBC) first aired a Canadian adaptation of *Howdy Doody* in 1954, efforts to make sponsor messages discreet failed because advertisers realized "it was much cheaper to bring in filmed commercial messages from sponsors' parent companies in the United States."[4] By the 1960s the US networks, which also garnered sizable Canadian audiences, discovered that Saturday morning was "prime time" for children and began filling the slot with cheap-to-produce cartoons. The commercial breaks in these cartoons brought considerable controversy as parent groups expressed concern over cereal, toy, and confectionary advertisers pitching directly to children.

Controversies reached a boiling point in 1969 when ABC aired a *Hot Wheels* cartoon that amounted to a half-hour toy commercial. The American consumer group Action for Children's Television (ACT) lobbied heavily to rid children's television of advertising. The efforts of groups like ACT resulted in several regulatory changes in the 1970s: the US Federal Communications Commission (FCC) prohibited television programs based on licensed characters; self-regulatory codes for children's broadcast advertising were developed in both Canada and the United States; and in Canada, the province of Quebec enacted a ban on all advertising directed at children under the age of thirteen, effective April 30, 1980. Quebec's ban was upheld in a Supreme Court ruling that justified the law as a reasonable limit to commercial free speech.[5] By the mid-1980s, however, the large cohort of baby boom–echo children, deregulation, and the penetration of cable specialty services helped turn children's television markets into a veritable feeding frenzy. The FCC's earlier policies were rolled back, resulting in both Canadian and American children enjoying "program-length commercials" like *G.I. Joe*, *Strawberry Shortcake*, and *Teenage Mutant Ninja Turtles* on major networks. Specialty cable services also fuelled children's television advertising in the 1980s. Joseph Turow argues that specialty media create "primary media communities," a kind of gated community that emerges when viewers feel "part of a family, attached to the program hosts, other viewers, and sponsors."[6] Turow identifies Viacom's Nickelodeon as the quintessential primary media community. According to Sarah Banet-Weiser, Nickelodeon offers an entire way of life for young viewers.[7] YTV, the subject of this chapter, was launched on September 1, 1988, and represents the Canadian answer to Nickelodeon. Indeed, for Canadian "Millennial" youth, YTV is more than a channel; rather, through "weird" and "gross-out" branding, it provides an attitude that speaks to children. Such viewer loyalty is extremely valuable to advertisers.

Hence, specialty cable services work in the interests of advertisers—not necessarily consumer choice—by delivering loyal niche audiences with similar demographics. A youth-oriented television channel like YTV fulfills an important role in larger children's marketing efforts. YTV touts itself as Canada's number one youth network and is seen in some eight million homes across Canada.[8] Although YTV claims to be an "expert" on youth, producing research in documents titled "Tween Reports," the channel's expertise also lies in targeting a tidy, relatively homogeneous demographic that is attractive to media buyers. YTV's audience is desirable because advertisers now charge children with three duties: (1) buy goods, (2) influence family buying decisions, and (3) become "good" future consumers. These three duties are rather uncritically described in Anne Sutherland and Beth Thompson's book *Kidfluence*. "Kidfluence" concerns not only the way in which children spend their own money, but also how they influence family purchases and develop life-long brand preferences. Consequently, during the children's marketing boom of the 1980s and 1990s new categories of advertisers, such as automobile manufacturers, suddenly took an interest in children's television. The YTV sales website proudly claims that Canadian children and tweens influence $20 billion in household purchases every year. These sales materials also suggest that "gone are the days when parents raised their kids to be 'seen and not heard' ... today's parents encourage their kids to participate in decisions that affect the whole family"— such as choices over restaurants, groceries, cars, electronics, and vacations. This rhetoric of a new and more "democratic" family dynamic also appears in Sutherland and Thompson's text.[9]

Although YTV might suggest its commercial approach liberates children from the shackles of authoritarian adults, the tenets of kidfluence, including discussions of "brand imprinting" at an early age, raise concerns over the exploitation of childhood by market forces. This debate is consistent with a broader theoretical dispute over the agency of children. As Buckingham explains, concerns over the "loss of childhood" have existed for decades; these concerns are manifested in both psychological "media effects" research, and even the writing of Neil Postman.[10] From this perspective, children are constructed as a passive, vulnerable media audience that can be exploited by advertising. The consumer groups and policy-makers who opposed sugary cereal advertising in the 1970s or program-length commercials a decade later generally shared this paradigm. In recent years, though, research that frames children by what they lack (i.e., rationality) and ultimately paints them as passive victims to consumer culture has been disputed. Several children's media culture scholars argue that children are far more media-savvy than many critics believe, and that media effects analyses ignore a host of other socialization factors. However, Buckingham nonetheless expresses caution in adopting a theoretical position that constructs children as an intelligent and active audience, smart enough to see through television advertising attempts. Buckingham describes the parallels between industry rhetoric and recent academic discourses surrounding media-savvy youth as an "uneasy coincidence."[11] The language of youth empowerment is foundational to both the Nickelodeon and YTV brands. Likewise, in their seminal *Kidfluence* text, Sutherland and Thompson explain how children are "neither gullible nor naive" and claim the best ads for children are ones that appeal to a critical—even cynical—audience.[12]

Conversely, Buckingham warns that advertising can still have a considerable impact on children. Parents, educators, and policy-makers, even if they do not consider children to be passive victims, still have justifiable reason to be concerned about television advertising. The totality of advertising on television acclimatizes audiences to a world of consumption. Advertising hails viewers as individual consumers, not as members of a collective citizenry. As Robert McChesney warns, advertising tends to produce cynicism and greed.[13] Likewise, television advertising contains a class bias. In order to attract advertisers, specialty television services develop programming for audiences with deep pockets. Niche targeting is also a process of excluding the "wrong" audience members. While *Sesame Street* was designed by the Children's Television Workshop to appeal to children of a lower socio-economic standing, specialty media outlets that rely on advertising revenue do not share this goal. It is television advertising as a system, not the persuasive intent of individual advertisements, about which Canadians should be concerned.

The structural problems of advertising fall into a policy and regulatory blindspot. Based on its May 2007 announcement beginning a process of deregulating television advertising restrictions, the Canadian Radio-television and Telecommunications Commission (CRTC) appears satisfied that commercial broadcasters and advertisers can regulate their own practices. Outside of Quebec, industry self-regulation is the primary way in which advertising to children is regulated in Canada. The Broadcast Code for Advertising to Children is enforced by an industry body, Advertising Standards Canada (ASC). All television advertisements targeted at children must be "pre-cleared" by an ASC panel. ASC clearance panels look at issues such as relative size, factual presentation, comparison claims, price, and purchase terms. While all of the above details are important to scrutinize, the ASC clearance system is fixated on factual advertising claims. The ASC tends to focus on making sure there are "batteries not included" disclaimers in advertisements, but fails to attend to the more pernicious forms of children's branding or the structural impact of advertising on children's culture. The structural problems of children's television advertising have little to do with the persuasive strategies of individual messages and have more to do with the way in which the imperatives of promotionalism influence many aspects of television. Because self-regulation offers scant help for those concerned about the totality of advertising, we must consider new policy and media literacy interventions.

Therefore, I seek to critically investigate "hypercommercialism," a recent and largely unregulated trend in commercial television whereby television channels become integrated, multimedia, multi-platform marketing vehicles for advertisers dissatisfied with the now-dated business of merely purchasing thirty-second spots.

Hypercommercialism

The traditional commercial break is losing its charm with advertisers and broadcasters alike. As a consequence of living in a world where promotional messages dominate so many spaces, advertisers are forced to go one step further to ensure their messages stand out. As McChesney and Foster argue, commercial clutter "has become a source of real concern for marketing firms, which find themselves forced to run faster and faster just to stand still."[14] Moreover, traditional commercial breaks can be bypassed with new technology and alternative methods for television consumption, including personal video recorders, DVD box sets, or portable devices such as mobile phones and iPods. Advertisers are adjusting their media buys accordingly. Procter and Gamble, the largest broadcast media buyer of the last century, made front-page headlines in 2005 when the company announced a cut in traditional commercial spending by up to 25 per cent.[15] The thirty-second commercial is equally problematic for private broadcasters. With dissatisfied advertisers and increasingly fragmented audiences, prices for television advertising slots are falling. Additionally, Canadian broadcast licences have historically limited the number of commercials that can be included during a program. As a result, television sales departments have a finite "inventory" of commercial time to sell. Although the CRTC has now loosened restrictions for conventional television,

YTV is bound by supplemental rules prescribed by the Broadcast Code for Advertising to Children. This industry code limits the amount of advertising time to eight minutes per hour of programming that is directed at children under twelve.

If the thirty-second commercial has lost its charm with both broadcasters and advertisers, "integration" might be a solution. Integration is a current buzzword among advertising agencies and Canadian television upper management alike. Integration refers to a blurring of boundaries between commercial messages and creative content. This process extends the branding of an advertiser beyond the traditional walls of the commercial break. Integration also concerns the extension of television brands beyond programming to construct non-broadcast entertainment platforms that are also hospitable to advertisers. Integration satisfies commercial television broadcasters because it means that there is no longer a finite inventory of advertising time to sell. Of course, integration also pleases advertisers by furnishing an innovative way to break through the clutter of thirty-second spots; brand messages might gain attention, authenticity, and legitimacy if they are deeply embedded within entertaining content. As Matthew McAllister contends, by the 1990s entertainment companies, facing new competition from a proliferation of channels and other technologies like the personal computer, began extensively branding, promoting, and cross-promoting themselves.[16] McAllister's research on American children's television demonstrates how a desire to break through advertising clutter and reach distracted viewers cultivates a televisual "commodity flow" where promotional messages become the dominant feature of television.[17] Integration therefore fits within the larger "promotional ethos" that is driving television and ultimately culture.[18]

John Caldwell, assessing the so-called "post-television" environment brought about by institutional and technological shifts, suggests that advertising and commercialism will be essential to television's continued survival.[19] Throughout the history of broadcasting in North America, instead of passively responding to changing media environments, "advertisers have been active lobbyists in the commercialization of media and in reorganizing them to suit their own particular needs and orientations."[20] For example, by the 1980s product placement became an industry unto itself, with specific agencies created to broker deals between advertisers and film and television producers. Likewise, William Boddy notes that in recent years, "advertising and television trade presses have been filled with calls for sponsors and broadcasters to develop advertising vehicles that would rebuff the expected assault from digital recorders."[21] To answer these demands, a new breed of sales department is appearing within the organizational charts of Canadian television corporations. Corus Entertainment's television division, which broadcasts over a dozen conventional and specialty channels including YTV, created a "Client-Marketing" department. This department offers services such as product placement, elaborate sponsorships, and multi-channel, multimedia integrated promotions across several Corus Entertainment assets. The Client-Marketing group functions as an intermediary between sales—responsible for selling traditional commercial time by maintaining relationships with advertisers and agencies—and all other television departments, including programming, production, and the websites for Corus Entertainment properties. Specifically, the YTV Client-Marketing website promises that the group will be "the connection between your brand and the YTV brand" through "the creation of award winning, innovative, multimedia communication programs."

I, however, do not want to rely on the industry's terminology of "Client-Marketing" or "integration." The industry's framing tends to make these practices sound like natural, inevitable, and innocuous business decisions that broadcasters and advertisers mutually undertake simply to stay afloat in changing times. Instead, I use the term "hypercommercialism," which can be defined as the way in which advertisers tend to colonize media spaces. Describing marketing integration as hypercommercialism avoids any positive connotations and also invites us to acknowledge the larger historical and political economic context that lies behind the blurring of boundaries between content and advertising. Hypercommercialism, in some respects, can be described as a step backwards in television advertising models. Following arrangements that date back to early radio, broadcasters, agencies, and advertisers were often co-producers of programming. By 1939 Procter and Gamble "produced" over twenty radio programs.[22] However, while today's hypercommercial television landscape has roots in the advertising models of early radio and television, McChesney and Foster contend "what is happening now goes far beyond what was done from the 1930s to the 1950s ... in both scope and intensity."[23] One significant difference between today's hypercommercial media and early broadcasting is the integrated multi-station, multi-platform promotions that blur content and advertising not only on-air, but also online, in print, and through live events. Furthermore, the "hyper" aspect of hypercommercialism occurs because the bombardment of promotional messages that characterizes contemporary television reduces the effectiveness of any single message, which in turn drives media corporations to dig even deeper for creative ways to further merge brand messages and content. Hypercommercialism is a downward spiral of sorts and can push children's television commercialism beyond early broadcasting models and even beyond what *G.I. Joe* accomplished in the 1980s.

We should be concerned about the political economy of hypercommercialism because it represents a change in the balance of power between advertisers and broadcasters. In contrast to critiques of advertising that focus on the ideological content of messages, I suggest that hypercommercialism is problematic because advertisers are penetrating more and more aspects of Canadian television operations. Media critics often argue that the "separation of media content from advertising" is integral in justifying "the existence of modern media systems in a democracy."[24] Hypercommercialism raises numerous concerns, because as television finds ways to insert brand messages into seemingly every minute of airtime, creative decisions and choices can be suppressed. Creative ownership is increasingly moving from the jurisdiction of producers and writers to the hands of advertising agencies or "Client-Marketing" departments—not unlike radio arrangements in the 1930s. A Canadian independent television producer understands that a show is much more likely to be green-lighted if it accommodates the "integration" needs of this new breed of sales department. Media content can change dramatically and creator autonomy is sacrificed as advertisers demand easily marketable entertainment platforms. This trend is particularly troublesome in children's television. Although children may grasp the persuasive attempt of individual ads, they may not appreciate how advertising shapes the television *system*. In fact, Buckingham's interview research suggests that while children understand what advertisements attempt to do, they know "much less about why they appeared on television in the first place."[25]

YTV and Hypercommercialism: On-Air

After-school and Saturday morning time slots are prime time for children's television and are described by YTV as "dayparts." A daypart is a period of time in a programming schedule that receives a relatively stable audience across multiple shows. Because these dayparts offer stable demographics, the entire block of time can be sold to advertisers. YTV's most recent dayparts menu consists of: *The Zone*, after-school viewing on weekdays; *Crunch*, a Saturday morning time slot chock-full of popular cartoons; and *Zapx*, a Sunday afternoon family movie programming block. These three dayparts are noteworthy because they feature hosted "interstitials" between programs. Hosted interstitials are unique to a post-MTV television environment and have a distinctive function on YTV. Because the Canadian Broadcast Code for Advertising to Children has tighter rules regarding the number of commercial minutes per half-hour of programming, children's programming produced for American and global markets runs short. To fill in an extra two or three minutes at the end of the show—time that could be used for commercials on American broadcasts—YTV relies on the hosted interstitial, which is cheap to produce and helps to maintain the "flow" of television. YTV hosts, who have achieved rock-star status in the eyes of many Canadian children, talk up programming trivia and YTV events, perform sketch comedy, and "throw" to the next show—not unlike an MTV or MuchMusic "VJ."

But *The Zone*, *Crunch*, and *Zapx* also mark an important shift towards hypercommercialism. YTV dayparts can be used for "fully integrated" sponsorship opportunities "to fit a big idea."[26] The YTV Client-Marketing website informs potential advertisers that *Zapx* offers product placement, customized segments, host mentions, and branded content. Hosted interstitials give YTV the chance to incorporate advertiser messages and products into creative content. The YTV hosts are consistently working brand names into their supposedly improvised banter. When Hasbro launched an iPod-like media player aimed at children in the fall of 2006, they teamed up with YTV's *Crunch* daypart to run a contest. An industry periodical described how *Crunch* host Ajay promoted the device for four weeks "by hyping the product's features (videos, photos, music)."[27] A "contest details" spot also aired regularly during the *Crunch* interstitials throughout this four-week promotional window. The YTV Client-Marketing website declares that this kind of sponsorship "integrates your products or services into a homegrown YTV production via product placement and/or branded content." The same sales materials outline how YTV has "created an environment that allows its clients to 'get in deep' with YTV properties and programming, thus creating a strong association between your brand and the equity of the program."

YTV Client-Marketing brags about how the sponsorship of hosted interstitials provides access to YTV's "prized assets." We might question, however, what or rather *who* these "prized assets" are. Are they the programs, the hosts, the viewers, or, given the dynamics of kidfluence, the parents? This question is worth considering in light of a recent Sunlight detergent promotion that was housed, interestingly enough, within YTV's *Zapx* Sunday afternoon movie daypart. The underlying philosophy of this campaign, according to Sunlight's Canadian brand manager, was "Dirty is Good." In typical marketing rhetoric, Sunlight claimed that every grass stain "tells a story" and YTV viewers were asked to submit stories outlining why they deserved a backyard makeover (the top prize).[28] Semi-finalists were then profiled in branded *Zapx* interstitials.

Simon, the host, asked viewers to vote on their favourite Sunlight semi-finalist. In a follow-up segment that aired as an on-location *Zapx* segment, Simon visited the winner to show the backyard transformation to viewers and to "officially acquire a grass stain in the new outdoor space."[29] Simon was marketed as YTV's resident movie buff, yet his interstitials were frequently used for showing this kind of "branded content" rather than discussing movie trivia with young viewers. These interstitials exemplify how Canadian children's television can longer be placed into neat categories of "programs" or "commercials." Yet, ASC clearance is only for commercial "spots." Because the current regulatory system presupposes a clear demarcation between content and advertising, many of YTV's on-air tactics fall into a grey area.

YTV and Hypercommercialism: Online

YTV programming, promos, bumpers, billboards, contests, and interstitials consistently direct viewers to ytv.com; conversely, ytv.com features direct web visitors back to on-air programs. Invariably, viewers are kept in a circular flow of the YTV brand's primary media community. Online advertising is without question big business, topping $1 billion in sales in Canada by 2006.[30] The most popular category of online advertising is called "display," which includes banner ads, contests, sponsorships, and microsites—all of which are available on ytv.com. At any given time, YTV is running half a dozen sponsored contests, with clients ranging from Kraft Foods, to Air Canada Vacations, to Hasbro's Furby animatronic stuffed animal. Links to contest microsites, which each include separate pages for prizes, the sponsor, and contest entry, are prominent on ytv.com. YTV also offers "advertorial" microsites housed within the larger ytv.com look and feel. In 2006 ytv.com created an "integrated advertorial" for Lego, targeting "web-savvy boys" ages six to eleven.[31] This microsite was nothing more than a product information page, but shared the look of other ytv.com features, such as message boards or blogs written by the various hosts. The ytv.com platform is a frontier landscape because there is virtually no limit to the number of commercial messages that can be delivered.

Perhaps the most notable example of ytv.com's commercialism lies in the realm of online games. Online games are now *the* big draw on ytv.com. While television executives defend games as making children empowered, from the perspective of advertisers, branded online games allow children to interact with advertisements instead of simply watching them. Branded games mark a territory where commercialism intersects with play. The ramifications of this are significant as "the expropriation of play by the forces of the market threatens a devaluation of the cultural meaning of play."[32] YTV games range from simple Flash-based puzzle games, to "massively multiplayer online games," which allow hundreds of Internet users to interact, team up, and compete in virtual worlds. While these games are promoted as being "free," they exist to serve the needs of YTV's advertising clients. A YTV game can furnish "highly-customized opportunities" including "unique integration opportunities within the game itself, providing clients with the ability to connect with their audience in truly innovative ways."[33] One of YTV's first massively multi-player online games was "Skittlization," a game that came complete with an elaborate back story, which served as an interactive advertisement for Skittles candy. The game took players to "Planet Rainbow" to join "the Flavour Force," five superheroes that represent the five flavours of Skittles candy, in an effort to thwart the evil "Dr. Bland," a "flavour-less fiend" who schemed to make the world "colour-less and tasteless." Once again, these advertising practices exemplify the myopia of ASC regulation. ASC enforcement is premised on factual product claims and on issues like "false" and "deceptive" advertising. We cannot fault a Skittles web game, for example, for providing "deceptive" or "false" claims because no objective product claims are presented.

A McDonald's campaign offered YTV's most unique branded game to date. The McDonald's and YTV "Go Active Film Festival" won a Canadian Media Innovation Award and was touted as empowering children, the target market being ages six to eleven, to generate their own ytv.com content. The film festival was a movie-making web-based program that allowed children to create their own short films by choosing between and combining a multitude of cartoon backdrops, characters, props, sound effects, and music. Children could submit their short films and vote on each other's work. The larger five-week campaign was promoted heavily through host mentions, a dedicated microsite, and point-of-sale advertisements in McDonald's franchises across Canada. The McDonald's brand presence was far from subtle. The winner received a "Golden Cheeseburger Award," in addition to other sponsored prizes. A press release described the Go Active Film Festival as an "integrated online and on-air promotion that empowered viewers to create a customized *'i'm lovin it' film* [emphasis added] showcasing physical activity in fun and creative ways."[34] With YTV and McDonald's facing increasing criticism over the issue of childhood obesity, both parties used this campaign to promote exercise. All entrants were supposed to celebrate physical activity in their submissions, and the grand prize winner in 2006 created a skateboarding mini-film. Commenting on the multi-platform contest, a McDonald's Canada marketing executive described the popularity of the promotion as "a great indicator that we've been successful in helping kids bring to life their passion for sports and activity in a way that appeals to them."[35] Likewise, a YTV executive claimed that the online movie-making program was an "empowering and creative initiative" that generated "excitement and positive responses from our audience in a forum that promotes balanced lifestyles."[36]

YTV and Hypercommercialism: Event Marketing

From brand name–dropping hosts, to sponsored online games, YTV has constructed a hypercommercial children's mediascape, both on-air and online. However, there is a third media "space" that YTV has conquered for advertisers: live events. YTV's website positions "Weird on Wheels" as a "high-energy, high-impact road show" that "allows thousands of kids nation wide to experience their favourite network in full colour and in 3 dimensions." Weird on Wheels trucks hit the road in summer, stopping in communities across Canada where children in attendance can play free interactive games with a YTV crew. Fitting in with YTV's overall "weird" appeal, the tour trucks, each nicknamed "Oooze," come complete with monster-like eyes and tentacles. According to the YTV Client-Marketing website, the vehicles unfold to "reveal an interactive environment that captivates and stimulates the senses." However, the Client-Marketing group also promises: "YTV gets kids and the [Weird on Wheels] Crew can act as the ultimate ambassadors for YOUR brand." With Weird on Wheels, YTV Client-Marketing delivers "an integrated, experiential program that will continue to build your brand's equity and deliver a positively memorable experience to your consumers."

What makes this advertising platform even more flagrant is the nature of the locations at which Weird on Wheels has recently appeared. While the tour predictably visited major family-oriented festivals and fairs—such as Toronto's Canadian National Exhibition or Vancouver's Pacific National Exhibition—the tour has also made stops in Toys"R"Us, Zellers, and Walmart parking lots. Nearly one in every five stops on the Weird on Wheels summer 2007 tour was simply a parking lot of a suburban shopping plaza, placing children close to a retailer offering the products they may have just sampled in the various Weird on Wheels "attractions." In 2007 the Weird on Wheels ytv.com microsite listed a total of six questions under a "Frequently Asked Questions" heading. One of these six questions asks, "Where can I purchase the products used at [Weird on Wheels]?" and was answered with a list of retailers like Walmart and Toys"R"Us.

For YTV advertisers, Weird on Wheels is a disguised sampling opportunity. For several years the Weird on Wheels Oooze trucks featured three or four "games" or "shows" for children. Year after year, a snack food producer has taken at least one of these slots. In 2006, General Mills created the "Fruit By the Foot Extend Your Fun Zone," which was described as a "branded fun zone for kids ages 6–14."[37] In the Fruit By the Foot Extend Your Fun Zone, children worked on a giant puzzle with the assistance of the Weird on Wheels crew and could win product samples. In 2005, Procter and Gamble's Pringles potato chip brand enjoyed a spot on the tour. Pringles dubbed their event the "Irresistible Taste Tour" and gave participants at each stop "a chance to test their knowledge in the Pringles Irresistible Taste Trivia Challenge ... and have loads of fun, while mingling with the Pringles Crew in the Pringles Party Lounge."[38] Another slot on the annual tour typically went to a toy manufacturer. The "Ultimate Nerf Challenge" was a star attraction in 2006. Likewise, and with the aim to "get kids to play in the tournament while at the same time providing opportunities for sampling," a Hasbro "Lazer Tag" tournament was a highlight in 2005.[39] Character marketing has been a long-standing issue among those critical of children's marketing practices. The Weird on Wheels event marketing tour allows cartoon brand mascots to come alive in three dimensions. Minute Maid offers a "Bibo" juice box drink and uses characters such as "Taka Strawberry," "Johnny Orange," "Paolo Peach," and "Jay Apple Jr." to market the flavours. These flavour "mascots" joined Weird on Wheels in the summer of 2003 to play the "Bibo Time Machine" game with children in person. With the help of Bibo's "zany" mascots, children had to "collect all the needed Bibo wedges to solve the Bibo word puzzle."[40] Similarly, in 2004, Kelloggs' "Tony the Tiger" joined the tour to play a "Who's Got the Moves?" soccer challenge with participants at each stop.

Situating Hypercommercialism in a Neo-Liberal Mediascape

Hypercommercialism is embedded in the problems of "big media" and monopolistic competition. Hypercommercialism cannot be separated from vertical and horizontal media concentration, the promotional ethos animating mergers and acquisitions, or the philosophy of corporate synergy, "whereby the whole of the corporation is greater than the sum of the parts."[41] McAllister and Giglio argue that the "synergistic strategies" of commercial media contribute significantly to the increased promotionalism on children's television."[42] Contemporary television advertising practices not only erode the line between programs and advertising, but also blur the lines between different media platforms and brands owned by the same parent company. It is sometimes difficult to break down hypercommercial practices by media platform, because campaigns typically utilize several of a media corporation's advertiser-friendly assets. YTV promotions often include an on-air element, an online presence, an event marketing component, and, in some cases, a print execution.[43] Moreover, campaigns can reach beyond the YTV brand. In addition to YTV, other Corus Entertainment cable and digital specialty television assets include Nickelodeon Canada, Discovery Kids, TreehouseTV, W Network, and CMT Canada. The aforementioned YTV Sunlight contest was also promoted, presumably to parents, with W Network contest spots and sponsorships. By the nature of Corus Entertainment's organizational structure an advertiser can negotiate a multimedia, multi-station promotional effort with a single phone call.

Corus Entertainment also owns Nelvana, a significant Canadian animation, publishing, and licensing company. Nelvana franchises, ranging from *Franklin* to *Beyblade*, are often based around toys, books, or other licensed merchandise. As was the case with the so-called program-length commercials of the 1980s, these franchises and their accompanying products are promoted on air with animating programming. However, by also falling under the Corus Entertainment corporate umbrella Nelvana represents a kind of "internal" advertising client. YTV's hypercommercial advertising opportunities can even benefit other divisions of Corus Entertainment. Nelvana properties like *Beyblade* have been promoted by YTV contests, web games, and Weird on Wheels event marketing.

Highly concentrated media are symptomatic of a deregulated neo-liberal media system, driven by the alleged "freedoms" that the market provides. Cuts to public broadcasting are also indicative of a neo-liberal media system. If YTV viewers tire of endless promotions, Canadian public television, either the CBC or provincial educational broadcasters, could provide a viable alternative where children's producers have more authority than advertisers. Public television can take more risks and potentially enjoys greater autonomy. However, in times of significant public broadcasting budget cuts, this may no longer be the case. F.B. Rainsberry's review of Canadian children's television cites funding as the most significant concern facing the CBC's children's unit throughout its history. Without sufficient public funding—an ongoing problem in a climate where public television is expected to "compete" like any other business—even public broadcasters begin to make children's programming decisions based on advertiser imperatives. For example, Rainsberry has documented how the CBC classified *Fraggle Rock* as "family viewing" in the "light entertainment" department just so it could be commercially sponsored.[44] Marketers might defend advertising on children's television by suggesting the revenue helps to create better programming. However this kind of neo-liberal discourse obfuscates the question of why children's television must turn to advertising for funding in the first place.

Advertising-supported television is neither natural nor inevitable. As Stephen Kline articulates, "our cultural amnesia makes it appear as if television advertising has always been like this—as if children have always needed the right action toys to play with their friends, the right hero on their pillowcase."[45] Significant policy action has been taken against children's marketers around the world, and even within Canada with Quebec's 1980 prohibition of children's advertising. Although blanket bans are potentially simplistic in the twenty-first century television environment, nonetheless, such measures show us that policy can be used as a tool to push back against the over-commercialization of children's television.

Caldwell argues that the "televisual form in the age of digital simply cannot be accounted for without talking about the institutional forces that spur and manage those forms."[46] I suggest that advertising is a dominant institutional force shaping English-Canadian commercial children's television. Through a close reading of YTV materials and industry reports, it appears that several extensions of YTV's brand have been constructed as advertiser-motivated responses to the crisis of the thirty-second spot. YTV's current advertising practices are symptomatic of a hypercommercial mediascape. However, as I have also traced, even the force of advertising can be located in much larger institutional practices such as media consolidation, neo-liberal approaches to public television funding, and a policy environment that trusts the advertising industry to self-regulate using a dated and weak code. The issue of hypercommercialism on children's television is significant for parents, educators, and policy-makers to consider because it escapes current regulatory boundaries and impacts public, private, and even supposedly "commercial-free" television.[47] Finally, the issue of hypercommercialism is worthy of attention because it complicates debates on whether children are passive victims or active critics of television advertising. Hypercommercialism requires new kinds of media literacy efforts, because even the most media-savvy youth may not recognize the totality of YTV's advertising practices and link them to the channel's commercial goals.

Notes

1 See Havens, Lotz, and Tinic, "Critical Media Industry Studies."
2 Materials were collected between 2006 and 2008 from a variety of publicly available sources, including YTV's main website (ytv.com), YTV's Sales and Client-Marketing website (http://www.corusmedia.com/ytv/), Corus Entertainment's website (http://www.corusent.com), and several Canadian media industry news sources, like Media in Canada (http://www.mediaincanada.com).
3 Buckingham, *After the Death*, 87.
4 Rainsberry, *A History*, 48.
5 See Jeffery, "The Supreme Court," for a detailed account of Quebec's policy.
6 Turow, *Breaking*, 4–5.
7 Banet-Weiser, *Kids Rule*, 113.
8 YTV's reach, however, is minimal in Quebec. "VRAK," owned by Astral, is a French equivalent of YTV. However, due to Quebec's restrictions on children's advertising, VRAK's reliance on advertising revenue is considerably less.
9 For example, see Sutherland and Thompson, *Kidfluence*, 17.
10 Decades of psychological experiments have attempted to assess whether children understand the persuasive goals of television advertising. For a literature review of some of this research, see John, "Consumer Socialization."
11 Buckingham, *After the Death*, 116.
12 Sutherland and Thompson, *Kidfluence*, 72.
13 McChesney, *Problem*, 166.
14 McChesney and Foster, "Commercial Tidal Wave," 2.
15 Flint and Steinberg, "Ad Icon," A1.
16 McAllister, "From Flick to Flack," 104–5.
17 See McAllister and Giglio, "Commodity Flow."
18 For a broader discussion of promotional culture, see Wernick, *Promotional Culture*.
19 Caldwell, "Convergence Television," 70.
20 Leiss, Kline, and Jhally, *Social Communication*, 152.
21 Boddy, "Interactive Television," 121.
22 Budd, Craig, and Steinman, *Consuming Environments*, 77.
23 McChesney and Foster, "Commercial Tidal Wave," 7.
24 McAllister, "From Flick to Flack," 101.
25 Buckingham, *After the Death*, 155.
26 "YTV Forks Up."
27 Kohl, "YTV Gives Hasbro."
28 Kohl, "Corus Gets Viewers."
29 Ibid.
30 Poulton, "Online Advertising."
31 "Starcom Unleashes."
32 Kline, Dyer-Witheford, and de Peuter, *Digital Play*, 244.
33 Kohl, "Corus Targets Tweens."
34 "Winner Announced."
35 Ibid.
36 Ibid.

37 "Hasbro Partners."
38 "Cruisin' across Canada."
39 "YTV Takes Weird."
40 "Croozing across Canada."
41 McAllister, "From Flick to Flack," 108.
42 McAllister and Giglio, "Commodity Flow," 29.
43 Although not discussed in this chapter, YTV also offers a quarterly print magazine, *Whoa!* that is distributed in Pizza Hut restaurants, Indigo bookstores, among other locations. YTV promotions often include a print element in *Whoa!*
44 Rainsberry, *A History*, 215.
45 Kline, *Out of the Garden*, 264.
46 Caldwell, "Convergence Television," 46.
47 For example, even though Astral's Family Channel cannot include traditional commercial breaks, the service does enjoy advertising revenue through countless contests and sponsored promotions. Corus's "commercial free" TreehouseTV, aimed at preschoolers, also enjoys advertising revenue through sponsored contests.

Part III

Contexts of Criticism

Genre, Narrative, and Form

6

Canadianizing Canadians
Television, Youth, Identity

MICHELE BYERS

To be Canadian is to live in the space between certainties, to dwell in the gap that separates conviction from speculation. To be Canadian, in other words, is to exist in a constant state of becoming.[1]

IN THIS CHAPTER, I interrogate several Canadian TV series—*Degrassi Junior High* (1987–89), *Degrassi High* (1989–91), *Ready or Not* (1993–97), *Drop the Beat* (2000–1), *Degrassi: The Next Generation* (2001–), and *renegadepress.com* (2004–)—that explore myths of Canadianness through the production of narratives about Canadian youth. It is hard to make an explicit claim that these texts are representative of youth television produced in Canada. It might be truer to say that they are representative of youth texts produced in Canada for Canadians, even though some have found success in other parts of the world. That is, I think they provide a relatively solid sample of the type of youth shows that have circulated in this country over the last twenty-five years.[2] In each case, the intersection of youth and the rights of citizenship can be located in the dramatic tensions created in representations of age, agency, and racial/ethnicization. That all of these series highlight social difference among teens is significant within the broader lexicon of teen TV, but even more so are the potential opportunities they offer for the disruption of myths about Canadianness as a social location.

By the disruption of myths I mean that in the pages that follow I will identify some of the ways in which these TV series produce particular visions of

Canadianness—how they Canadianize particular subjects and/or subject positions—that participate in the production and dissemination of discourses through which contested terms like "youth" and "Canadian" enter into everyday life. I do this by looking at three main themes. The first theme examines the way in which middle-class and white/white-ethnic parents come to represent the lie that all Canadians are equal and that Canadians are not racist. It is in rejecting their parents that (some) young people are able to adopt their rights as Canadian citizens. The second theme displaces racism from the dominant social group onto individual members of marginalized groups, suggesting that young people on the margins must learn to love themselves for their "outsider" identities. In theme two, as in the first, racism is represented as an individual issue, rather than a reflection of historically entrenched structures of oppression, which aligns with the neo-liberal values that have been dominant during this period of production. The third theme looks at representations of youth, particularly marginalized youth in urban settings, as cultural producers. These examples, in which youth are represented as having some power to write/speak back to various forms of structural dominance, re-imagine the relationship between young people and popular culture in innovative ways.[3]

Why study Canadian teen TV? The first reason relates to the need to take teens, teen TV, and Canadian teen TV seriously. We must acknowledge that youth are both powerful consumers and negotiators of cultural meanings and largely absent as producers of mainstream media. Though adult producers may draw on the experiences of young people—the Internet, for example, provides a context in which young people can be "heard" and offer ideas to cultural producers—teen texts are still largely produced *by* adults *for* youth. These are adults who, as Glyn Davis and Kay Dickinson remind us, produce texts with a wide variety of social agendas, including education, entertainment, the creation of citizens, and the instillation of ethics.[4] I believe it is important to champion representations of youth, especially those young people—for example, queer and trans, immigrant and refugee, poor, rural, racialized, and so forth—long invisible in the popular public sphere. But it is also crucial to acknowledge that the youth in question are the mediated constructions of adults and to consider who is constructing, where, how, and for what possible ends.

Canada produces a lot of teen TV series. Most of these could be considered "quality teen TV"; unlike other quality teen series, however, these are unlikely to represent "teenagers as mature, reflexive, and 'adult,'" or to cast adults to play teen roles.[5] Many of these series have been critiqued for their emphasis on conventional values and moral lessons.[6] And yet they rarely offer unified moral positions, refusing the narrative closure that was long a trademark of many genres of television fiction (although, admittedly, this has changed significantly in the last decade). These choices are related to the way Canadian television has historically told stories differently, in distinctive voices that do not altogether differ, but are highly differentiated, from those produced in other national contexts.[7] This makes Canadian teen TV highly visible/marketable on the global stage, but has also tended to erase Canada's unique contributions to the genre, which is often considered almost exclusively American.[8]

A second reason to study these texts relates to the need to examine Canadian TV within the broader contexts of local production and global distribution, and to produce more critical discussion that can add to debates about TV that tend to be very US-centric. TV dramas are highly conventionalized, deeply rooted in the socio-cultural, political, and economic landscapes of their production; we need to study these texts because to date they have been so little studied. At the same time, everything in a TV drama is constructed; we must not assume that what is being shown is a transparent rendering of a particular social reality. This is especially important in the context of Canadian TV—with its long documentary roots—about which claims of "authenticity" are often made.[9]

Lack of study, distribution, and systematic archiving means that many Canadian series not only run under the radar, but are in danger of being erased from the cultural map.[10] But these series offer points of disruption in a global media matrix that we often imagine flowing only in one direction; Canadian teen series are just one example of how "we have become adept at producing idiosyncratic variations of longstanding and successful cultural forms."[11] We are also, at times, the original producers of those forms; I would point here to the centrality of the *Degrassi* series in developing the contemporary teen TV genre.[12] We must challenge Canadian TV's status as an imitation of something more authentically produced somewhere else.

A third reason to study Canadian teen TV relates to the way in which dramas comprise structures and practices through which questions about identity are addressed, and through which subjectivities are made visible in complex and contested ways. Canadian television has often been seen as attempting to manage a perceived crisis of Canadianness by staging authentic subject positions for Canadians to occupy. These offer particular, and often limited, landscapes that viewers can engage with fiercely as they struggle to make texts meaningful based on the unique (and at times uniquely Canadian) identities and experiences they bring to bear on what they see onscreen.[13]

Finally, Canada's particular national history, including its state-funded and -regulated media and multicultural policies, makes studying these media texts important. Melanie Ash writes: "There is an ironic coming of age for all Canadians of colour: the moment when you first have to justify your presence in your country in a way that white Canadians, and even newly-arrived white immigrants, never will."[14] Augie Fleras, writing in the same volume, insists that official multiculturalism reinforces, through a kind of intentional myopia, an endemic racism all its own.[15] Wendy Brown's recent work deals with the resurgence in the last decades of the idea of "tolerance";[16] we might consider state-sanctioned multiculturalism in Canada—and as it circulates in the texts studied here—a discourse of tolerance par excellence. We might ask, through what particular "modalities," "codes," or "practices" of tolerance is the racializing work of multiculturalism set in motion in these texts?[17] Consider that central to the myth of multiculturalism in Canada is the elision of white supremacy. For the myth to come to be seen as an inherent national value it must be constantly reiterated, "cover[ing] over the constitutive conventions by which it was mobilized."[18] It is thus important to study texts in which social differences are centrally represented and which provide moments in which these constitutive conventions may be at least partially problematized.

The ways in which we engage in processes of mediated consumption are ambivalent. While the theoretical tradition of searching for "good" images in the media persists, it is more productive to "seize aesthetic and pedagogic potentialities in a wide variety of cultural practices," in this case televisual.[19] At best, this type of work can lead to a "popular multiculturalism" that "articulate[s] itself through a politicized understanding of cultural representation."[20] This is a move away from a multiculturalism that is state-sanctioned, highly formalized, and embedded in "the myth of Canada as a benevolent, caring and tolerant nation."[21] To dispel this myth is to challenge what it means to be Canadian. Each of the texts studied in this chapter takes up the challenge of representing youth in narratives that complicate our understanding of how age and social difference intersect to produce landscapes of citizenship and belonging. In doing so they provide us with opportunities to think through the ways we come to know and be Canadian.

"My Momma Says ..."

Degrassi Junior High was shot in Toronto between 1987 and 1989 and aired on the CBC. It began as a grassroots pedagogical project; issues of identity and difference are central to many story arcs and are raised in relation to core characters. No character is reduced to a single facet of identity. In "Black and White" (3014), Michelle (Maureen McKay), who is white, struggles to confront her parents' discomfort with her desire to date BLT (Dayo Ade), who is black.[22] Initially, Michelle cannot make the link between her parents' rejection of BLT and racism, because their racism works against her common-sense understanding of her parents as good Canadians. Several scenes in the episode position Michelle and her family within a familiar visual iconography of middle-class whiteness, where boundaries of gender, race, and class are well maintained. There are several shots of their well-kempt, two-storey brick home, as well as interior shots where we can see how well, if not lavishly, appointed it is. Michelle's father is shown as a brusque man in a three-piece suit; her mother is softer and gentler, but still professional.

Michelle can find nothing in her parents' firm location as middle-class Canadian citizens to hang the hat of racism on. It just doesn't fit. So she asks some friends: Alexa (Irene Courakos), who is Greek, L.D. (Amanda Cook), who, like Michelle, is presented as generically white, and Lucy (Anais Granofsky), who is bi-racial (white and black). The discussion takes place in the cafeteria, one of the prime spaces where the characters congregate and where we can observe that the series' players are predominantly white and visually quite similar. This is true of the four girls at the table too. Although they represent different racialized and ethnicized identities, the visual coding of them through the way they are dressed, the way they talk and gesture, includes only small differentiators (Lucy is "hipper," L.D. is a "tomboy," Michelle and Alexa are "girly"). Overall, the effect is to reduce the visual reading of difference within the scene and to highlight instead the similarities of the young people in the school, no matter what their particular racialized, ethnic, or class identities are represented as being.

Back at the table, Alexa's suggestion that BLT is a good dancer and athlete because he is black is met by incredulity from L.D. and Lucy, who chastise her for the racist implications of her common-sense perceptions. Alexa responds that her parents would never accept her dating someone who was black; in fact, they would prefer she only date Greek boys, as is the custom in their small town in Greece. L.D. and Lucy insist that this is prejudice, but Alexa just shrugs, suggesting that it may well be, but that it is an inevitable part of her ethnic (and her parents' immigrant) experience. Michelle is positioned as watcher rather than participant in the discussion, as if trying to reconcile what she hears with her own experience. This scene locates the roots of racism in ethnic otherness constituted in cultural difference sanctioned by the state.[23] Alexa reiterates her immigrant parents' racist views; her girlfriends, who are "purer" Canadians, reject them.

Later, Michelle confronts her mother, asking very directly if the reason she cannot go to the dance with BLT is because he is black. Her mother acts surprised, insisting that she is not racist, but that she is protecting her daughter (and BLT) from *other people's* racism. Michelle's mother constitutes racism as a position that cannot be articulated by people like herself: she cannot be racist because her identity precludes racism. This is made more problematic when she suggests that if they date, Michelle and BLT will run into problems because of their different cultural values, demonstrating the way racialization is used to police "Canadian" identity;[24] BLT's blackness overwhelms the very myths of multiculturalism and diversity Michelle's mother invokes. In the end, Michelle rebels and goes to the dance with BLT, showing that she has not inherited—has in fact rejected—her parents' racist views. They date for several years of the series.

A similar story arc appears on *Ready or Not*, a 'tween series shot in suburban Toronto between 1993 and 1997 that aired on Global. The series focuses on the friendship of Busy Ramone (Lani Billard), who is Italian, and Amanda Zimm (Laura Bertram), who is Jewish. In the first-season episode, "Black or White or Maybe Grey" (1010)—note the similarity in the episode titles—Busy encourages her father (Sam/Gerry Mendicino) to hire her friend Troy (Omari Moore) at the family butcher shop, failing to mention that Troy is black. When they meet, Sam is nonplussed: "This is your friend? Uh, look, I don't know what Busy told you, but uh, we're not hiring anybody." Busy is confused, but Troy insists that Busy just won't see the truth behind her father's behaviour.

This scene mirrors the lunchroom scene on *Degrassi* because it equates racism with ethnicity, in this case with the Italian immigrant father. If we take a wider look at the episode, we can see how central Sam's ethnicization is to his construction as racist. A secondary story arc involves Busy's brother Manny (Joseph Griffin), who wants to go on a motorcycle trip rather than work in the family business. Throughout the episode, the scenes involving Troy are intercut with scenes in the family home, usually the kitchen, in which the father tries to assert his authority. Sam's frustration and anger are linked to the changes happening at home, in the theme and structure of the episode. His desire to see his racist beliefs *come true* is connected to the idea that this will prove that his desire to keep the world unchanging (to maintain his status/control as family patriarch) is "right."

Sam hires Troy. This offers the possibility of narrative closure: Sam will learn not to be racist by working with Troy.[25] However, Sam points the finger at Troy after twenty-five dollars goes missing from the cash on Troy's first day. Busy is incensed and insists to her mother (Lucy/Diana Reis) that Sam is a bigot: "those people" one reads about in "social studies."[26] Troy is fired. When he insists that he has the right to know why and to be paid for the work he did the previous day, he is humiliated and thrown out of the store. Immediately after this the money is found, but Sam is so invested in being "right" about Troy that he refuses to apologize or offer Troy his job back. Troy tells Busy: "People like that don't listen. They decide things about you long before they've even met you." Busy apologizes and insists that she is not like her father. Busy and Troy wander off together.[27]

Both of these narratives are highly ambivalent in their attempts to negotiate with issues of racism in the Canadian context. Both suggest that racism is part of an "ethnic" rather than Canadian tradition.[28] The *Degrassi* narrative is perhaps more challenging, in that it articulates the difficulty of attaching racism to those whose identities are most hegemonically Canadian—white and middle-class—and because Michelle's parents are both racist, it does not link racism exclusively with masculinity. Both series allow their young characters to speak (back) to parents about their racist beliefs and to challenge them, and do not offer easy moments of closure in which the parents suddenly "see the light" and change. At the same time, neither narrative offers the possibility that young people are racist, suggesting that if Canadian racism does exist it is something that belongs to the past. This is interesting because the teen TV texts of this period are ones that for the first time really move focus from the family (or student/teacher relations) to the peer group. The parents, in a sense, can be invested with racism because they are not the anchor of enculturation they had been represented as in the past. These texts, both situated in the Toronto of the late 1980s and early 1990s, offer visions of youth who, despite their differences, look remarkably similar to one another and thus represent a unified peer group: it is the parents who are outsiders here and who must be rejected in order to truly become Canadianized.[29]

"I'm Sick of Myself ..."

Airing on CTV starting in 2001, *Degrassi: The Next Generation (TNG)* was produced for a private broadcaster in a period of neo-liberal ascendancy in which television production practices were increasingly shaped by global competition, audience fragmentation, privatization, deregulation of broadcasting standards, and the general decline of the viability of public, national broadcasting. It was also shaped by the phenomenal growth and formalization of a youth TV culture, with its attendant professionalization of the genre and its performers.

The new series does, however, continue to highlight discourses about social issues that are rooted in earlier—welfare-statist—discourses, although they find themselves increasingly entangled with neo-liberal strategies of representation. The characters are more firmly middle-class than on the older *Degrassi* series, and perhaps for this reason the series has not focused much on issues of racialization and ethnicity.

One exception is found in the second-season episode "Don't Believe the Hype" (2011), in which Hazel (Andrea Lewis) acknowledges her Muslim identity. This episode points to the context of production in that it aired after 9/11/2001. In this episode, the Degrassi Community School holds "International Day," an event that celebrates the cultural diversity of its students. Hazel leads everyone to believe that she is Jamaican, but a Muslim classmate, Fariza (Jacqueline Rose), who is Iraqi and is identifiable as Muslim by her hijab, recognizes that Hazel's name, Aden, is Somali. When Fariza's display is defaced with the word "terrorist," Hazel, though innocent, is the prime suspect. Hazel eventually "comes clean" by giving a presentation that reveals "the truth" about herself.

Interestingly, this episode is constructed around the visual style cultures of teens and the style cultures of racialized and ethnicized identities. The episode opens with Hazel and Terri (Christina Schmidt) standing at their lockers. Their friend Paige (Lauren Collins) comes up and gives one of the girls a "fashion police" ticket for wearing last year's jeans—on this series, like the earlier ones discussed, the general cast members tend to look "the same," with some notable examples, such as Fariza; visible difference is most marked through consumable style cultures. Hazel looks down the hall and sees Fariza. She grabs a ticket from Paige and then places herself in front of the girl in the hijab, intoning: "Your crime? Terrorist chic." Fariza tries to ignore Hazel, but Hazel blocks her path until the other girl takes the ticket. Even Paige and Terri look embarrassed and uncomfortable. It must be understood that it is in this context—and in the context of Hazel standing with her girlfriends in the hall, in their identically trendy clothes, hair, make-up, and accessories—that Hazel makes her (episode-)closing remark that she does wear a hijab when she goes to mosque but that "to take it on full time [as Fariza does], it's a personal and important decision.... Unlike you guys, I was ashamed of who I am." The issue of style cultures also comes up in the representation of the school celebration as an opportunity to "dress up" and to "display" culture through flags, pictures, food, and clothing. Hazel understands intrinsically that she can "be" Jamaican rather than Somali simply by bringing in jerk chicken and wearing a knit hat in Jamaican colours. That is, she can pass easily within the context of a school where no one else seems to be Jamaican (or Caribbean for that matter). The only people who question her are Fariza—who is thus a real threat to Hazel—and the Jamaican man who sells her the chicken. Being Jamaican is like being cool; it involves being able to hold cultural or social capital and pass it off as one's own.

At the end of the episode Hazel insists that she is no longer ashamed of being Muslim. The last image on screen is of Hazel, almost facing the camera, while behind her, taking up the other half of the screen, is her own projected image, in profile, wearing a hijab. This suggests a reconciliation of her identities, but we never hear about it again. It is noteworthy that it is Hazel, not Fariza, who is a core character in the series; the issue of the hijab as part of everyday life disappears.[30] Although parents are not central to the series, the elision of Hazel's parents is a missed opportunity to interrogate questions about racialization/ethnicization in the Canadian context. For instance, in the relationship Hazel has with Jimmy (Aubrey Graham) in seasons three and four, the issue of their different religious/ethnic backgrounds is never raised, presumably because they are both "black." Not making Fariza a more central, recurring character is also a loss. She is interesting here, because she is represented as quite tough and I would have liked to see where the series could have gone with her character's development. In one scene in this episode, Hazel tells Fariza that she stopped wearing the hijab after she was badly beaten by some girls at her old school, girls who also called her a terrorist. Rather than allow this to be a bonding moment, Fariza simply says, coldly, "you sure learned from them."

While the episodes of *Ready or Not* and the earlier *Degrassi* series focus on questions of community, the lesson learned on *TNG* is much more individualistic and neo-liberal. Though other students voice various opinions, Hazel's self-hatred is the centre of this narrative. Like the suggestion that racism comes from ethnic groups and new immigrants, here racism comes from inside the Muslim community. The challenge of the episode is thus ambiguous: the anti-racist message is directed into the community against which the racism is also directed. The ambivalence is clear in a scene in which the class as a whole debates the defacement of Fariza's display and the curtailing of the rights of Muslims and Arabs more generally. The students know the correct way to respond but are not clear about how this is linked to more pervasive, and state-sanctioned, oppression. Finally, because the culprit is revealed to be an extra, the core cast is more or less excused from the label "racist," which is further emphasized by Hazel's remark that she is the only one who was ashamed of her cultural heritage.

A somewhat similar narrative appears in *renegadepress.com*, a series set in Regina that began airing in 2003 on TVO and APTN.[31] The series follows a group of students who run an online video newspaper. One of the unique aspects of this series is that two of its core characters are urban Aboriginal youth, a group particularly marginalized within the Canadian media. In "Skin Deep" (1004), Crystal (Rachel Colwell) decides that since she is starting a new school she is going to pretend that she is not First Nations. This requires that her brother Jack (Bronson Pelletier), who has recently moved in with his father and sister after living on a reserve, not acknowledge that they are related, or even know one another, so she can be known as "herself."

At the start of the episode, Jack and Crystal are walking to school together. Jack asks if she is going to attend a community feast, to which she responds that she is tired of going to community events and hates bannock. Jack says: "What kind of Indian are you?" In the cafeteria Crystal and her friends talk about a recent spate of locker break-ins. Two of Crystal's friends suggest that it is probably the work of "Red Clan," an Aboriginal gang. Crystal looks uncomfortable. On the way to class a third friend, one who knows she is Native, reminds Crystal that they would speak more carefully if they knew who/what she really was. But Crystal isn't interested. Further, she tells her friend: "I'm tired of being the Native expert." Her concerns are shown to be justified when, in her next class, the (white) teacher calls on a Native student to elaborate on a story he is telling about a historical Cree leader. The student responds: "How should I know, I'm Ojibway."

Crystal decides to take action in the class's family history presentations, which she and her friends mock as being "so grade three." They do not deny the differences that are plainly visible in their hallways; they seem to be mocking the clash between the lived reality of these differences and events that focus on their most superficial aspects. Like the other series I have discussed thus far, *renegadepress.com* highlights similarities among the student characters, especially in the way they talk and dress, with the exception of the Native gang members, some nods to subcultural style, and minor class differences that can be discerned in what the characters wear.[32] Crystal and Jack look and speak like their peers who are of a variety of racial, ethnic, and class backgrounds. In this episode, Crystal decides to pretend her roots are Italian and Portuguese. She does this simply by saying that it is so. With her long, straight brown hair and eyes, and the pizza she brings to class, when she says: "I'm a mutt. It's cool. I can be whoever I want. I like Italian best," her classmates appear to believe her (at least, no one offers a challenge). When Jack hears about this, he accuses Crystal of being ashamed. But she insists: "I know who I am, okay. Telling people I'm Native, it's not gonna make me more me."

At the end of the episode, we hear the following in voice-over: "There are so many pictures on TV and in magazines of how we're supposed to look." This emphasizes the relationship between identity and popular representation, complicating how we are positioned to read this series as well as pointing to the lack of popular representation of young Native people. This episode does not resolve Crystal's discomfort, because it is not clear how we are to read her discomfort: is she ashamed of her identity or does she want to shield herself from the pressures and ignorance of others? Are these different? The suggestion remains that Crystal's ambivalence is a product of herself rather than anything systemic. This comes out in an arc in the episode discussed in the next section, about Josh (Daniel Maslany), the boy Crystal has a crush on. Crystal thinks that Josh starts ignoring her when he finds out that Jack is her brother, and thus that she is Native. Enraged, she confronts him in the cafeteria, where he admits he has been avoiding her, but because he wanted to ask her out and was embarrassed about how to do it. Finding out about Jack was just coincidental. Now Crystal is embarrassed, and it is suggested that her fears of being rejected because of her social identity are unfounded.

Both of the episodes discussed in this section highlight the value of cultural difference and pride. But they also present us with the problematic reality of the way different identities are valued in Canada. Neither Hazel nor Crystal tries to "pass" as a white, Anglo-Canadian girl, but both are narrated as choosing ethnicized identities that they feel are more generically Canadian than their own. Both girls articulate the way marginalized identities can be written across their bodies, either by the scorn of others or by their relentless curiosity. In both cases, the series highlight the fact that these girls have legitimate reasons to be concerned. And yet, the truly problematic relationship to difference is, in both cases, represented as internal. Crystal and Hazel are the ones who are most intolerant of their own differences. In this way, racism is presented as something that comes from within and which is not explicitly tied to histories of marginalization and oppression even as the deep ambivalence represented in both characters challenges the myth that *all* identities serve us equally in Canada, as Canadians.

"Where Did You Learn to Act Like That?"

In the *renegade* episode "Some of My Best Friends Are Indians" (1007), the school goes into a crisis when a middle-class white boy (Ricky Turnbull) is found dead. While the cause of death is reported to be a heart attack, rumours begin to circulate that the boy and his friends had been "sniffing." Jack (Bronson Pelletier) investigates; he tells his best friend Zoey (Ksenia Solo) he wants to do a piece about the incident on *renegade*, to dispel the myth that only Native kids sniff. Zoey is protective of the family, neighbours she has known since childhood, even after Ricky's brother Andrew (Michael Sterling) reveals that Ricky *was* sniffing.

Jack is thrown back in time to the death of his best friend on the reserve and tries to explain to Zoey why it is so important to tell the truth about Ricky. He reminds her that the incident on the reserve was covered extensively on the national news, that newscasters got into the faces of the Aboriginal youth in a way that they never can with middle-class white youth. He says: "I did some research on the Net. Turns out 12–15 year-old white males are most common sniffers. Oh what? You thought it was only Native people?" Zoey responds: "Didn't you?" This scene addresses the desire to see the Canadian news media as presenting "the truth" and, through this truth telling, as serving as a vehicle for helping marginalized peoples. What is offered instead is a vision of the news media as central to the constitution and continual recirculation of myths about Otherness.[33] The episode highlights the different amounts of power different social groups have and their ability to use, and/or avoid being exploited by, the media.

While the characters on this series are represented as visually similar, the series is highly concerned with differences in urban spaces. As the series moves between storylines, the viewer is treated to a blurred scan of various locations within the city of Regina, which highlights the urban-ness of the landscape, but also the way space is marked along class (and hence racialized) lines. This is integral to the way sniffing, and Jack and Zoey's negotiation of their relationship, are represented in this episode. In one scene, Jack follows a friend of Ricky's into a posh—Zoey's and Andrew's— neighbourhood. A white woman jogging sees him, a young Native man in a hoodie, following a young white boy. A few moments later the police arrive and challenge Jack's presence there.

Zoey begins to look more closely at Ricky's death but meets resistance from her mother, Linda (Wendy Anderson). Zoey's questions disrupt the safety Linda feels she and her daughter are entitled to because of who they are. The privilege of these women is highlighted when they stand in front of the Turnbull's front door in their beautiful clothes and flawless hair and makeup. In another scene, Jack's father, Wayne (Lorne Cardinal) tries to keep Jack from writing the story because of a complaint from Mr. Turnbull. Wayne encourages Jack to shift his focus to the damage sniffing is doing to *his* people. Jack explodes: "It's been done." Wayne seems to be protecting Jack from what he sees as the inevitable response of the "white community," but his words cannot contain Jack's anger and frustration at the way the media, via those with power, manipulate the "truth." These scenes provide a strong visual contrast in terms of the representation of the characters and the physical spaces they do and can inhabit. The last scene of the episode encapsulates this even more strikingly: Andrew comes to Jack's house to talk about his brother for the story. On the street are a group of multi-racial children playing street hockey. The contrast between this street, though certainly not poor, and the street where Andrew lives (and the houses the two boys live in) cannot help but be noted.[34] Andrew and Jack sit on the back steps; where the street in front of Andrew's house had been quiet in both earlier scenes in which it appeared, here we can hear sirens in the background. The two boys sit close together: the red-haired Andrew wears blue jeans and a black wool coat; Jack, black-haired, wears black jeans and a grey canvas coat. As they talk the sound fades out, and Jack puts his arm on Andrew's shoulder for comfort.

A different critique is made on *Drop the Beat*, a short-lived series about a hip-hop radio show in Toronto that aired on the CBC in 2001. "Battle Royale" (1003) deals with a violent eastend/westend rivalry involving Toronto hip-hop artists. Like *renegadepress.com*, *Drop the Beat* is explicitly concerned with urban spaces and communities, and with the way social difference is constituted within those spaces. It is one of the few Canadian texts I have ever seen in which the actors onscreen at any one time are predominantly Afro- or Caribbean-Canadian.[35] One of the first scenes takes place in the bedroom of Dennis, aka Ballistic (Merwin Mondesir), a young DJ. A group of young men listen to and talk about music and the politics of the street. The room is messy and covered with posters. The young men are represented within a very urban, racialized iconography of style, including a lot of tattoos and jewellery. As they exit the room, Dennis's mother, a professional-looking woman with a Caribbean accent, looks on with unmasked displeasure.

Dennis invites westend friends (Mega, Blade, and Lefty) to the station where he is the DJ. The scene is complicated because two of the other young people who work at the station (Divine/Michie Mee and DJ Craft/Shamann) are eastenders. Jeff, aka Vizion (Mark Taylor), the other host, is more excited about his guest, Maise Jones, an American cultural theorist and his idol. Dennis is not impressed. The two hosts are contrasted physically: Jeff is more conservative, while Dennis sports a backwards baseball cap, a white undershirt, earring and chain. In the studio, the east and westenders begin to quarrel. Jeff tries to keep things on track, but before he can do more than introduce

Jones, Lefty and Blade invade the studio and end up in an altercation with Craft and Divine. Dennis tries to keep the peace by inviting them to square off live on the show and to have the audience call in to decide who is the best. Jeff tries to keep the focus on Maise and to draw Maise's attention to the uniqueness of Toronto's hip-hop culture:

> Jones: I'd like to talk about what's going on up here. In my article in *The New Yorker* I talk about cultural transportation, and this is a classical example of it. You guys are taking on a beef that started between the east coast and west coast rappers in the States and you're making it your own.
> Dennis: That's typical American-negro-centric theory talking. We have our own culture here and we got our own shit to deal with.
> Jones: Yeah, but cultural imperialism is called that for a reason. It's very powerful. You may think that it doesn't affect you, but it does.
> Jeff: Yeah, I mean, how many times do you see brothers front like they're straight out of Brooklyn, when they're straight out of Rexdale?[36]
> Dennis: Yo, this is all starting to sound like a broken record.... I mean, the more you hear something the more you start to believe it.

Here the voice of cultural authority calls into question the legitimacy of Canadian hip-hop culture. Jeff yearns for the kind of recognition that Jones has achieved, a translation of hip-hop culture into intellectual/business success, and is more willing to accept his views. As the "expert" Jones thinks that he is the only one who can see the "truth"; only through him can Canadian youth be set free. But Dennis rejects that what he produces somehow belongs to someone else, somewhere else; he recognizes that this rhetoric also acts as a colonizing discourse that discredits his voice and those of other Canadian youth.[37] This is interesting in terms of the way the show itself was received: "a TV news report on the Canadian TV industry cited this series as an example of a show geared toward the American market ... Why? ... how is it *not* Canadian? Surely not because the leads are black and it focuses on inner city/Hip Hop sub-culture?"[38]

The eastenders and westenders square off against each other. The screen feels cramped and claustrophobic. The lighting is dark, which it often is on this series. Maise looks impressed by the young DJs' unique voices and evocations of the particularities of their experiences. The calls, which Dennis refuses to screen, provoke the duelling rappers further. Eventually everyone but Jeff heads outside; a melee has broken out. Dennis brings his cellphone and provides commentary that Jeff transmits live from the studio. There is a continuous cutting between Dennis watching the intensifying fighting and Jeff listening in the DJ booth with his head down. Circling back to Maise, Dennis asks his listeners, but really the young people on the street: "We just mindless clones imitating all this violence ... Biggie and Tupac? We're not down south. We should be proud of our own stuff!" Dennis looks baffled; we get a shot of the switchboard lighting up.

This episode asks us to look at Canadian cultural production within a global sphere often understood as American. As Rinaldo Walcott argues, albeit in a different context, Canadians may "borrow from an African American model, [but] it seems clear that black Canadians reinvent what they borrow for local purposes."[39] This episode levels a critique at the imposition of a theoretical model that assumes that Canadian cultural products and lived experiences are pale imitations of American ones. Public reaction to the series, as indicated above, posits that black Canadian youth are incapable of creating authentic media texts or of having authentic media texts created about them; this episode challenges that line of thought.

In both of these episodes, Canadian youth are featured as media consumers *and* producers. As consumers, they are positioned as savvy, but also, in a sense, at the mercy of a media marketplace that offers little authenticity. Jack knows that only Native kids will likely be the focus of news stories about sniffing. Dennis sees his own invisibility as anything but a subject to be colonized by the American media. Jeff's adulation of the American hip-hop model is presented as ambivalent, if for no other reason than because the narrative constantly thwarts his conversations with Jones. As producers, these youth are represented as marginal because they are young, but also because what they have to say is problematic, both because of what they say about Canadianness, but also because they *are* Canadian. And yet, by representing youth as cultural producers at all, these series challenge the ways Canadian youth can be imagined.

Possibilities for Disruption?

In this chapter, I have examined representations of young people struggling to articulate a sense of themselves as Canadians. They are often earnest, idealistic, and pedantic; the young people produced in these series are positioned as more open-minded than adults, but also as more critical; as distanced from racist impulses even as they come to realize that racism exists in the most unlikely places. None of these images are inherently positive or negative; they are ambivalent. Each of these texts offers possibilities for disrupting myths about Canadianness by offering up narratives about youth who are Canadian and yet who are often at the margins of Canadianness. Many are in the process of experiencing the ironic coming-of-age moments described by Ash earlier, of realizing that "to be black [or Native or Muslim ...] and at home in Canada is both to belong and not belong."[40]

The episodes from the early *Degrassi* series and *Ready or Not* offer that mundane forms of racism are wrong and should be challenged, and that the most unlikely people, except maybe young people, can be racist. They may also suggest that racism and intolerance are most prevalent in traditional, immigrant cultures, whose views are tolerated within state-sanctioned multiculturalism but do not represent what "real" Canadians think. In the episodes from the new *Degrassi* and *renegadepress.com*, the function of the narrative appears less as a challenge to racism than as a suggestion that equality can be found in the restoration of pride in a particular character's heritage. The community at large is not challenged because the community is not represented as racist. By shifting focus from the community to the individual, these representations articulate a neo-liberal concern with personal responsibility and the ability to narrate the self that hides the histories of racism through which the Canadian nation has and continues to be constituted. Finally, the episodes from *renegadepress.com* and *Drop the Beat* critique the silencing and marginalization of voices of youth as cultural producers, suggesting that there are ways for youth to use the media as venues for the constitution of alternative notions of nationhood and identity. All of these representations are ambivalent. In the end, each character is represented as having a body they have to live in, one moving through Canadian spaces in which they "both belong and [do] not belong."[41]

In this chapter I have been considering series that produce narratives about Canadian youth, and where dramatic tension is created at the intersection of representations of age, agency, and racial/ethnicization. A lot of what circulates in the Canadian media is performative of an anterior investment in a mythic idea of Canadianess in which "Canadian" is a unified subject position that is open to everyone. The texts studied here reveal our investment in these myths but also offer challenges to them. In this way, they are productive moments articulated within a deeply contradictory space of both pleasure and constraint[42] and very much worth the time and effort of our critical scrutiny.

Notes

The author would like to thank both anonymous reviewers of this essay for their careful reading and insightful questions. Thank you to the editors of this volume for their tireless commitment to getting this book to print. This work was support by grants from SSHRC.

1 Pevere and Dymond, *Mondo Canuck*, viii.
2 There are other shows that could have been included here, such as *Edgemont, Northwood, Madison*, or *Straight Up*.
3 There is no space to cover all the points that could be touched upon in an analysis of these series, or even these episodes. While the focus I have chosen is on racialization and ethnicization, this intersects with various others aspects of identity through which the characters in these series are constructed. Where possible I have touched on these, but I recognize that my analysis is necessarily limited and partial.
4 Davis and Dickinson, "Introduction," 3.
5 Hills, "*Dawson's Creek*," 65.
6 Nicks, "*Straight Up* and Youth Television," 141–57.
7 This is the result of historical and contemporary differences related to the socio-political realities of different nations. The kinds of stories that can be told on Canadian television are often quite different from those than can be told on youth series in the United States, for example. See Grant and Wood, *Blockbusters and Trade Wars*.
8 *Beverly Hills, 90210* is almost always posited as the first "teen" television series of the contemporary period, despite the fact that *Degrassi* began airing earlier. See Moseley, "The Teen Series," 41–43.
9 Hogarth, *Documentary Television in Canada*.
10 The same observation has been made about series produced in Australia and Britain, which have been similarly undertheorized, even by their "own" scholars. Some good discussion of this can be found in essays in Davis and Dickinson, *Teen TV*. The lack of scholarship in this area is particularly pronounced given that there has been a recent explosion of critical work focusing on American television series, including *Buffy the Vampire Slayer* (Kaveney, *Reading the Vampire Slayer*; Wilcox and Lavery, *Fighting the Forces*; South, *Buffy the Vampire Slayer and Philosophy*), *Sex and the City* (Akass and McCabe, *Reading Sex and the City*), *Beverly Hills, 90210* (McKinley, *Beverly Hills, 90210*), *The Simpsons* (Irwin, *The Simpsons and Philosophy*), *The X-Files* (Lavery, Hague, and Cartwright, *Deny All Knowledge*), *The Sopranos* (Lavery, *This Thing of Ours*; Greene and Vernezze, *The Sopranos and Philosophy*), and *Seinfeld* (Irwin, *Seinfeld and Philosophy*). The literature on contemporary Canadian television is limited, and includes Miller's three volumes on Canadian drama (*Turn Up the Contrast*; *Rewind and Search; Outside Looking In*); several chapters from Flaherty and Manning's *The Beaver Bites Back?*; Nicks and Sloniowski, *Slippery Pastimes*; Byers, *Growing Up Degrassi*; and Druick and Kotsopolous, *Programming Reality*. It is notable that more volumes are now appearing that deal with television from other national contexts.
11 Straw, "Dilemmas of Definition," 95–108.
12 Note, however, that in Canada we have a history of rejecting our own products until they have attained success elsewhere. Frank Manning writes about Canadian football: "The game is a striking distillation of typically Canadian conflicts (east versus west); compromises (English tradition versus American innovation); and ironies (an export to the

U.S. that was later re-imported and may be exported again)." Manning, "Reversible Resistance," 16.

13 Bodroghkozy, "As Canadian as Possible," 566–89.

14 Ash, "But Where Are You REALLY From?" 398–409.

15 Fleras, "Racialising Culture/Culturalising Race," 429–43.

16 Previously understood by many to mean "mannered racialism." Brown, *Regulating Aversion*.

17 Ibid., 3, 1.

18 Butler, *Excitable Speech*, 51. Here I refer to the problematic notion that Canadianness is a privilege equated with whiteness.

19 Shohat and Stam, *Unthinking Eurocentrism*.

20 Bannerji, *The Dark Side of Nation*, 5.

21 Walcott, "'Keep On Moving,'" 32.

22 I note the problematic nature in which I have reinscribed "whiteness" as a monolithic identity, as well as how I have created a linguistic binary—white/not-white (or white/black)—that does not disrupt assumptions about the meaningfulness of these categories. It is difficult to find a way to articulate these complex relations without resorting to problematic linguistic references. I use them here with this always in mind, and, where possible, have tried to problematize them explicitly.

23 There is a deep resonance to this image, as the popularity of Canadian Nia Vardalos's *My Big Fat Greek Wedding* clearly indicates.

24 And it is worth noting that in almost none of the texts I studied were there examples where cultural differences *did* come into play beyond the standard way described in this section (to highlight the slow enculturation of the parental generation).

25 We might have expected something like this in the *Degrassi* scene where Michelle goes to her mother as well.

26 Note the idea that bigot and bigotry are not systemic, but something arcane that one finds in scholarly textbooks.

27 In another scene, Amanda talks to Busy about how cute Troy is, which is narratively linked to a scene that follows in which Sam brings up his real concern, that Troy might be interested in Busy. Busy demands to know what the problem would be if she wanted to date Troy, and her father finally expresses his racism explicitly: "He's a black boy. Are you blind?" Troy does become Busy's boyfriend the next season. See note 29.

28 Bannerji, *The Dark Side of Nation*.

29 Both of these episode focus on white girls, and the threat suggested is in the sexual relationship that could burgeon between themselves and their black (boy)friends. The theme of white girl/black boy, and the racism of white parents, is a familiar media trope. Recasting the story to offer a less familiar focus—a different racialized pairing or the minority parents' experience of their child's interracial relationship—might complicate the reading of the issue of interracial dating represented here. For example, it might be interesting to see how parents of white male youth are represented as responding to their sons' choice of dating non-white girls, or to see how the parents of a young black woman respond to her choice to date a white boy (leaving aside the heterocentrism of all of these narratives for the moment). See Byers and Haines, "The White Girl from *That Show*."

30 Although this is taken up in other narratives, such as on *renegadepress.com*.

31 The series very recently (2008) started airing on Global TV, which is exciting news for a show that never had a space on one of the national broadcasters.

32 As I will show in the next example from this series, however, issues of class and racialization are much more explicitly represented in the way the urban landscape is framed and moved through by a variety of characters.

33 See Jiwani, *Discourses of Denial,* especially her reading of the murder of Reena Virk.

34 For a series that deals with poverty in one urban (also Regina) Canadian Aboriginal community, see *Moccasin Flats*.

35 A more recent example of a series focusing on black Canadian identities is *Da Kink in My Hair*, a comedy created by Trey Anthony and Ngozi Paul that ran on Global for two seasons in 2007–9.

36 Rexdale is a working-class suburb in northwest Toronto.

37 Some might read these conflicts as somewhat superficial, which might then substantiate a reading of them as examples of "cultural imperialism." Of course every close reading reveals something different. However, I do not think that these two points are antithetical. It is true that the beefs between the groups are superficial—some might argue that this is true of many such disputes no matter where they take place. And yet they do devolve into violence, suggesting that despite the superficiality there are material consequences to this conflict. Further, the scene I describe takes an ambivalent position on the cultural imperialism thesis, offering up three points of view, one that insists upon the thesis, one that rejects it, and one that takes up a middle ground. In this, the scene mirrors recent debates within Canadian TV studies that have attempted to destabilize a similar media imperialism thesis, which was, for a long time, foundational in the discourse of Canadian TV studies (e.g., Attallah, "Reading Television").

38 http://www.pulpanddagger.com/movies/d4_b.html.

39 Walcott, *Black Like Who?* 146.

40 Ash, "But Where Are You REALLY From?" 147.

41 Ibid.

42 Gray, *Watching Race*, 3.

7

How Even American Reality TV Can Perform a Public Service on Canadian Television

DEREK S. FOSTER

REALITY TV IS popular television fare. And while the content of reality television may not always be edifying or enlightening, it is important to recognize that Canadians can be enlightened by the public debate surrounding reality programming on Canadian television. We learn about ourselves not just from representations on television but also from the discourses surrounding it. In turn, reality TV provides an excellent case study for questioning the nature of public broadcasting and broadcasting that serves the public interest. Regardless of its place of origin, it is, for the most part, tainted with the "ideology of mass culture."[1] Fear and loathing of the genre is especially pronounced in Canada, where popular punditry is characterized by frequent arguments against lowest-common-denominator cultural products like (American) reality TV that threaten to take over Canadian airwaves and cultivate non-Canadian attitudes and sensibilities.

Too often, I argue, Canadians present "cultural nationalist" arguments that seek to establish an authentic Canadian cultural counterpoint as a means of highlighting the supposed uniqueness of our national appetites and as a way of creating a beachhead against the influx of American debasement. The CBC's decision to not program "reality TV" but to feature "factual entertainment" is emblematic of this trend. The latter term is a desultory label more or less accurately summing up the hybrid nature of the genre but also meaning more or less the same thing as the former term. Of course, discourses of "factual entertainment" are really debates about entertaining television in general. In turn, debates about public broadcasting and the perpetual struggle between educating and entertaining the public are, of course, reinscribed in the subject of reality TV/factual entertainment.

This is especially the case in Canada, where questions of culture and nationalism seem coterminous with broadcasting and the too-easy association of American culture with "bad" culture. By avoiding the negative connotation of "reality TV," the CBC seems to suggest that the genre can somehow contribute to Canadian identity. This implies, of course, that the CBC itself contributes to Canadian culture and Canadians' identities (and that American culture or mass popular culture such as reality TV threatens or denigrates them). I argue, on the other hand, that culture and identity are never so straightforward and we would be wise to understand how (Canadian) popular culture does more than hail Canadian consumers, but also helps constitute Canadian citizens. Citizenship is constituted not simply through media consumption but by circulation of and contestation within discourses surrounding media content. Thus, I argue for the need to focus on the public debates over Canadian television (inspired by and focused upon the content of reality programming) rather than the content of Canadian television itself. While the discourse of reality television programming is important, it must be contextualized within wider discourses of the institutions that produce reality TV and the wider discourse of both real and potential "television publics." I wish to focus attention upon reality TV publics instead of reality TV audiences. While broadcasters and advertisers value reality programming for the audience it generates, the social value of such programming comes from the discussion it stimulates among Canadians. This wider public discussion, in turn, performs a pedagogical function that revitalizes or reconfigures the reality of public service broadcasting.

To be clear, citizens can learn something from reality television in Canada, but only by acknowledging that Canadians exist both as audiences *for* television programming and as publics based *around* television content. Clearly, as we justify our viewing decisions and as we criticize network programming choices, we negotiate what we value and display our rhetorical vision of ourselves and our country in our public declarations. We act when we watch television but we act more meaningfully when we engage in debates about series or programming choices, sometimes even without having seen the specific content that may be in question. Thus, my focus is not on the texts of Canadian reality TV as much as it is on the context in which these televisual texts are mobilized to mean different things for different people.

Others, of course, have devoted considerable study to both the content and the context of reality TV programming. Some focus on fan commentary on websites in order to investigate how viewers become participants in the wider socio-cultural drama surrounding reality TV.[2] Such an approach, while valuable, confines its focus to fans of certain series. While fans may be the most active of audiences, many viewers of reality television are casual consumers, and many others may have something to say about reality programming without even having seen it. These individuals are members of the "reality TV public." Their proclamations about the genre help constitute public opinion about it even as they may not be audiences of certain series or consumers of the genre. As has been noted elsewhere, "with a narrative peopled by broadcasters, journalists, public intellectuals, participants, viewers and academics, the debate around reality TV has been as visible as the emergence of the form itself."[3]

Focusing on these discourses about reality television can give viewers and non-viewers alike clues about how television can be used to advance a participatory media culture. By focusing on the publics that arise around contested forms of television such as reality television, we can understand the potential for audience agency and the possibility of media citizenship, which is to suggest a level of engaged involvement that goes beyond media consumption.[4] My contribution to this debate is the suggestion that even "bad" TV can be good for Canadians as they participate in sometimes contested discourses about what constitutes Canadian programming, what appeals to Canadian audiences, and what political and regulatory measures ought to be instituted. I focus on debates unique to Canadian (public) broadcasting and the programming of reality TV, extending and further focusing earlier suggestions that the television audience could amount to a kind of cultural commons wherein its textuality may act as "a site for new forms of cultural engagement and even civic participation through which emergent forms of citizenship could be discerned."[5]

CBC as "Good" TV—Reality TV as "Bad"

Why does the issue of reality TV on Canada's national public broadcaster provoke such controversy? Public service broadcasters typically embody the values of comprehensiveness, pluralism, and cultural uplift, and their programs are expected to meet and maintain standards of impartiality, ideological balance, and good taste.[6] Contrarily, reality television is not, generally speaking, perceived to be an expression of good taste. Admittedly, it is notoriously difficult to consistently describe what "is" reality television.[7] In part, this is because, like Jill Godmilow suggests regarding the label "documentary," "everybody thinks they know what the term means, because everybody has seen some television programs labeled [as 'reality']."[8] In Canada, as is the case in every territory where reality formats have proven popular, "reality TV is a catch-all category that includes a wide range of entertainment programmes about real people."[9] A similarly broad definition suggests, "as a genre, reality television involves placing 'ordinary' people before the camera and deriving some entertainment value from the perception of their activities being unscripted."[10] We can see, then, that regardless of how one defines the genre, "the primary impetus [is] to entertain."[11] Of course, this does not simply describe the genre of reality TV; it is true for the medium of television in general: "Everything in the system tends to take second place to entertainment.... It fits a dominant image of how people supposedly use their television sets, looking most of the time for instant gratification, relaxation, excitement, and escape."[12]

Because of audiences' assumed appetite for entertaining rather than educational television, one of the great charges against television in general, even during its earliest days, has been its "purported massive poor taste and/or its taste-debasing effects."[13] Reality TV is the latest genre to be subjected to this long-standing critique.[14] People use "'reality TV' to describe popular factual [content], as the term is instantly recognizable and instantly categorises programmes as a particular type of television, usually cheap, tasteless, and compelling."[15] This widespread recognition was reinforced when, at the end of 2005, then CBC president Robert Rabinovitch declared, "There are certain types of programming that we don't have to do, or shouldn't do. For example, we don't do reality television.... If we just were chasing audiences, or just were chasing rating points, we could do reality programming ... But we don't do that."[16] This statement is consistent with the belief that, while the CBC is certainly in the entertainment "business," a public broadcaster is intended to be an institution of democracy and "should not apply commercial principles as the primary means to determine its programming."[17]

Overhauling Public Broadcasting

Just eight months later, after the president's strong stance against reality television, the CBC created a "Factual Entertainment" division. This was responsible for "talk shows, game shows, lifestyle and reality programs, as well as the acquisition and adaptation of formats of this type."[18] Still, Rabinovitch insisted that the CBC's version of reality TV would not "stress plastic surgery, sex and humiliation [and the] eating of insects."[19] Subsequently, far from denying that the CBC "did" reality TV, CBC spokesperson Jeff Keay noted that reality TV was a long-standing feature on the network. "CBC has always been involved in producing reality TV. Back in the 1950s, it was Front Page Challenge."[20] In 2008, Kirstine Layfield [later Stewart], CBC-TV's then executive director of network programming, defended CBC's current reality offerings as television that reflects Canada back to Canadians and that is meant to get Canadians to think critically about their world: "These are shows that are culturally relevant, all of them. We always try to make sure there's some value to them. They're part of the CBC convention; they remind people of shows they've watched on CBC in the past."[21]

However, even with their attempts to program compelling television that is not tasteless, the CBC has weathered criticism for its pursuit of larger audiences with commercial fare such as reality television. As such, it has been accused of reneging on its tradition of public service. This was most obvious in the widespread denunciation of the CBC's 2006 decision to broadcast *The One: Making a Music Star*. The series was a production of the US commercial broadcaster ABC that the CBC chose to air in the hopes of building an audience for a subsequent home-grown series called *The Canadian One*. The expected negative response to foreign reality programming on the CBC was magnified by the decision to simulcast the ABC version given that, in some parts of the country, the CBC was then forced to reschedule *The National*, the network's flagship news program. Such programming outcomes were short-lived, however, as *The One* generated very little viewership and was pulled from the air in just its second week of existence.

While American audiences quickly dismissed the series, the Canadian public could not. US commentary about the show tended to be preoccupied by its "quality." Representative comments include: "The worst piece of trash ever foisted on the American viewing public," and "this sucked a lot. *The One* tried to combine the pop savvy of *American Idol* with the rock edge of *Rockstar* but really turned out a 2-hour dull crap-fest instead."[22] In Canada, however, commentary was decidedly political: the Alliance of Canadian Cinema, Television and Radio Artists (ACTRA) issued a statement saying it was "shocked": "We support the CBC's desire to air programming that appeals to Canadians, but to spend money simulcasting a U.S talent show in search of ratings and revenue is a sell-out of its mandate as Canada's national public broadcaster."[23] A former dean of journalism at the University of Western Ontario suggested that bumping the news for a US reality show was "a deathly tactic for the CBC to try."[24] Two years after the fact, a letter to the editor of the *Globe and Mail* invoked the debacle when protesting the removal of *Marketplace* from the CBC's fall 2008 schedule in order to simulcast the American game show

Jeopardy. It sarcastically suggested, "the brain trust at CBC didn't learn their lesson ... when they punted *The National* to make way for *The One*."[25] In Canada at least, popular discourse about the series circulated for far longer than the televisual content that provoked it in the first place.

Cultural Nationalism and the Threat of Reality TV

The backlash against foreign reality programming on the CBC was clearly an acknowledgement of the special role the public broadcaster is supposed to have within the (Canadian) public sphere. Of course, all broadcasting provides audiences with potential material out of which they can constitute themselves and locate themselves in a wider cultural field of meanings (for example, what it means to be Canadian, or more prosaically what it means to prefer a particular show over others). But public broadcasting carries with it the weight of certain expectations. As Graham Spry declared, in his support for the institution of public broadcasting, "Broadcasting ... is no more a business than a public school system is a business.... Broadcasting, primarily, is an instrument of education in its widest significance, ranging from play to learning, from recreation to the cultivation of public opinion."[26]

We can use the term "cultural nationalists" to describe those who defend such a vision of a unique and strong public broadcaster, tied to a sense of a unique Canadian culture. Cultural nationalist sentiment is expressed most clearly during those occasions when something such as American reality television threatens to intrude upon and damage Canadian public television. Television in Canada always seems to operate within the matrix of cultural nationalism, an understandable context given Canada's geographical proximity to the United States and Canadians' ongoing appetite for popular culture. In fact, it has been suggested that "Canada is not a nation-state but a nationalist state."[27] In Canada, a "cultural nationalist public" is evident in the public proclamations of those who "look with anguish upon the popularity of American television and seek to wean Canadians from it and induce them to watch their own television."[28] Such proclamations are regularly heard in the claims making of ACTRA, the Canadian Media Guild, the Writers Guild of Canada, politicians and bureaucrats in Heritage Canada, and otherwise invested individuals such as CBC employees and Canadian film and television producers. This cultural nationalist discourse is not constrained by but is given additional institutional backing and public prominence by advocacy organizations such as Friends of Canadian Broadcasting and interest groups such as Our Public Airwaves.

The mission of Friends of Canadian Broadcasting is to "defend and enhance the quality and quantity of Canadian programming in the Canadian audio-visual system." Though officially not affiliated with any broadcaster or political party, its members frequently "fight for a strong CBC and the presence of Canadian content on radio and television."[29] Similarly, Our Public Airwaves advocates for Canadian public broadcasting that delivers "excellent programming that is a true alternative to the limited offerings of commercial networks; programming that taps the creative energies of Canadians to provide voice for their ideas, a window on the world and a reflection of themselves, their diverse cultures and their common values, locally, regionally and nationally; programming that is informative, independent, universally accessible, democratic, publicly accountable and free of commercial influence; and programming that sets the standard for quality and innovation."[30]

Within this context, there are two major criticisms that cultural nationalists levy against reality television in Canada (especially against reality television on CBC-TV). The first is that reality TV displaces drama and other programming designed for "cultural uplift," replacing it with lesser, more disposable fare. In this capacity, when focused on reality television especially, members of the cultural nationalist public tend to worry about the triumph of style over substance and reproduce entrenched fears of mass culture that once characterized widespread moralizing about the emergence and popularity of television in general. Just as Newton Minow warned of television's potential as a "vast wasteland" over a half-century ago, some still worry that the marvellous world of the ordinary and the basest of entertainments will drive viewers to distraction and fill their heads with empty spectacle instead of discourse related to substantive issues of the day. This is evident in a *Toronto Star* editorial that referred to "the cultural wasteland that is reality television."[31] While private broadcasters like CTV, Global, and CityTV have no problem scheduling foreign reality programming in order to attract audiences and their concomitant advertiser dollars, the CBC has found itself attacked for similar decisions. In the wake of its decision to reschedule *The National*, a spokesperson for Friends of Canadian Broadcasting declared, "We don't want public broadcasters going around trying to emulate our private broadcasters."[32] Similarly, former CBC journalist Knowlton Nash argued: "If the CBC really wants reality TV, let people get the reality of what's happening in the world by turning on *The National* at 10 p.m. every night."[33]

The second criticism is tied to the traditional complaint that Canadian broadcasting ought to ensure programming that is "Canadian" in content and character and which maintains and strengthens Canadian identity. As the national public broadcaster, the CBC is tasked with documenting the nation, more so than any private broadcaster. Thus, it is questioned when it programs reality-type shows that do not resonate with traditional themes of Canadian culture and particular Canadian identity. Specifically, Canadian nationalists indict the CBC for presenting a Canadian reality that is (1) not "Canadian" and (2) by being indistinguishable from its private competition is not particularly edifying for Canadians. Tied to both of these criticisms is the fear of encroaching commercialism that satisfies the basest of desires with cheap, entertaining programming. Taken together, both of these criticisms suggest that reality television is a perfect exemplar of how "the category of the public sphere has been eroded by the mass media and the tyranny of the popular, which leads subjects to passivity, rather than toward dialogue, discussion, and debate."[34] This is the reason why advocacy organizations such as Friends of Canadian Broadcasting have lamented foreign reality television on Canada's public broadcaster.

The fear that the genre of reality TV is lowest-common-denominator fare is clearly one of the reasons why the CBC has framed its own forays into the genre as serious, unifying, or somehow edifying content. By foregrounding the social value of their programming, the public broadcaster might mollify cultural nationalists who contend that the CBC ought to rebel against the erosion of public knowledge rather than contribute to it. Cultural nationalist discourse typically supposes that the CBC's role is to reach out to and cultivate an educated citizenry, demonstrating to them the proper use of reason, broadcasting content that ought to contribute to rational debate rather than undermine it. However, this critique of (reality) television "is based solely on what is produced, and not how diverse publics do use it."[35] Obviously, the culture-consuming audience can also be a culture-debating public.

Public Discourses and Public Broadcasting

While television and commercial media in general are frequently condemned for perverting the ideals of the public sphere, it should be noted that rational-critical debate can spring up around television, even if it is not the typical subject matter of much popular television programming. Beyond the cultural clamour that sprung up around *The One* in Canada, a clear example of this can be seen in the "official" Facebook group dedicated to *Triple Sensation*, the CBC acting, singing, and dancing talent search series. Though there are many groups dedicated to social networking around the series and its performers, the largest forums for such discourse are featured via links on the CBC's web page for the show. While the series was promoted as an attempt "to elevate reality TV" that was "important for the cultural health of the country,"[36] *Triple Sensation* did not include any explicit political content about the need to support the Canadian performing arts community. This type of political commentary did, however, take place in the public discourse about the series. The discussion board in the Facebook group dedicated to the second season of the series featured an invitation to write for the website www.publicbroadcasting.ca, while members of the group also encouraged protests against Bill C-10, federal legislation that could revoke tax credits for film and television productions deemed offensive.

The texts produced by this television public supplement the televisual text on the show itself. This demonstrates how even reality TV, sometime source of debasement and constant flirt with the tyranny of the popular, can do more than entertain. Even this most lamented genre of commercial television can be yoked to public broadcasting's ideals and continue the promise of a media-based communicative democracy where viewers are more than consumers; they are active participants in media culture, questioning and using television's representations, becoming "media-citizens": "Just as the popular press of the nineteenth century was responsible for the creation of the mass reading public, and hence the public, so TV became the place where and the means by which, a century later, most people got to know about most other people and about publicly important events or issues."[37]

To understand how this television-based public takes shape, we should understand that there are at least three different discursive contexts that we can pay attention to: (1) the institutional discourse of the CBC (forms of public address that define the corporation and the government policies that shape it); (2) the discourses of the programming on the CBC (the content of the shows themselves); (3) the discursive practices surrounding these texts (the critiques and interpretations, often contested) and the things said by audiences for this content. The vernacular public sphere, manifest in newspaper columns, letters to the editor, blogs, online discussion boards, and face-to-face interactions, is the site where differently situated publics interact, evaluate, and make sense of these discourses.

Consider how the show *Dragon's Den* provides examples of the three discursive contexts. First, Julie Bristow, executive director of CBC's factual entertainment division, contextualized *Dragon's Den* as "programming that's smart, that informs people and also entertains."[38] Within an institutional discourse of public broadcasting, reality TV is one way to continue to present distinctively Canadian content and supposedly contribute to shared national consciousness and identity (and therefore remain consistent with the Broadcasting Act, which governs its operation). At the same time, it is clearly part of a "large-scale retooling of CBC-TV's primetime schedule" defined by the naked pursuit of ratings fuelled by then CBC vice-president Richard Stursberg's desire for "more 'fast-paced,' 'escapist' and 'positive and redemptive' programming."[39] Second, the discourse of *Dragon's Den* itself seems to reinforce this desire to be both educational and entertaining. Promotions for season two visually played with the idea of contestants getting "burned" and going down in flames due to the "Dragons'" caustic feedback: "*Dragon's Den*—where bad ideas get torched and good ideas get a piece of over 3 million dollars." The season's premiere episode highlighted the possibly edifying pleasures of voyeurism when it hailed viewers at the outset: "High finance is a spectator sport.... Sit back and watch how money is really made." Finally, vernacular discourse surrounding *Dragon's Den* has been varied. It was classified as "an odd foray into reality TV ... watchable enough for those who like this kind of thing,"[40] lambasted as "peculiarly uninvolving,"[41] and hailed as "one of the greatest shows now on television."[42] Even as the deal making and decision taking on the series are critiqued (by frequent unflattering comparisons with the BBC version), much information is shared online in order to assist like-minded venture capitalists. One of the "Dragons" who could not agree on contractual terms with the CBC and did not return after the fifth season took the opportunity to both compliment the possible pedagogical value of the series[43] and critique its tendency towards carnivalesque, "whack-a-mole," "Simon Cowell-type commentary."[44]

Conflicted discourse in the vernacular public sphere characterizes all "reality" programming on the CBC. When citizens publicly protested the CBC's simulcasting of *The One*, they engaged in more than simply publicly sharing their private opinions of the series. They exchanged their views on public concerns such as CBC policy, public programming choices, and larger issues of Canadian identity. For instance, on the online TV discussion forum Viewers.ca, a user named "Tripster" opined, "Waste of bandwidth these Idol clones," and speculated, "I imagine it soured their taste for picking up reality shows from the US."[45] Blogger McNutt used the opportunity to hypothesize about "the purpose of a crown corporation in a progressive capitalist society."[46] As Hauser argues (and as these postings indicate), each such exchange "opens a discursive space that exceeds the boundaries of entirely personal and private matters. Across time these multiple exchanges include us as participants in the social conversation by which we learn and also contribute to themes that inculcate shared motives."[47] To crassly but accurately summarize this Canadian context, "Recently, the CBC has shifted its focus away from an abstract cultural mandate to a narrower ratings-driven approach, and in the process pissed off countless employees, confused its audience and set off yet another debate about the role of public broadcasting."[48]

It could be argued, then, that there are few things more "Canadian" than debating the role of public broadcasting in Canada. And, with each mandate change at the CBC, the never-ending conversation continues. Thus, the *Toronto Sun* reported that Richard Stursberg was fired in August 2010 as executive vice-president of English-language services "apparently because he was too good at getting more people to watch the programming that Canadian taxpayers subsidize to the tune of $1 billion a year." The article reported that TV ratings increased by 52 per cent and CBC television's overall market share grew 34 per cent during Stursberg's appointment.[49] Yet the drive toward commercial programming was seen at odds with the CBC's traditional public service mandate. In essence, Stursberg's tenure at the CBC ended because the CBC became more popular. As one commentator noted, "Ironically, as CBC became more successful in terms of ratings, the clarity of purpose of the organization became more confused."[50]

The CBC president Hubert Lacroix suggested that Stursberg's departure coincided with the implementation of a new strategic plan and a new vision of what the public broadcaster brand stands for.[51] In turn, the *Globe and Mail*'s TV critic reported that any potential programming shifts were likely to be incremental instead of radical, "a slight tilt upwards. Toward the more Canadian, the somewhat more upscale and the cross-cultural."[52] And indeed, in her first major address as executive vice-president of CBC English Services, Stursberg's successor Kirstine Stewart announced that the CBC would be reducing the amount of US programming on the main network, calling its reliance on foreign imports "a crutch."[53]

This idea that the CBC is more "Canadian" or more "cultural" than its competition or even previous versions of itself is also a crutch. It does not accurately reflect the impossibility of clearly or positively defining Canadian audiences or even Canadian culture. It also falls into the trap of assuming that "real" Canadian culture should not be influenced or unduly coloured by American or commercial culture. This was evident in comments by Carmel Smyth, the president of the Canadian Media Guild when she called for the CBC to become "a really public public broadcaster." She appealed for a less commercial approach with "programming that's made in the public interest as much as for the potential 'eyeball' numbers."[54] Such comments reinforce the notion that public interest and a large viewing public might not be incompatible but also suggest that commercial, popular (or populist) programming is not likely the means to achieve it. This demonstrates how discourses of and about the CBC continually vacillate between accusations of either cultural populism or cultural nationalism in an attempt to defend or vilify something that confounds easy categorization. Maybe, as was noted earlier, the real significance of broadcasting lies in the cultivation of public opinion. However, we ought to focus less on how the content on Canadian TV screens influences or cultivates Canadian culture and more on how Canadian debates about broadcasting content cultivate a sense of what Canadian culture might actually mean for Canadian citizens.

Reality TV—Popular Culture as Public Knowledge-Building Project

By paying serious attention to the public discourses surrounding popular programming, we can shift analytical focus away from what counts as Canadian culture or Canadian citizenship and examine how culture is contested and, via these debates, how citizenship takes place.[55] Television provides resources for citizenship—providing citizens with access to content that allows them to make sense of their lives, informing them and entertaining them alike, and making them agents of potential change. The CBC can be valuable because of the subject positioning that it may enact, and it may have a potential ideological effect as it encourages national socio-cultural identity. However, perhaps even more importantly, reality television on the CBC has a political effect evident in its power to open up new discursive spaces. Audiences actively question and interrogate the material being shown on the national broadcaster and, through their activity (of debating CBC content, rather than simply viewing it), they participate in and perform Canadian cultural identity rather than just consuming it. The politics of programming lies not only in what is shown, but in how it is received and in the rhetorical contests about these shows—in the public sphere of discourse that exists around them.

In its paradoxical status as being the most widely condemned yet also the most widely watched of television programming, reality television underscores how "we must recognize that the conversation of the culture is centered not in the *New York Review of Books* but in the television experience."[56] Even in the wake of interactive and narrowcast technologies, we ought to "recognize the TV screen as the contemporary shape of the public sphere."[57] In other words, new spaces for politics and citizenship arise out of a people's mediated existences, and the idea of a public sphere of rational discourse about "proper" issues of public concern ought to be supplemented by the idea of "the public screen" in which technologies of television, film, photography, and the Internet bring new topics and new forums, and indeed new voices and new ways of talking, into public circulation. Given its popularity and its pervasiveness, reality television can play a significant role in this updated mediasphere.

Clearly, dismissing reality television as a cultural wasteland does not account for how some audience members might use the content and the medium for something other than individuated consumption. This is not to suggest that all content can produce rational-critical debate. But, obviously, we do have such debate *surrounding* reality programming, mostly centred around the type of content that would never actually feature such debate *in* its programming. It is easy to see content such as the news, political debates, and town hall forums as a mediated theatre of democracy, calling forth citizens' engagement and provoking attachments with various causes and ideologies. What does reality television offer by comparison? Rather than invitations to dialogue, reality television simply disseminates spectacular visions of society that do not presume to offer insights or enlightenment. Instead of edification, we have simply dissemination.

However, the idea of the public screen "starts from the premise of dissemination, of broadcasting. Communication as characterized by dissemination is the endless proliferation and scattering of emissions without the guarantee of productive exchanges."[58] And this is why cultural nationalists are worried by content such as reality television (on Canadian television screens in general, much less the national public broadcaster). "The public screen supports the view that visibility is potentially good regardless of the type of visibility."[59] The metaphor of the public screen suggests that meaning (much less communion) can never be guaranteed. Audiences might be guaranteed, but the normative ideal of Canadian stories or images meant for deliberation by carefully consuming audiences is not. This uncertainty does not pose a problem for commercial broadcasters, but the CBC is held to a higher standard. This standard is, I suggest, arbitrary and artificial. Foreign reality programming on the CBC need not be seen only as yet another onslaught of American commercialism. Though objectively not "Canadian content," it can still be content that Canadians use to define themselves as Canadian. Instead of viewing reality television as the expression of cultural attitudes, we can learn more about ourselves if we view them as nodal points in ongoing conversations about our cultural circumstances. Content on the CBC need not represent Canadian culture, nor even attempt to define it; yet Canadian audiences can still use it as an excuse to have these debates among themselves. This is the difference between seeing television as rhetoric and taking a rhetorical perspective on television.

Reality television (much less all television) is implicitly rhetorical. Rather than being explicitly persuasive, it acts as symbolic inducement, "using techniques that direct attention, shape interpretation, and foster identification or division."[60] Typically, Canadian nationalists want their TV to be rhetorical—they want it to appear to be Canadian, to perform a service for Canadians that is explicit. However, I suggest that even non-nationalistic programming, content that is not meant to cultivate Canadian identity or to conjure up concrete ideas of Canadian-ness, still performs an implicit service. It gets us talking. *Battle of the Blades* is not "Canadian" because it features former NHL hockey players. Rather, its value is its capacity to stimulate Canadian public debate. And in this capacity, shows such as *The One* generate new public forums, new excuses for Canadian nationalists to reinvent and recirculate their discourse and for all Canadians to debate whether or not this is a good thing. These shows are rhetorical in that they provide the grounds for the production of such discourse.

The CBC need not broadcast "challenging" material to challenge Canadians. Even if cultural nationalists are loath to admit it, the public sphere consists, in part, of debates about reality television in addition to (or instead of) traditional political subject matter. Reality television, like all television, is always political. It has a capacity to both elevate and enervate viewers. Yet arguing that reality television contributes to the televisual public sphere could be a contested claim. This is because when we are told that "the public screen includes the pundits on talking head TV ... the staged campaigns of electoral politics ... sitcoms and other entertainment TV where national 'discussions' take place,"[61] the public screen is still associated with the broadcasting of eminently "political" content (even if it is sometimes presented in irrational forms). On the other hand, I want to suggest that the often obviously irrational content of reality television that is designed more often than not to drive audiences to distraction rather than contemplation ought to be seen as part of the public screen too. Such content provides citizen-publics with the opportunity to express themselves through public rhetoric and to discuss political issues. This public discussion can (and does) focus on debates over Canadian policy, what constitutes "Canadian" content on Canadian TV, and what it means to be Canadian in the first place. Obviously, US-based content need not be political for it to be politicized by Canadian interests. Hence, cultural nationalists need not seek to protect Canadian audiences from themselves when "bad" American television is taken up by Canadians as a source of conflict and tension to be negotiated in public discourse. By this measure, even American reality shows such as *The One* can productively engage Canadians in public debates.

This essay does not present the reader with an in-depth analysis of reality programming on Canadian television. Instead, it invites readers to analyze television programming in general by focusing on the discourses surrounding such television programming. It provides a model for understanding "citizen's reactions" to specific instances of discourse, something rhetorical critics rarely take into account.[62] Reality TV enjoys a certain cultural currency. It thus behooves cultural critics to take the genre seriously, especially since "serious" broadcasters such as the CBC do so too. The goal of this essay has not been to present the best or the only interpretation of reality TV on Canadian public television, but to demonstrate the rhetorical power of such programming. Reality TV on the CBC, or anywhere for that matter, does not explicitly persuade or even influence audiences as much as it invites people to consider its content as symbolic equipment for living. Whether or not they watch it, citizens form subject positions, not so much in the image of reality TV's content, but out of the interstices of public opinion circulating in official forums and vernacular discussions.

Reality television on the CBC need not represent a slide in broadcasting standards or the decline of Canadian culture. Rather, the controversy over factual entertainment on the CBC provides the opportunity for "new modes of intelligence, knowledge, politics, rhetoric, in short, new modes of being in the world."[63] Viewing reality television in the context of public broadcasting mandates emphasizes how we must move beyond an examination of reality television's representations and assess discourses around reality television in Canada. We ought to examine not simply how Canadian culture is represented (or not, as the case may be) but also how all television provides opportunities for public fashioning and revaluing of what Canadian culture is or ought to be. The fact that there are no easy answers to these questions should provoke further research into communication media and programming content that may be otherwise overlooked, material that is easily dismissed but whose banality is the source of both its condemnation and its popularity.

Notes

1 See Ang, *Watching Dallas*, 86–116.
2 Wittebols, "Reality TV."
3 Holmes, "When Will I Be Famous?" 8.
4 See Hartley, *Uses of Television*, 157-165; Ouellette and Hay, *Better Living*, 204.
5 Hartley, "From Republic of Letters," 388, 407.
6 McCauley, "The Contested Meaning of Public Service," 209.
7 Simon, "The Changing Definition."
8 Quoted in Edwards, "Chasing the Real," 254.
9 Hill, *Reality TV*, 2.
10 Smith and Wood, "Introduction," 2.
11 Holmes and Jermyn, "Introduction," 2.
12 Blumler, "The New Television Marketplace," 206.
13 Meyersohn, "Social Research in Television," 345.
14 See, for instance, Nichols, "Reality TV and Social Perversion."
15 Hill, *Reality TV*, 46.
16 Zerbisias, "TV Misguide."
17 McChesney, *Rich Media, Poor Democracy*, 226.
18 IndieNewsQuebec, "Appointments."
19 Canadian Broadcasting Corporation, "Heritage Committee Grills CBC Bosses."
20 Reveler, "Drabinsky Looks to Elevate Reality TV."
21 Strachan, "CBC's Fall Announcement."
22 Realitytvmagazine.com, responses to "The One—Who Will Go Home First?"
23 Canadian Broadcasting Corporation, "Nash Slams CBC."
24 Peter Desbarats, quoted in Brioux, "CBC Kerfuffle No National Emergency."
25 Moore, "Wrong Turn at the CBC."
26 As cited in Dale and Naylor, "Dialogue and Public Space," 207.
27 Collins, *Culture, Communication and National Identity*, xiii.
28 Attallah and Foster, "Television in Canada," 179.
29 Friends of Canadian Broadcasting, "About Us."
30 "*The One* Not the One,"*Stratford Beacon Herald*, editorial.
31 "Curling Gets Glitzy," *Toronto Star*, editorial.
32 Lofaro, "A Short, Not-So-Sweet Run."
33 Canadian Broadcasting Corporation, "Nash Slams CBC."
34 Mackenzie, *Screening Quebec*, 38.
35 Ibid., 41.
36 Reveler, "Drabinsky Looks to Elevate Reality TV."
37 Hartley, "From Republic of Letters," 411.
38 Davidson, "CBC Enters the *Dragon's Den*."
39 Whyte, "CBC Taps American to Craft New Shows."
40 Dillon, "CBC in Ratings Tailspin."
41 *Globe and Mail* TV critic John Doyle, quoted in Turner, "CBC-TV's Nemesis."
42 Menon, "These Dragons Light My Fire."
43 Köhler, "In Conversation: Brett Wilson," 15.
44 Leong, "W. Brett Wilson Leaves *Dragon's Den* with a Challenge."

45 See the online postings at http://www.viewers.ca/discuss/showthread.php?t=26 and http://www.viewers.ca/discuss/showthread.php?t=40.
46 See the post at http://mcnutt.wordpress.com/2006/07/31/in-which-mcnutt-wonders-what-the-hell-cbc-was-thinking/.
47 Hauser, *Vernacular Voices*, 65.
48 Bell, "Boob Tube."
49 Akin, "CBC Axes Exec Despite Ratings Success."
50 Dvorkin, "Why Is Managing the CBC So Damn Difficult?"
51 Lacroix, "CBC President Sets the Record Straight Following Stursberg's Departure."
52 Doyle, "The Post-Stursberg CBC: Tilt Goes the Tightrope."
53 Szklarski, "CBC-TV to Reduce Reliance on Foreign Programs, Be 'More Canadian.'"
54 Smyth, "Richard Stursberg: Early Thoughts about a Demonized Man and His Impossible Job."
55 See Asen, "A Discourse Theory of Citizenship," 191.
56 Gronbeck, "Rhetoric, Ethics, and Telespectacles," 235.
57 Deluca and Peeples, "From Public Sphere to Public Screen," 126.
58 Ibid., 130–31.
59 Schutten, "Invoking Practical Magic," 335.
60 Blakesley, *The Terministic Screen*, 17.
61 Deluca and Peeples, "From Public Sphere to Public Screen," 146.
62 Brummett, "Rhetorical Theory as Heuristic and Moral," 102.
63 Deluca and Peeples, "From Public Sphere to Public Screen," 147.

8

Television, Nation, and the Situation Comedy in Canada

Cultural Diversity and *Little Mosque on the Prairie*

SARAH A. MATHESON

THE OCTOBER 22, 2007, issue of *Maclean's* magazine featured a striking cover photo that depicted a Muslim woman wearing a hijab and a Caucasian man clad in a business suit. They stand side by side, facing forward, yet peering at each other out of the corner of their eyes, their respective glares suggesting unease and distrust. The article title, "Canada: A Nation of Bigots?" provided a clear context for interpreting this image, which is unmistakably suggestive of anxieties surrounding cultural difference and national identity in Canada, framing difference in terms of suspicion and opposition. It also dramatically conveys the classed and gendered tensions that can often be located within these discourses. The accompanying article by Martin Patriquin describes a climate of growing intolerance towards immigrants and cultural and religious minorities in Canada. He cites the recent public hearings in Quebec on "reasonable accommodation" as an example of an escalating and increasingly vocal racism. He writes: "Since it was enshrined as official policy in 1971, multiculturalism has been worn by Canadians as a badge of honour even as its consequences have remained happily abstract. But if tolerance has long been one of the touchstones of Canadian identity, there is reason to believe our cherished multicultural tapestry is fraying."[1] Among the telling signs of this unravelling he identifies (and that is communicated vividly in the cover photo) is the growth of anti-Muslim sentiment, most disturbingly evidenced in the increase in hate crimes against Muslims in Canada. These include, Patriquin notes, vandalism of mosques in Toronto and Edmonton and assaults against Muslim students on Canadian university campuses, events fuelled in part, he argues, by post-9/11 anxieties and fears. The article expresses concern about how well multiculturalism is working in Canada, shedding light on events and popular sentiments that reveal racism to be a reality in Canadian society, a revelation that he worries raises questions about a core aspect of Canadian national identity.

This *Maclean's* issue appeared on Canadian newsstands just three weeks following the launch of the second season of the CBC sitcom *Little Mosque on the Prairie* (WestWind Pictures, 2007–), a gentle "culture clash" comedy which focuses on a Muslim community in the fictional prairie town of Mercy. Amid the press surrounding the series' return, it was announced that the program's creator, filmmaker Zarqa Nawaz and producer Mary Darling were to be presented with the "Search for Common Ground" human rights award. Previous recipients have included Bishop Desmond Tutu and former US president Jimmy Carter. In a statement Darling responded: "This is a very humbling award to receive and it feels like a confirmation of our vision ... we wanted to create a show that would allow people to laugh while hopefully breaking down stereotypes. We felt that comedy would be a great way to inspire people to dialogue together and to build understanding of each other no matter what their beliefs."[2] The sale of *Little Mosque* internationally has been framed in similar terms. The title of an article in the *Edmonton Journal* about the program's sale to Canal Plus ("Can Little Mosque's Message of Tolerance Help Heal Racially Divided France?") expresses an analogous bridge-building ideal.[3]

From its initial debut, *Little Mosque on the Prairie* has been praised for its representation of multiculturalism and its message of understanding across cultures. Reviewer Kate Taylor suggests that "its success reflects back to Canadians the multicultural and ultimately tolerant image of themselves that they like to see."[4] Similarly, *Little Mosque* cast member Zaib Shaikh sees the show as a "metaphor for Canada": as "a small community of people, where lots of diverse cultures, all sorts of traditions, come together."[5] Nawaz herself noted the way the series has been taken up as an emblem of nation. She says: "In Canada ... we've become like the poster child for everything that's right about our country, about multiculturalism, about assimilating different groups of people and what's successful about our nation."[6] Indeed, throughout the critical response (in newspaper articles and in letters to the editors), the series' apparent celebration of cultural diversity, its earnest tone, and themes of coming together of the community were often claimed as aspects that reflected and reaffirmed a national self-image of Canada as a tolerant, multicultural nation.

In this context, *Little Mosque on the Prairie* appears as both answer and antidote to the problems and questions raised in "Canada: A Nation of Bigots?" In the popular press, for some the program seems to offer reassurance that, despite the conflicts that mark the post-9/11 era, Canadian multiculturalism works. At the same time it has been ascribed an important role in working towards larger social change, as a potential solution to current conflicts at home and abroad. The series and the dialogue surrounding it address these wider popular discourses about cultural diversity and national identity. They also suggest particular ideas about the relationship between television comedy and social change. In particular, this discourse suggests that comedy may be used as a means of tackling and dealing with larger social anxieties and conflicts.

Implicit in the dialogue surrounding *Little Mosque on the Prairie* is the notion that television may not only reflect aspects of a society, culture, or nation but can actually enact change (in this case, for instance, may operate as an instrument of healing). Scholar Beverly Rasporich describes humour as a "sociocultural and group phenomenon."[7] As a group phenomenon it can, she argues, tell us a lot about collective life. It can reflect a group back to itself; it can speak to collective concerns, feelings, shared anxieties; and it can work to affirm the identity of the group.[8] My analysis of *Little Mosque on the Prairie* begins with this idea of comedy's potential social role and its relationship to identity. I limit my attention to the series' first season, which provides an opportunity to trace how its debut was greeted in the popular press and to identify how, as the series established its premise and launched its initial episodes, its significance was discussed and debated. Within this context, I consider the following questions: What ideas about Canadian citizenship, national identity, and nationhood are being communicated in *Little Mosque*? How does the series negotiate issues of cultural diversity in ways that may echo wider debates and tensions? What strategies are deployed to provide a sense of reconciliation and how does the sitcom form specifically work to help support this?

In his analysis of the representation of African Americans on US television, Herman Gray argues that different portraits of black life can be read in the context of a history of representation where new images are often responding to or are in dialogue with previous depictions. At the same time he demonstrates how specific programs represent cultural difference within and through the dominant and hegemonic discourses on race and race relations that mark specific eras.[9] Likewise, *Little Mosque on the Prairie* can be first situated in terms of a larger history of representation and in relation to dominant discourses on cultural diversity in Canada.

In a broad sense, *Little Mosque* reflects the mandate of the CBC, outlined in the Broadcasting Act, which stipulates that its programming should, among other things, "reflect Canada and its regions to national and regional audiences," "contribute to shared national consciousness and identity," and "reflect the multicultural and multiracial nature of Canada."[10] Comparing it to CBC Radio's *Dead Dog Café,* Margaret Wente argues that "*Little Mosque* fits squarely into the CBC's mission of building mutual understanding between all Canadians."[11] The program bears a further resemblance to another successful CBC series, the 1970s sitcom *The King of Kensington*, which has been similarly praised as a program that attempted to bring Canada's multicultural "mosaic" to life on the small screen. Both series rely on familiar, light-hearted "culture clash" scenarios featuring immigrant characters, and both depend on the conventions of the situation comedy to support their general themes of reconciliation.[12] Nawaz has described *Little Mosque* in ways that suggest its potential to operate as a corrective to previous representations of Muslims in the media.[13] It can also be viewed as a program that, through its familiar approach, displays a consistency with earlier series such as *King of Kensington*, fitting in with the CBC's larger history and nation-building mandate.

The negotiation of issues surrounding cultural diversity in *Little Mosque* is also framed by the larger circumstances surrounding the impact of 9/11, as it directly confronts the Islamophobia that pervades this era. In this context, it taps into dominant discourses surrounding cultural diversity and multiculturalism in Canada. According to Banting, Courchene, and Seidle, Canadian policy has traditionally approached the challenges presented by diversity through "the twin agendas of recognition and integration," which form the basis for concepts of shared citizenship.[14] This rests, on the one hand, in support for the acknowledgement, expression, and accommodation of diversity, and on the other on "integration, seeking to bring minorities into the mainstream, strengthen the sense of mutual support and solidarity, and reinforce the bonds of a common community."[15] Underlying dominant discourses of cultural diversity therefore is what Richard Day describes as a "fantasy of unity,"[16] where the symbol of the Canadian mosaic visually communicates this seemingly paradoxical ideal of "unity within diversity."

In a recent study assessing the state of citizenship and diversity in Canada, Soroka, Johnston, and Banting situate Canadian multiculturalism in the context of a wider perceived crisis facing other Western democracies that are struggling to balance the two agendas of recognition and integration. They cite the 2005 riots in Paris and Australia, the intense and divisive debates that have erupted over immigration policies in the United States, fears about the increase in Muslim extremism, and the increased security agenda spreading across many countries in the wake of 9/11 as events that raise questions about how well multiculturalism is faring internationally and how governments are responding to diversity.[17] They suggest that while Canada stands in stark contrast to these other nations, "cracks in Canadian equanimity seem to be appearing."[18] The study frames its appraisal of Canadian policies in the context of national and international events that have impacted debates about multiculturalism and citizenship in Canada. Within this framework, Canada is presented as a nation potentially facing an uncertain future as the appearance of specific "warning signals" suggest that a reassessment of current policies may be warranted. Significantly, new anxieties fuelled by 9/11 and surfacing within contemporary conflicts here (such as the debates surrounding Sharia law in Ontario), position Islam and anxieties about social integration as key focal points within this dialogue.[19]

Little Mosque emerges within and is shaped by this larger context, and as a popular response offers its own "fantasy of unity." Its themes of compromise, community participation, and bridge building work to reaffirm this ideal, which may explain the popular impulse to read it in ways that support dominant discourses surrounding nation and Canadian multiculturalism. The series uses humour to defuse tensions that arise around cultural differences and works to provide narratives of reassurance, comfort, and affirmation. Its dependency on traditional sitcom conventions helps support the program's confirmation of this ideal as it provides a lighthearted response to an insistent question that lies at the core of discourses of diversity: in the absence of a common national culture, "How are we to live together?"[20]

Little Mosque and the Politics of Representation

Little Mosque on the Prairie debuted on the CBC on January 9, 2007, and its premiere attracted 2.1 million viewers (an impressive viewership for a homegrown series). It won awards for best television series and best writing at the Roma Fiction Fest in Italy in July of that year and was sold for international distribution in France and in markets in Finland, Israel, Dubai, and Turkey.[21] Creator Zarqa Nawaz had been making short films since the early 1990s that were comedic treatments of Muslim issues and life in North America. *Little Mosque* fits within her larger body of work and was inspired in part by her own experiences as a Muslim woman who moved with her husband and children from Toronto to Saskatchewan.

The first season begins with the arrival of Amaar Rashid, a young Toronto lawyer who gives up his practice to become the imam of the new Mercy Mosque, which is housed in the basement of the town's Anglican church. The mosque's diverse congregation is a collection of affable yet quirky and offbeat townspeople with different cultural backgrounds and varied views on Islam. The mosque's members include the Hamoudi family: Yasir, the founder of the mosque who also owns a local construction company, daughter Rayyan (a feminist and also the town's physician), and his wife Sarah (a convert to Islam who works for the mayor). Other members are the bumbling Baber Siddiqui (the congregation's most conservative member), his teenage daughter Layla, and Fatima Dinssa (a woman from Nigeria who owns the local diner). Rounding out the cast are Mercy residents Fred Tupper, a right-wing radio host who views the mosque and its members with suspicion, Anglican minister Reverend Magee, who becomes Amaar's friend and confidant, and Mayor Ann Popowicz. In the first season, the storylines centre on Amaar's struggles to manage disputes within his congregation and his efforts to bring together Muslims and non-Muslims in the community, all the while trying to adjust to life in rural Canada. The comedy revolves around a number of different central conflicts that include disagreements within the Muslim community, tensions between Muslims and non-Muslims in the town, domestic and family conflicts, as well as gender and generational conflicts.

The launch of *Little Mosque* was initially framed within an enthusiastic discourse that loudly announced that this series represented something innovative, daring, and groundbreaking. Prior to its debut on Canadian television, *Little Mosque* generated unprecedented international news coverage. CNN, MSNBC, ABC News, National Public Radio, BBC Radio and *The New York Times*, for example, all featured reports on the series, which was repeatedly referred to as a "controversial" new Canadian comedy program. The media frenzy surrounding it suggested that the controversial nature of the program was due to its focus on Muslim characters and its humorous treatment of post-9/11 tensions. Some commentators wondered if comedy was the appropriate form for dealing with these very serious issues (was it trivializing them, was it too soon to poke fun in this way, was this offensive or in bad taste?). Others wondered if there was a possibility of a brutal backlash against the series and its creators, with one journalist citing the controversy surrounding the depiction of the Prophet Muhammad in political cartoons published in Denmark as an example of a potentially violent response.[22] Still other journalists considered the potential of the program to ease political tensions and soothe social conflicts. In an article in the *Edmonton Journal* for example, one critic suggested that *Little Mosque* could possibly operate as a means of assimilation for Muslims in North America, where humour could help make them "seem less peculiar."[23] Similarly, in a roundtable discussion led by Paula Zahn on CNN, a panel of guests debated the role of comedy in combating intolerance. They agreed that television comedy such as this could not only entertain, but could be used to teach and to debunk negative stereotypes.[24]

In the midst of this media attention, Nawaz seemed to distance herself from any specific political objectives associated with the series. While she stated that she anticipated that the series might be considered controversial, she seemed reluctant to frame the series' goals in overtly political terms and tended instead to emphasize her desire to just entertain. In an interview in *Maclean's*, for example, she says "We don't want to be political; we just want to be funny."[25] Elsewhere she comments, "To me, this is not a political show, this is not about the Iraq war, it's not about 9/11. First and foremost it's entertainment."[26] In another interview she suggests her aspirations in similar terms, seemingly detaching herself from the notion that she had a larger social or political agenda in creating the series. She is quoted as saying:

> My biggest hope is it is treated as a comedy, like any other comedy, that we become like *Everybody Loves Raymond*, a comedy that people of all ages, faiths, and backgrounds watch ... We want them to watch because it's a funny, entertaining show that just happens to have Muslims in it. We hope the viewers will be able to relate to the characters and the situations because they're all very universal. I want them to tune in because they want to watch a really funny show and they want to laugh. Ultimately, that is my goal, to make people laugh.[27]

Producer Mary Darling echoes a similar sentiment saying, "It really is a show that focuses on relationships and families; it's not about terrorism," adding, "but we're not afraid of introducing those issues."[28] Despite generally downplaying a political agenda, Nawaz's comments do suggest a hope that the series will enact positive change, and like these other critics she links this with a view of comedy as an instrument of social change. She says, for example, "Laughter is a universal language, so I'm hoping it will help bring people together and heal some of the misunderstanding."[29] Interestingly, Nawaz distinguishes between political humour and situation comedy, a distinction that, as I will argue, has an importance to the way cultural difference is addressed in *Little Mosque*. She says, "*Little Mosque on the Prairie* is a sitcom, not a political satire. I want people to find the hilarity in the show and recognize similar issues that appear in all our lives. It's important to normalize the community within the greater community so as not to be seen as 'other' but to recognize that we all have universal themes that exist in all communities.

I simply want people to laugh with Muslims like they would laugh at anyone else and feel comfortable doing so."[30] Nawaz has described her hope that the series would offer a contrast to media representations of Muslims and would help clear up popular misconceptions about Islam. A greater sense of understanding, she suggests, could be engendered by emphasizing universal themes and characters. The evocation of Day's notion of a "fantasy of unity" is evident in Nawaz's description of these universal themes which suggest that there are things that connect all of us, which can be traced across communities and cultures and can conceivably raze barriers between people. She evokes an image of an interconnectedness that exists beyond cultural differences, a notion that is central to the image of nation that official multiculturalism supports.

Despite Nawaz's repeated contention that *Little Mosque* is "just a sitcom," scholarly work into the politics of representation has made clear the explicitly political nature of all representation. In his groundbreaking work on the representation of sexual minorities in the media, Larry Gross has exposed the relationship between representation and power in mass culture, where, he argues "non-representation maintains the powerless status of groups that do not possess significant material or political power bases."[31] His concept of "symbolic annihilation" describes how exclusion from mainstream media works to sustain existing power hierarchies. At the same time, Gross argues, "When groups or perspectives do attain visibility, the manner of that representation will itself reflect the biases and interests of those elites who define the public agenda."[32] In short, visibility in itself may not be enough to secure social power; it matters who is speaking for whom. As Gross notes, "The most effective form of resistance to the hegemonic force of the dominant media is to speak for oneself."[33]

The frequent characterization of *Little Mosque on the Prairie* as "controversial" and the corresponding debates about the series' relationship to post-9/11 tensions point to the political stakes associated with the representation of Muslim characters on television. Providing visibility for a "misrepresented or under-represented" group is an expressed aim of the program according to Darling.[34] And, the series can also be considered an important act of self-representation as this biographically inspired scenario works to provide a counter-image to dominant media representations of Muslim communities. It provides an important forum where aspects of Islam are explained and debated and asserts the place of Muslim communities in Canada and on mainstream television. At the same time, Nawaz's descriptions of the series' "normalizing" goals raise questions about how "normal" is being defined and mobilized here in order to contest the "othering" of Muslims and specifically which "norms" are suggested, challenged, and/or reaffirmed within this process.

Sitcom Formulas and Culture Clash Narratives

While *Little Mosque* was initially greeted as a series that represented something radically different on television, as the first season unfolded Canadian reviewers began to point out that, aside from the fact that the characters were Muslim, it all seemed very familiar. Its stock character types and "fish out of water" and "culture clash" storylines, they noted, could be found in a number of other programs. Its prairie setting also evoked connections with CTV's *Corner Gas*, a similarity that led one reviewer to refer to it as "Corner Mosque."[35] Many critics commented on its essentially predictable and formulaic structure and its generally soft manner and earnest tone, aspects which seemed to conflict with its characterization as an innovative and controversial program. For example, reviewer Vinay Menon writes, "for all the talk about edgy, groundbreaking fare, *Little Mosque on the Prairie* is oddly anachronistic, fervently blind in its devotion to traditional sitcom-making."[36] Another critic noted the "wholesome, aw-shucks feeling" that it shared with *Corner Gas*, describing it as "a generally good natured show, neither complicated nor threatening."[37] In a similar vein, reviewer Barbara Kay from the *National Post* criticized the series' seemingly outdated approach. Aside from Amaar, she writes, "the rest of the cast is stuck in the pre-ironic 1950s model sitcom, like *Father Knows Best*, *My Three Sons*, *Ozzie and Harriet* and *Leave It to Beaver*, where characters are cardboard cutouts, the reigning mood is earnestness where nobody is really bad (although many are somewhat simple), everyone's intentions are good and whatever minor conflict serves to propel the plot forward is resolved with a kind word."[38]

With a few exceptions, there was a general agreement among reviewers that the series failed to deliver the controversial, dark, edgy comedy they were expecting. Most seemed disappointed and surprised that *Little Mosque* seemed so mundane, so true to traditional sitcom formulas, and so gentle in its approach. Michele Byers describes her response to the series as "proud disappointment"; proud because it is made in Canada, that "there was room for such a vision" and pleased that it "breaks with the tradition of representing Muslims as secondary characters introduced to teach others about the perils of racism, or as terrorists ... or even as necessarily urban." But she was disappointed by its simplicity, its polite and familiar humour, and its one-dimensional characters.[39] Some critics expressed a similarly conflicted reaction, acknowledging the larger importance of the program in terms of offering a more positive portrait of Muslim life and sometimes seeing its mere appearance on Canadian television as evidence of Canadian multiculturalism at work. While many praised its reflection of a culturally diverse Canada, others expressed disappointment in its safe and familiar approach.

Therefore, while there was an impulse to claim *Little Mosque* as an emblem of Canadian multiculturalism, at the same time there seemed to be a general dissatisfaction with the way this was enacted. Its predictability and adherence to formula were used by critics to demonstrate the failings of the series. However, when considered in a different light, this is critical to supporting the larger objectives associated with the series. An appeal to the "ordinary" is an important part of working towards these "normalizing" goals and its reliance on convention a central part of the way the program resists situating the Muslim community as "other."

In an interview, Nawaz has asserted that *Little Mosque* presents Muslims as "normal people who are fathers and mothers and kids ... husbands and wives, people who raise their kids and pay their bills and just have a normal life which all of us do."[40] Her frequent references to her desire to "normalize the community," to present Muslim characters as "normal" or "ordinary" or just like "anyone else," takes on an added significance when one begins to unpack the issues of power that underpin definitions of "normal" and "ordinary." Far from neutral concepts, they imply modes of classification and exclusion and point to the operations of power that are enacted through their mobilization. Through their naturalization, they are used to define and "fix difference," to exclude "others," and obscure the inequalities of power that they support.[41] These terms also have specific relevance to ideas about citizenship and national identity. For example, Eva Mackey writes about the notion of the "ordinary" or "Canadian-Canadian," which, she argues, serves as the neo-conservative, "ideal" Canadian citizen.[42] According to Mackey, the "notion of the 'ordinary Canadian' was mobilised politically in a number of co-exiting sites" and was used, she argues, "to re-define citizenship and to naturalise the exclusion of some citizens from notions of national belonging without direct reference to culture, race, sexual preference and gender."[43] The "ordinary" Canadian, Mackey notes, is both "white and unmarked." where "the state of being unmarked (and therefore 'normal' or 'ordinary') is both constitutive of, and an effect of, structural advantage of power, and the cultural authority that that power brings."[44]

Therefore, an implied objective associated with aligning Muslim characters with notions of the ordinary or the normal is to problematize the racial and ethnic coding these concepts often suggest (as an effort to perhaps unhinge this fixing of difference) and to contest the ways they are used to endorse this process of "othering." "Ordinary" in this context is also used to suggest forms of connection, shared values, and aspects which unite people across divides. In *Little Mosque* this is aided by its adherence to formula and specifically its reliance on the conventions of the domestic sitcom genre, which disrupts conventional images of Muslims on television (as terrorists or exotic or dangerous "others"). As Darling points out, "On the news all you ever hear are voices from the extreme end of the spectrum, [*Little Mosque*] gives voice to ordinary people who look just like other ordinary people."[45] By situating Islam in the context of comedy, the series effectively resists the sensational and violent depictions typical of news coverage and found in dramatic actions series such as *24* and *Sleeper Cell*. Moreover, the characters are located within the familiar and conventional milieu of the domestic situation comedy, which includes the central importance of everyday, "ordinary" settings of domestic life and focuses on family and neighbour relationships. Nawaz's description of the "normal" aspects of Muslim life evokes an image of family that perfectly corresponds to the central concerns of the domestic sitcom genre.

The sitcom formula also provides a structure which enables and supports the series' overall themes of reconciliation and unity. As David Marc has pointed out, it is possible to identify a basic "narrative architecture" characteristic of the sitcom form that, he argues, has remained fairly consistent since the radio period: "episode = familiar status quo → ritual error made → ritual lesson learned → familiar status quo."[46] This "problem/resolution format" is a key trait of the sitcom that offers a straightforward, repeatable framework for each episode's storylines. Jane Feuer adds that this structure has an "ideological flexibility" that makes the sitcom "the perfect format for illustrating current ideological conflicts while entertaining an audience."[47] On the one hand, the sitcom form provides space for the articulation of a variety of conflicting viewpoints, while the problem/resolution convention (the re-establishing of order) offers a familiar and perhaps comforting sense of reconciliation. The storylines in *Little Mosque* demonstrate this "ideological flexibility" as each episode tackles a topical issue, typically centred on aspects of Islam, and through its ensemble of characters a variety of perspectives are defined and expressed. Key conflicts are identified and the "culture clash" narrative provides a familiar framework for working through potentially divisive issues.[48] On the one hand, the series foregrounds and humorously explores tensions surrounding cultural differences; however, its conventional character types, familiar settings, and predictable narrative patterns become an important part of the "fantasy of unity" it presents as it works to reconcile the disruptions of difference that arise.

Culture clash narratives and fish-out-of-water storylines are commonplace in television, representing a prevailing device for depicting the collision of cultural difference or the arrival of an outsider to an unfamiliar milieu.[49] As such, they often depend on a structure of opposition, where differences are set in contrast and humour is elicited from the misunderstandings that arise through lack of knowledge or miscommunication. Following the traditional sitcom formula and its reliance on a problem/resolution format, culture clash narratives on television typically offer temporary resolution by depicting the overcoming of the obstacles to communication and by settling conflicts in ways that emphasize compromise and suggest that a greater sense of understanding has been achieved. New conflicts in subsequent episodes replay the same basic pattern with minor variations.

In *Little Mosque*, the culture clash narrative presents a timely take on the formula, using it as a way to engage with the so-called "clash of civilizations" argument that has been used by some to explain the attacks of 9/11 and the wars that have followed. This argument seeks to explain international relations between the "Western" and "Islamic" worlds as an essentialist clash of cultures.[50] Following suit, *Little Mosque* begins by establishing an Us-Them structure setting the Muslim and non-Muslim communities in contrast, with each viewing the other with distrust and suspicion. The culture clash narrative provides a straightforward, well-worn, and easily recognizable framework for engaging with these large and complex issues. In the opening episode, the characters are introduced against a backdrop of fear and paranoia that explicitly references the central misconceptions and stereotypes surrounding Muslims that have emerged in the aftermath of 9/11. The Muslim presence in the town is presented as something viewed by many Mercy residents as unusual and unsettling. The new Mercy Mosque opens in secrecy as Yasir worries about how the community will react and fears that Reverend Magee will shut them down if he finds out that the hall he's rented is being used as a mosque, not just as an office for his construction company. When a local town handyman stumbles upon the congregation in prayer he flees in fright and in panic dials the "terror attack hotline" to report what he has seen. Meanwhile, as a result of a wacky misunderstanding, Amaar becomes a victim of racial profiling and is detained for questioning at the Toronto airport. When he finally arrives in Mercy he is greeted by a frenzied journalist from the local newspaper who demands to know if he has a connection to al Qaeda. Distrust in the mosque is represented by Baber, who, in his last sermon before the new imam arrives, comically rails against the enemy that lurks in their kitchens. He says, "Wine gums, rye bread, licorice ... Western traps designed to seduce Muslims to drink alcohol." This first episode, therefore, establishes this Us–Them culture clash premise by depicting the relationship between the Muslim and non-Muslim communities as one primarily defined by the after-effects of 9/11.

True to formula, each episode replays the culture clash premise and provides narratives that work through these conflicts by deploying a number of strategies (similar to what Stuart Hall refers to as "trans-coding strategies")[51] that work to complicate and redefine the Us-Them opposition in ways that reinforce its themes of compromise, community togetherness, and the promotion of greater understanding across cultural divides. It depicts forms of connection that provide bridges between communities and individuals. For example, the friendship between Amaar and Reverend Magee suggests a friendly cross-faith understanding with each man facing similar challenges managing their congregations. Bitter rivals Fred Tupper and Fatima begin to establish a kind of love-hate relationship as they discover a shared distrust of conventional medicine (pitting them as allies against Rayyan) and Fatima heals his back using traditional remedies from Nigeria. Rayyan considers dating a non-Muslim when she becomes attracted to a handsome local firefighter. And, in the season finale ("The Archdeacon Cometh"), the mosque members come to the aid of the Anglican Church, posing as Christians in order to help save the church from being closed due to shrinking attendance. All of these examples demonstrate the series' emphasis on alliances and connections across the Us–Them divide, stressing camaraderie, shared goals, friendship, and co-operation.

Another key strategy used in *Little Mosque* is reversal, narratives that flip the dynamics of dominance and subordination that typically underpin Us-Them oppositions. The season finale offers an ideal example. In preparation for a visit from the archdeacon, Sarah (as a former Anglican) agrees to teach the mosque members about aspects of Christianity so that they may be more convincing in their impersonation. During her presentation on communion, she is heckled by Yasir and the others who find the rituals strange and funny. Yasir wisecracks, "My seat smells. Is that why they call it a pew?" In mock repulsion at the idea of eating the body of Christ and drinking his blood, Fatima screams, "I will not engage in cannibalism!" Everyone dissolves in laughter, finding Christianity both baffling and hilarious. While offering a narrative of inter-faith co-operation, this simple reversal also serves to situate the dominant in the position of the "other," subjecting it to light-hearted ridicule, and through the eyes of the "other" (with whom the audience identifies), it appears strange and different. It works to reveal, in a safe and humourous way, the absurdity of dominant perceptions of "otherness."

Another predominant strategy used in *Little Mosque* is demystification. Each episode offers information about various aspects of Islam, using its culture clash premise to display Muslim culture and to engage with questions surrounding it, especially as they relate to women. The characters take up different perspectives on issues, and a variety of conflicting perspectives and ideological positions are expressed. Among the issues explored are Islamic holidays and traditions, modesty and dress for Muslim women (including the meanings surrounding the wearing of the hijab), courtship and marriage customs, and so on. While all of the episodes contain scenes which provide information and explanation, episode three, "The Open House," takes this up more literally. The mosque opens its doors to the Mercy community, setting up different kiosks designed to introduce the public to aspects of Islam with the goal of promoting better relations with the larger community. This provides moments which are almost didactic in tone, teaching visitors (and viewers) about Islam, and the culture and traditions surrounding it. Mercy Mosque is portrayed as a community reaching out, working towards peaceful coexistence and dedicated to active civic participation, things that are stressed throughout the series. Through these gestures of demystification, the series works to familiarize audiences with Islam. Popular misconceptions are confronted and disarmed by providing explanation and addressing disagreements and debates that arise within the Muslim community, effectively disrupting the representation of Islam as a homogeneous and mysterious "other" set in opposition to mainstream society.

At the same time, issues are often located to the domestic sphere, and the family becomes a familiar trope for working through conflicts and highlighting the "universal" aspects of the situations. As Nawaz states, "It would be great if people could get a sense that Muslims have so many similarities to non-Muslims ... It's the same issues, you know, a father and his rebellious teenage daughter and how she dresses; just because you're Muslim your standards may be a little bit different, but they're still the same issues."[52] Focus on the family therefore becomes a key form of connection which provides a bridge across cultural differences. The second episode, "The Barrier," offers a useful example for analysis. The episode focuses on the issue of barriers in mosques that separate men and women while they pray. Baber has decided that a barrier is needed, arguing that women are a distraction. This sparks a controversy in the mosque as many (but not all) of the women object to being separated from the rest of the congregation. Each character takes up a different perspective on the issue: Baber campaigns to get support from Yasir and the other men; Rayyan is vehemently opposed to it, arguing that it is sexist and has no theological justification; Sarah supports her and tries to pressure Yasir to endorse their efforts to remove the barrier (denying him sex until he agrees); Fatima supports the barrier, arguing that it protects the women's privacy as well; and Amaar is caught in the middle and struggles to find a way to mediate the conflict. Meanwhile, Fred Tupper rails against the barrier on his radio show, declaring it evidence of the sexist nature of Islam. This sparks a controversy in the town, prompting a feminist group to picket the mosque. The issue is ultimately resolved through Amaar, who declares that half the barrier will stay—those who want to pray behind it can, and the others do not have to. Yasir and Sarah rekindle their romance and peace is restored in their marriage and in their family. This is a good example of how the series uses the traditional formula of the domestic sitcom to deal with the potentially controversial issues it introduces and works towards this universalizing and bridge-building agenda that Nawaz describes. The episode works to acquaint audiences with the issue and define the different viewpoints surrounding it. The core issue of the barrier is then recast as a domestic issue, transported into the domestic sphere and worked through in a familiar and conventional way (as a playful battle of the sexes); it is refigured as a conflict between husband and wife, father and daughter, and is ultimately resolved through compromise. The family appears to operate as a site of "normalization" where "universal" themes of family, marriage, and parenting are emphasized even as the episode tackles a culturally specific conflict.

The resolution of conflicts through compromise is fundamental in the series, which serves to balance the range of perspectives that are offered and communicate themes of co-operation within and between communities. Overall, moderate positions are emphasized and extreme viewpoints within both the Muslim and non-Muslim communities are cast as ridiculous, comically absurd, or the result of the ignorance of misguided (although basically harmless) individuals. The series appears to continually reach towards this sense of common ground, where disagreements can be settled, fears can be overcome, and commonalities can be unearthed. In doing so, *Little Mosque* does not dismantle the Us-Them framework but rather seems to position their relationship in ways that support notions of integration that underpin discourses of Canadian multiculturalism. According to Richard Day, "integrated identities occupy a paradoxical position as simultaneously both Us and Them, both problematically 'distinctive' and canonically 'participating.'"[53] *Little Mosque* emphasizes cultural difference as a recurring dilemma in the series, which seems to tap into anxieties surrounding social integration and multiculturalism. However, the "fantasy of unity" that it evokes is not an assimilationist vision; rather, it seems to balance recognition and integration, diversity and unity in ways that support dominant discourses on Canadian diversity.[54] Through these various strategies, forms of connection, and familiar narrative patterns, *Little Mosque* works to reconcile the disruptions posed by the culture clash and affirms the compatibility of diversity and notions of togetherness.

The Limitations of *Little Mosque*

In his discussion of the landmark series *The Cosby Show*, Herman Gray notes the ways blackness "was mediated and explicitly figured through home life, family, and middle-classness."[55] He writes, "*The Cosby Show* strategically used the Huxtables' upper-middle-class status to invite audience identifications across race, gender, and class lines ... it was impossible simply to laugh at these characters and make their blackness an object of derision and fascination. Rather, blackness coexisted in the show on the same discursive plane as their upper-middle-class success."[56] In referencing Cosby's own intention to offer a different image of African Americans on television (in particular, than those dealing with the black underclass), Gray notes, "The Huxtable family is universally appealing, then, largely because it is a middle-class family that happens to be black."[57] A striking correspondence can be identified here with Nawaz's comments that she wanted to emphasize universal themes and produce "an entertaining show that just happens to have Muslims in it." In *Little Mosque* the family, the core of the domestic sitcom, becomes one mechanism by which *Little Mosque* is able to reframe issues around the concerns central to the genre: specifically its frequent focus on relationship and parenting issues. As I have argued, the representation of the family in *Little Mosque* plays out larger debates about aspects of Islam in the context of a familiar family milieu, linking these with more banal and seemingly more universal domestic situations.

However, its so-called "normalizing" of Muslim life is enacted not only by adhering to a predictable narrative pattern and locating itself within a familiar domestic setting, but also by naturalizing middle-class life. Yasir and Fatima are successful business owners, Sarah has a career in public relations, Rayyan is a doctor, Baber is an economics professor. Their large single-family homes evoke the comforts of material affluence. The characters' conformity to middle-class norms likewise mediates the series' depiction of difference. The families are situated within a comfortable middle-class environment where affluence and the luxuries of middle-class life become part of their "ordinariness." The concept of the "ordinary," as Mackey notes, may exclude others based on race or cultural difference but can also be suggestive of other forms of exclusion as well (such as sexual preference, gender, class). It is not surprising then that Barbara Kay would note the show's evocation of 1950s series such as *Father Knows Best* and *Leave It to Beaver*. These fifties series provided an idealized portrait of the family, naturalizing the image of the white middle class and working to define it as the so-called "average" American family. As Mary Beth Haralovich points out, this image depended on various kinds of exclusion that contributed to the narrow image of family that these programs supported.[58] While *Little Mosque* challenges these racial and ethnic exclusions, it maintains this naturalization of middle-classness, which restricts the complexity with which it is able to engage with the questions of difference that are posed throughout the program.

As Gray argues, *Cosby* offered an image of black life that had not been seen on US television; however, he notes, "while effectively representing middle-class blackness as one expression of black diversity, the show in turn submerged other sites, tensions, and points of difference by consistently celebrating mobility, unlimited consumerism, and the patriarchal nuclear family."[59] While *Little Mosque* obviously emerges within and responds to different discourses surrounding race and cultural difference that circulate within these two very different national contexts, it does seem to display similar limitations (which may result in part from their shared generic roots). The series' culture clash narratives allow for issues of racism and intolerance to be addressed; however, its naturalization of the middle-class lifestyle suppresses a consideration of the larger systemic nature of discrimination that includes economic and other barriers to social mobility and integration. The effects of discrimination are therefore presented as conflicts that are individualized, personalized, and easily surmounted through education and compromise, rather than something that impacts their everyday material circumstances. It portrays an image of success and equality and confirms the narrative of progress that is often found within discourses of multiculturalism which suggest that within immigrant families each generation is marked by increasing prosperity and greater economic and social integration.[60] However, this narrative is often out of step with the realities of Canadian experience. According to Banting, Courchene, and Seidle, current research is revealing that since the 1980s, income levels for new immigrants have declined and their overall economic success has worsened.[61] They further suggest that "the intergenerational mobility enjoyed by the children of immigrants who arrived before the 1980s may be at risk."[62] Likewise, in their critique of Canadian multiculturalism, Fleras and Elliott write: "All the deeply ingrained myths in the country cannot disguise the obvious: Canada remains a racially stratified society where differences because of race and ethnicity continue to make a difference in terms of who gets what and how much."[63] The naturalization of middle-class privilege in *Little Mosque* smoothes over these realities and in effect suppresses a consideration of how class may intersect with the issues surrounding diversity that it tackles.

In her assessment of *Little Mosque,* journalist Paula Simons writes: "Anyone looking to *Little Mosque on the Prairie* for a fresh, edgy, take on 21st century Canadian multiculturalism is in for a disappointment."[64] I agree with Simmons in the sense that *Little Mosque* does not appear to interrogate, dismantle, or radically challenge current and dominant discourses on Canadian multiculturalism. Despite the anticipation of controversy surrounding its premiere, the program has not been considered especially controversial. I would argue that this is because its representation and negotiation of issues surrounding cultural difference are in keeping with dominant discourses on multiculturalism and the twin agendas of recognition and integration that underlie Canadian policies. In reaffirming dominant understandings of nation and national identity, it is also consistent with the objectives of public broadcasting in Canada and fits with CBC's history and its nation-building mandate. It arrives during a moment seemingly marked by an anxiety about Canadian multiculturalism and social integration, where Islam is often positioned at the forefront of public dialogue. Backlashes such as those seen in Quebec over reasonable accommodations have brought to public attention the xenophobia that exists in Canadian society that conflicts with a national self-image based on tolerance and multiculturalism. In this context, *Little Mosque on the Prairie* represents an important and interesting popular response, using the conventions of the sitcom to construct narratives of affirmation and reconciliation. It successfully challenges dominant representations of Muslims on television and effectively uses the culture clash narrative to reinforce themes of cooperation and compromise. However, in affirming the "ordinariness" of Muslim culture through an appeal to middle-class norms, the series also reveals some of its most significant limitations.

Notes

1 Patriquin, "Canada: A Nation of Bigots," 16–22.
2 CanWest, "Little Mosque Earns Big Honour," C3.
3 Goodman, "Can Little Mosque's Message of Tolerance Help Heal," D3.
4 Taylor, "The Little Mosque That Could," R3.
5 Quoted in MacDonald, "Allah in the Family," R11.
6 From Jesse Hirsh's interview with Zarqa Nawaz, *3D Dialogue*.
7 Rasporich, "Canadian Humour in the Media," 84.
8 Ibid.
9 Gray, "The Politics of Representation in Network Television," 439–61.
10 Sections m (ii), (vi) and (viii). 1991 Broadcasting Act, http://laws.justice.gc.ca/eng/acts/B-9.01/.
11 Wente, "Little Mosque: Way Too Cute," A15.
12 In an analysis of *King of Kensington* I have suggested that the series was explicitly shaped by discourses surrounding Canadian multiculturalism in the 1970s. I argue that "through its efforts to smooth over conflicts, deflate tensions and work towards reconciliation, the series appeared to be involved in both redefining the meaning of nation and providing a sense of stability and reassurance during an era of uncertainty." Although shaped by a very different historical context, *Little Mosque* uses the conventions of the sitcom form to achieve similar ends. See Matheson, "Ruling the Inner City," 47–48.
13 This is similar to the way Gray describes *The Cosby Show* which, he writes, "quite intentionally presented itself as a corrective to previous generations of television representations of black life." See Gray, "The Politics of Representation in Network Television," 446.
14 Banting, Courchene, and Seidle, "Conclusion: Diversity, Belonging and Shared Citizenship," 648.
15 Ibid., 647.
16 Day, *Multiculturalism and the History of Canadian Diversity*, 9.
17 Soroka, Johnston, and Banting, "Ties that Bind?" 1–3.
18 Ibid., 3.
19 Ibid., 3–4.
20 Ibid., 7.
21 Dixon, "Little Mosque Hits the Middle East," R1.
22 Pellerin, "Equal Opportunity Humour," A10.
23 MacFarquhar, "A Sitcom's Perilous Premise," C1.
24 Zahn, "Out in the Open."
25 Quoted in Intini, "It's a Good Hijab If You Can Get It," 67.
26 Quoted in Doyle, "Little Mosque Is Gloriously Canadian," R1.
27 Quoted in DeDekker, "Mercy! 'Little Mosque' Breaking New Ground," A6.
28 Quoted in Duff-Brown, "Sitcom Tackles Sensitive Religious Divide," L3.
29 Quoted in Dube, "Muslim Comedy Debuts in Canada," 09a.
30 Quoted in Rubinoff, "Muslims Take Their Satirical Turn," B3.
31 Gross, "Out of the Mainstream," 406.
32 Ibid.
33 Ibid., 418.

34 Quoted in Worboy, "Little Mosque Lands Big New Deal," F5.
35 Simons, "Little Mosque on the Prairie Not Such a Stretch," B1.
36 Menon, "Little Mirth on the Prairie: Under the Veil Is an Old-Style Sitcom," D5.
37 Murray, "Little Mirth on the Prairie," K1.
38 Kay, "The Joke's on Us," A19.
39 Byers, "*Little Mosque on the Prairie*: The Life and Times of the CBC."
40 From Jesse Hirsh's interview with Zarqa Nawaz, *3D Dialogue*.
41 Burton, referencing Stuart Hall, *Talking Television*, 174–75.
42 Mackey, *House of Difference*, 33.
43 Ibid., 34.
44 Ibid.
45 MacFarquhar, "A Sitcom's Perilous Premise," C1.
46 Quoted in Feuer, "Situation Comedy, Part 2," 69.
47 Ibid., 70.
48 Ellis, "Television as Working-Through."
49 As mentioned, *King of Kensington* also relied on culture clash narratives to address issues surrounding multiculturalism. Other series (Canadian and US) that used a similar narrative premise include *Due South, Northern Exposure, Perfect Strangers, True Colors, Chico and the Man, Aliens in America, Men in Trees.*
50 Ellen Seiter references the "clash of civilizations" argument in her analysis of US policy and the American sitcom *Aliens in America* and notes how emphasis is often placed on the "'cultural' nature of the assumed conflict between the US and Islamic world." See Seiter, "A Place at the Table."
51 Hall, "The Spectacle of the Other," 340.
52 McGinn, "We're Not Looking for a Purely Muslim Viewership," AL1.
53 Day, *Multiculturalism and the History of Canadian Diversity*, 196.
54 According to Gray assimilationist television discourses in the United States can be found in programs that "celebrate racial invisibility and color blindness." Examples include *Julia, I-Spy, Mission Impossible*, and *Room 22*, which "integrated individual black characters into hegemonic white worlds void of any hint of African American traditions, social struggle, racial conflicts, and cultural difference." See Gray, "The Politics of Representation in Network Television," 451.
55 Ibid., 447.
56 Ibid.
57 Ibid.
58 Haralovich, "Sitcoms and Suburbs: Positioning the 1950s Homemaker," 128–29.
59 Gray, "The Politics of Representation in Network Television," 448.
60 This narrative of progress was discussed by Lily Cho in her presentation, "Citizenship and the Materiality of Affect," at the Canadian Association of Cultural Studies Conference in Edmonton (October 27, 2007).
61 Banting, Courchene, and Seidle, "Conclusion: Diversity, Belonging and Shared Citizenship," 658.
62 Ibid., 659.
63 Fleras and Elliott, *Unequal Relations*, 117.
64 Simons, "Little Mosque on the Prairie Not Such a Stretch," B1.

9

"Come On Eileen"
Making Shania Canadian Again

SCOTT HENDERSON

> *It's possible, of course, that the life story of Shania Twain, surely familiar enough to anyone who might care, could make a decent biographical movie for fans. This isn't it. In fact,* Shania: A Life in Eight Albums *is repetitive, disjointed and riddled with the showbiz clichés that have been around since* Broadway Melody of 1936. *There are the struggles, the setbacks, the callous producers who won't let Shania do her own songs. There's the pushy stage mama and plenty of siblings. There is poverty and pain. There is a terrible family tragedy. There are men of various levels of sophistication, none of whom are quite right for our girl, until she runs into mega-producer Mutt Lange, the man who would become Mr. Shania Twain, a biographical fact that's somehow missing in this film.*[1]

MARC HORTON'S REVIEW of Jerry Ciccoritti's 2005 biopic *Shania: A Life in Eight Albums*, which aired on the CBC, is fairly typical of the generally negative response that greeted the film, both in print and online. Yet, at the same time, Horton manages to identify many of the key components that would appear to be central to Ciccoritti's strategy with the film. Twain's story, as Horton notes, is "surely familiar," and its component parts would easily allow it to be treated in a generic, clichéd manner akin to any Hollywood rags-to-riches story. That Ciccoritti avoids this tendency is one of the key aspects of the film's approach to its subject material. While Horton laments that the film avoids expected plot points such as Twain's relationship with Mutt Lange, and that its structure is not linear, but rather disjointed, he is also critical of the inclusion of so many formulaic components of the showbiz rise-to-fame story. Both Horton's review, in his desire for a more typical narrative and in his deriding of the use of clichés, and Ciccoritti's film, in its denial of the former and abundance of the latter, come across as contradictory. It is the intent of this chapter to unravel these contradictions in order to address the manner in which *Shania: A Life in Eight Albums* provides an example of assuredly Canadian television and underscores Ciccoritti's importance as a creator of uniquely Canadian television programming. The goal here is not necessarily to valorize Ciccoritti as a television auteur, but rather to illustrate that it is possible to employ familiar television codes and styles in a manner that underscores connections to nation. Shania Twain may be a global superstar, but this movie brings to the fore her Canadian connections in an overt, if frequently clichéd, manner.

Jerry Ciccoritti and the Materiality of Television

It would not be unfair to suggest that Ciccoritti has specialized in the historical biopic. While the history involved tends to be more recent than the concept of a historical biopic might suggest, the attention to period detail in Ciccoritti's films is significant. Among his films *Shania: A Life in Eight Albums* covers a time period from the early 1970s to the early 1990s; the two-part *Trudeau* biopic of 2002, of course, reaches back a bit further in time but is most notable for its depiction of the 1960s and 70s; *Net Worth*, which first aired on CBC in 1995, is set in the late 1950s; the 2008 CBC film *Victor: The Victor Davis Story* is set primarily in the 1980s; and his more recent film for CTV, 2008's *The Terrorist Next Door*, addresses events involving an al-Qaeda sleeper cell in Montreal in 1999. In an interview, Ciccoritti notes of the latter film, "just a decade ago cellphones were a novelty, there were no BlackBerrys, Europe still seemed very far away, the Internet was still a bit of a mystery. It was fun to make the movie this way, almost as a period piece."[2] Even where Ciccoritti is not dealing with the past, his television creations have offered an impressive degree of verisimilitude. His Gemini Award–winning direction on the youth-focused series *Straight Up* is described by Joan Nicks as placing "its teen characters in a Toronto core that is never directly named, but alluded to as urban-familiar through visual anchors (The Pickle Barrel, Sam the Record Man), thematic motifs (the ubiquitous arcades, a Yonge Street, fast-food hangout named A-J's that appears to operate around the clock), and the settings of prior CBC series (*Degrassi*, *Street Legal*)."[3] Nicks suggests that this is done, in part, to enhance the series' focus on youth subjectivity by allowing "*Straight Up*'s youths [to] imaginatively and serendipitously occupy spaces that can be scanned, felt, penetrated, tested and, in [Robert] Kroetsch's terms, uninvented to reveal something subjective, primal and apart from peer, parental or social scrutiny."[4]

In addition to his attention to period detail it is notable that so many of Ciccoritti's television films have involved biographies of Canadians. What is striking about these works is that they have avoided typical aspects of the docudrama. Ciccoritti's style is one that seems to interrogate the events being represented. These are not straightforward dramatizations of events. Instead, chronology is frequently ignored in favour of fractured timelines that reinforce thematic connections or repeat key incidents in order to permit a search for greater meaning by making viewers look anew at sometimes familiar historical moments. The meanings that emerge from this approach are ones that often reinforce the Canadian-ness of the stories being told. This Canadianness is rarely explicit but tends to be drawn more from a combination of character and setting.

Characters are identified explicitly as Canadian and normally offer traits and values that are positive, while settings are familiarly Canadian, reinforced via the intimacy of television's image. Ciccoritti's telefilms make express use of the materiality of television, particularly its pared-down nature, segmentation, and immediacy. The shallow focus and tighter framing of television's less expansive (than cinema) screen space are frequently exploited by Ciccoritti in frequent close-ups of familiar, and often iconic, everyday items. These serve to locate his films in particular places and spaces. Ciccoritti's films are often filled with highly stereotypical and, in their evocation of the past, nostalgic representations of Canada and Canadians. These serve as a form of televisual shorthand in that the sorts of images and ideals are ones that have been frequently called upon as part of Canadian self-representation. Ciccoritti's use of these suggests that there is a realization that his audience will recognize these often-overt references. Given the above-mentioned attributes of televisual representation, such obvious stereotypes, visual and attitudinal, help to ground these stories as recognizably Canadian by adhering to a familiar Canadian representational landscape. While it is true that such stereotypes belie more complex negotiations of meaning that may lie beneath the representations, their function in these films is as visual and aural signposts, in keeping with common tendencies in television representation. Of course Canada is not only the "great white north," and Canadians are not always polite, though it is equally true that New York is not solely the Statue of Liberty and a ferry ride from Staten Island, or Las Vegas the hotel strip, or Miami pastel-coloured art deco beachfront buildings; however, such iconographic signifiers are a staple of television production that quickly aid viewers in recognizing locales, themes, and meanings. Ciccoritti exploits this aspect of television in foregrounding the Canadian aspects of his films.

The opening scenes of *Victor: The Victor Davis Story* are typical of the rather complex manner in which Ciccoritti employs such structures. The film opens with a shot of a lake and the surrounding landscape. It is, for all intents and purposes, what for many Canadian viewers, familiar with national archetypes, represents a typical Canadian cottage scene, firmly rooting the story as Canadian from the outset. A second shot provides a close-up of a coffee mug and swimming goggles on a table, with the same lake visible through a window in the background. The scene then alternates from shots that serve to emphasize the beauty of the stereotypical Canadian surroundings, and close-ups of coffee being poured and the goggles being picked up as a man prepares to go swimming. This lone figure then walks along a lakeside dock with his back to the viewer, adjusts his swimsuit and puts on the goggles as he prepares to dive in the water. Before the identity of this figure can be revealed, the setting shifts to the 1982 World Aquatic Championships in Guyaquil, Ecuador. It was at this event that Victor Davis first came to prominence in capturing the men's 200m breaststroke in a world record time. The camera focuses on a large Canadian contingent in the crowd, their nationality made visually, and excessively, apparent through their waving Canadian flags and being dressed predominantly in red and white. Shots of Davis (Mark Lutz)[5] capture the Canadian flag and the country's name on his swim cap. Intercut with the race scenes are shots of the separate homes of Victor's father (Peter MacNeill) and his mother (Debra McCabe). Once again, the attention to detail provided by Ciccoritti is significant as furnishings, decor, clothing style, and so forth firmly root these scenes in what is evidently Canadian suburbia circa 1982. As Victor swims to his record, the fact that this is a Canadian success is reinforced aurally as the race announcer underlines Victor's nationality. The film's chronology is then further disrupted as the following scene is set during Victor's childhood, as his exhausted mother delivers Victor to the door of her ex-husband's apartment, acknowledging that she can no longer look after her son, who has too much energy. The young Victor's ambitions are then revealed as he is shown planning his rise through the ranks of world swimmers, starting with a local rival and eventually aiming to topple the world champion. This cockiness and confidence are shown to have followed him into his adult life, as the next scene returns to Guyaquil for a post-race interview session where Davis openly flirts with a female reporter. Yet this behaviour is countered by the following scene, which takes place on the night of Victor's death in a hit-and-run incident. After two young women (one of whom will later be revealed to have been Davis's girlfriend) are verbally harassed by a carload of young men, Davis nobly stands up for them by confronting the men only to be struck by their car as it bears down on him.

Within this sequence of events are small factors such as a salesman who abandons any attempt at his sales pitch to join Victor's mother and brother in viewing the race and celebrating the victory. Similarly there are scenes of Victor's father rushing outside to hug a multicultural collection of neighbours. While traits such as friendliness and community are hardly exclusively Canadian, the film's overt reinforcement of setting at this early stage does link these positive attributes with the time and place being presented, Canada in 1982.

All of this takes place before the first commercial break. The extensive recounting is offered here in order to demonstrate the complex nature of Ciccoritti's storytelling methods. A great deal of information is imparted, and numerous narrative threads and time frames are established in a relatively short period of time. This is a notable aspect of Ciccoritti's style. His films are made to accommodate but also exploit the rhythms of television. In 1995's *Net Worth*, a film exploring the role of Ted Lindsay in improving labour conditions for NHL hockey players, the film itself takes on the pace of a hockey game. Using the pacing tied to the need for commercial breaks, Ciccoritti is able to create a rhythm akin to the sport. The early part of the film has longer sections between commercial breaks, but as the tension in the film escalates, and the battle between players and owners heats up, the frequency of ads is increased, mimicking the frequent stoppages and excitement generated in the closing stages of a hockey game. This remains evident even on later DVD copies of the film, as there is a distinct fade to black between scenes where ads had appeared on its initial (and subsequent) CBC broadcasts.

The timing of ad breaks is not the only element of television's style and structure exploited by Ciccoritti. As already suggested, he makes use of television's pared-down visual nature. The scenes in Guyaquil are filled with images of Canada such as flags, t-shirts, and Davis's aforementioned swim cap. Prior to his press conference, Davis pulls a Canadian flag from a wall and wraps himself in it for the duration of his interview. Frequently in the film, particularly during race scenes, the colour red is dominant, a subtle reinforcement of the Canadian focus. It is the combination of these sorts of stylistic and structural traits, along with thematic aspects of the story that serve to reinforce stereotyped values such as friendliness, plurality, and neighbourliness as Canadian. While the film also displays elements of Davis's brash behaviour on the world stage, it in effect works to reveal the "Canadian" within Victor Davis. Despite problematic aspects of his personality, including an often cocky, unsporting attitude while in the pool, or infamous actions such as kicking a chair across a pool deck with the Queen in attendance during the Commonwealth Games, the film ultimately redeems him as possessing values that are so often valorized as being intrinsically Canadian—as Canadian as the maple leaf Davis has tattooed over his heart. The better-known image of Davis is one that is not normally represented as characteristically Canadian. Through firmly establishing positive character traits, in Victor and in others, and visually tying those traits to Canada, the film does work to create a positive Canadian image. The conclusion of the film reveals that the lone male figure in the opening shots was Claude Jacques (John Stoneham Sr.), the recipient of Victor's heart, a result of Davis's wish to donate his organs after his death. That Jacques is able to enjoy such a quintessentially Canadian moment, and then share this space with his family, as is seen in the film's concluding moments, reinforces the positive attributes the film ascribes to Davis as a Canadian.

Such melodramatic flourishes in combination with the reliance on verisimilitude in settings, helps to firmly locate Ciccoritti's efforts within the genre of docudrama, a genre that is fairly well established as part of Canadian television's traditions. In identifying the popularization of the docudramas that occurred in the 1970s, Seth Feldman suggests that they "came to operate as ritual. Events, persons, or even prominent works of fiction were *recognized* (in both senses of the word) by repeating them in another medium. The idea was not only to achieve further insight by scrutinizing the subject a second time ... as it was to affirm the subject's worth with additional attention."[6] Giving such recognition and affirming the subject's worth is significant in terms of what Ciccoritti does, as his films give value to Canadian experiences within a globalized culture where Canadian television is dominated by stories from elsewhere, predominantly the United States. Feldman goes on to note that "the act of seeing the recreation after being taught the history, reading the news, or living through the period is essentially narcissistic; we are looking at something that is already part of ourselves."[7] It could be argued, however, that in the Canadian experience these same actions may not have the same degree of narcissism. Canadian airwaves are dominated by American stories, often accompanied by American histories and myths, so that Canadian docudramas are offering "something that is part of ourselves," but in many cases it is something that may not have been acknowledged or recognized. Feldman says as much in noting, "for audiences used to American genre conventions, an accurately depicted courtroom, detective, or city becomes a building-block for self-recognition. At the same time, the recognition of a Canadian issue as being worthy of re-enactment or illustration through re-enactment creates the groundwork for collective awareness and a claim for control in setting the national agenda."[8] Ciccoritti takes this a step further. His docudramas tend to focus on events that may be known by Canadians, particularly those drawn to the subject matter. Hence, his films do not merely recreate the known events, but use the knowledge of those events to offer up more meaningful representations exploring Canadian experience and identity. Victor Davis's brash public persona and the tragic manner of his death may be known facts for Canadians viewing *Victor*. Ciccoritti is able to use this story to allow Canadians to see what they believe to be themselves, and their values, particularly in the familiar forms in which they are offered. In his recreation of the past, he brings a stereotyped Canadian way of life to television screens, offering the sorts of depictions that Feldman refers to as building blocks for self-recognition. These are not always "accurate" in the manner described by Feldman, but in his invoking of familiar tropes regarding Canada's image, Ciccoritti succeeds in making them feel familiar. At the same time, in recognizing themselves, Canadian viewers can recognize the values that they believe they cherish, allowing for a collective awareness of who they are, particularly as distinct from other globalized representations.

Shania: Reclaiming a Canadian Icon

The same approach as that found in *Victor* is also at the heart of *Shania: A Life in Eight Albums*, which could be seen as a televisual reclamation project in which the international music star, Shania Twain, is reclaimed as Canadian. Here is a story that is known to most Canadians, even those who may not be fans of Twain. Her stardom makes her a familiar icon within Canada, as well as beyond. Yet Ciccoritti's film is not focused on Twain as a superstar. Instead, it concentrates on her early struggles as Eileen Twain, her first attempts to break into the Nashville music scene, the tragic death of her parents that led Twain to put any career ambitions on hold in order to help raise her younger siblings, and finally her efforts to restart her career, which led to her meeting with Mutt Lange, her Svengali-to-be and future husband.

Even this narrative is not constructed as might be expected within a docudrama. As alluded to in Horton's review at the outset of this paper, *Shania: A*

Life in Eight Albums offers a mix of overt genre stereotypes related to the rags-to-riches showbiz narrative alongside a structure that breaks genre expectations. The narrative is not organized in a formulaic manner, despite the prescribed nature of Twain's life story. Instead, the film is organized around a thematic series of "albums" that break the film into eight sections, starting with "A Future Star Is Born.' While this "album" begins as one might expect, with a young Eileen (Riva Timbers) being pushed into singing by her mother Sharon (Megan Follows), the time frame then shifts to a teenaged Eileen (Shenae Grimes) attempting to get herself by train to Toronto to appear on the *Tommy Hunter Show*. Later albums pick up the threads of the different time frames, interweaving the young Eileen, the teen version, and the older version in her early twenties (Meredith Henderson).

The albums are a reworking of television's dominant aesthetic form, segmentation. As John Ellis initially described in writing about television in 1982, "segments are organized into groups, which are either simply cumulative, like news broadcast items and advertisements, or have some kind of sequential connection, like the groups of segments that make up the serial or the series."[9] While television has changed quite substantially in the intervening years, Ellis's basic premise has held true and segmentation still remains a central component of television structure. In *Shania*, however, the way in which segments are organized differs. Rather than being purely sequential, as Ellis describes for most narratives, any sequence is fractured in *Shania* by the primacy of thematic links between segments. In the album titled "Girl from the North Country," two separate events are contrasted. The first involves the younger Eileen learning aspects of Ojibwa culture. Here, her Native ties are offered as positive. The girl from the "north country" is connected to the iconographic landscape. This specific segment ends with Eileen at a gathering with her Native family members accompanying two young men, playing guitar and singing with them with confidence. In contrast, the other storyline addressed in this album deals with the teen Eileen. Here, her Ojibwa ties become a negative factor as her father Jerry (Eric Schweig) is laid off from his job, with her mother commenting that it is always the Natives that are let go first. While the segment does include some positive representations of Jerry and his efforts to cope with his situation, in contrast to the first half of "Girl From the North Country" this segment takes place predominantly indoors, in poorly lit, small, crowded rooms. Again, television's pared-down image aids in the film's addressing of themes. The positive is associated with the outdoors, with nature, while the negative is tied to the indoors as Eileen deals with the differing realities of life in the north country.

This shifting between time periods means that any narrative sequence needs to be reassembled by the viewers, though this is likely to be aided by their familiarity with Twain's story. Such familiarity may be part of the motivation for Ciccoritti's structure. A straightforward retelling of the story might capture Feldman's notion of "seeing the recreation after being taught the history," but given Shania's international stardom and the affinity of her biography with so many American success stories, it would not be viewed as a "Canadian issue worthy of reenactment." By placing the focus on thematic connections, this treatment of Twain's story shuns the mythic (possibly American, certainly generic) aspects of the story in favour of dwelling on its apparent Canadian-ness.

Given the manner in which nation is foregrounded in Ciccoritti's approaches, it is important to locate his work in the wider realm of contemporary Canadian television and the challenges it faces. Such a focus on nation and national identity may appear atypical in an era of increased globalization. Indeed, as Brenda Longfellow observes, "for most globalization theorists, the supranational spread of corporate empires and global reach of new technologies and media culture has been read as signalling the obsolescence of the nation and the dissolution of discrete and parochial forms of identification and belonging."[10] However, defining the nation still remains significant in Canada and in Canadian media. This is a point stressed by Longfellow: "What is curious and perhaps anomalous in Canada, however, is that against this backdrop of increasing 'global' rationalization of our economy and culture, issues of national identity have lost none of their resonance and seductions."[11]

This continued concern over national identity within Canadian media may be tied to an ongoing sense of colonization, whereby representations of Canada, and within Canada, are so frequently derived from outside the nation's borders. Mike Gasher stresses: "The decolonization of the Canadian imagination demands the affirmation of Canadian cultural values and the validation of Canadian cultural expression. The imagination is decolonized when the imagined possible is self-generated rather than externally imposed."[12] Ciccoritti's avoidance of the clichéd telling of Twain's story allows him to stay away from accepting the externally imposed structures tied to such a narrative. Similarly, the ideals foregrounded in *Victor* (and also in *Shania* as will be shown), and linked to being Canadian, provide the "affirmation of Canadian cultural values" anticipated by Gasher, even if these values function more as stereotypes than as truth. While both Gasher and Longfellow were writing over a decade ago, prior to the rapid rise of digital culture and the changes that it has brought to the television landscape, particularly in terms of availability of global productions, their core arguments remain relevant. These are issues that do not seem to go away. As Christopher Gittings identifies, "drawing a direct correlation between what they read as an erasure of Canadian cultural identity and increasing American domination of Canadian cultural production, the Canadian Film and Television Production Association warned in 1991 that 'If Canada hopes to survive as a sovereign nation, it must take steps to repatriate its culture.'"[13] Gittings cites a 1999 *Maclean's* magazine poll that acknowledges the continuity of these concerns as "increasingly, some Canadians feel they are being assimilated into a dominant United States monoculture" as "Canadians continue to register the homogenizing effect of a US-dominated global culture."[14] Greater cultural choice has not necessarily led to a greater cultural diversity in terms of the types of media images available to Canadians. The multi-channel universe in Canada does not necessarily offer more Canadian choice. A cynic might suggest that the time-shifting aspects of digital television, where Canadian network affiliates from across the country are available in all time zones, simply gives most Canadians the opportunity to avoid Canadian programming more frequently. PVRs and Internet streaming have eroded the importance of "appointment television," so that viewers are no longer tied to the whims of programmers and an abundance of American and international options are always available to tech-savvy Canadian audiences. Bart Beaty and Rebecca Sullivan posit that the "business model adopted by Canadian broadcasters can only be defined through their apparent need to play it safe, avoid risk, and minimize costs. Leave programming decisions to the American networks and produce only low-cost, low-risk local programming for the Canadian market, while launching specialty channels that are carbon copies of successful American channels."[15] While Beaty and Sullivan's position glosses over some of the unique aspects of Canadian programming, even that found on some of the carbon-copy stations, the notion that national identity is secondary to placating audience demand is well taken.

Of course, issues of national identity need to be carefully negotiated. While the ever-present threat of colonization, be it by American culture or globalization, does mean that there is a further danger of losing a sense of national identity, the specific attributes of the nation are not necessarily etched in stone. Given Canada's diversity, notions of national identity are understandably fluid. The goal is not some quasi-Griersonian top-down enforcement of a prescribed national identity; instead, the invocation of such familiar representations permits Canadian viewers to know that they are seeing themselves and each other on their screens. Beaty and Sullivan make the point that "arguments for a distinctly Canadian television culture, which is usually defined simply as one free of American influence, tend to follow on the heels of the multicultural defence of Canada."[16] The result of this, they suggest, is that "'Canadianness is, in fact, one of the least understood and least clearly articulated concepts in the nation's lexicon. The result is a kind of reluctantly guilty commitment to a notion of Canadian culture in theory, but not in practice."[17]

Ciccoritti's docudrama treatments of familiar figures, in conjunction with his use of stereotyped attributes of Canada, both iconographic and behavioural, suggest a level of self-consciousness that allows his films to evade being seen as totalizing accounts of Canadian-ness, thus avoiding the problems raised by Beaty and Sullivan. Instead his work is more about acknowledging the need for Canadians to see themselves represented through familiar, instantly recognizable, and often stereotypical versions of themselves. Ciccoritti offers Canadian-ness that is knowingly representational; it is nation recognizing as opposed to nation defining. His docudramas provide a mix of highly artificial representations alongside the more exacting recreations of different eras of Canadian history. As already noted, these films fully exploit the mix of melodrama combined with verisimilitude that is part of the docudrama genre. In *Shania* there is again a use of this in conjunction with the structures of broadcast television. Returns from commercial breaks in *Shania* frequently highlight the specifically Canadian setting of the film through obvious stereotypes, particularly those tied to landscape. In fact, the film is filled with numerous landscape shots. This may seem unusual for television, given the importance of the pared-down image and the lack of cinema's screen space to exploit panoramic images. Here, however, these shots are a form of pared-down image, an iconographic reminder of locale and nation. On one return from a commercial break this tendency is made explicit. A wide shot revealing northern forests, occupied by tree planters working for the Twain family's new business, is accompanied on the soundtrack by noted (and notably) Canadian country singer Stompin' Tom Connors's rendition of "C.A.N.A.D.A. (Cross Canada)," itself a song filled with iconographic references to Canada as nature.

This image of "Canada as Nature" is one of three images Paul Rutherford identifies as recurring in constructions of Canadian identity. It is, he claims, "an inexact phrase that can incorporate related images of the Great North, the land of empty spaces, or wilderness Canada."[18] Despite the fact that the image may only be partially based in reality, it has been a pervasive stereotype of Canada. Peter Harcourt suggests that this image is part of a "recurring nostalgia for a rural past that has never actually existed. There is a yearning for the pastoral, which seems incongruously inappropriate both for the severity of our climate and for the harshness of our terrain."[19] Yet both Harcourt and Rutherford underline that this iconography has played a large part in Canadians' imaginings of their country's identity. Its use as a blatant stereotype, one to be manipulated in a melodramatic manner, is then a seemingly self-aware construction in Ciccoritti's films, as evidenced in both *Victor* and *Shania*.

Rutherford's other two images are also recalled by Ciccoritti's work. His first image is that of "Canada as a peaceable kingdom, devoted to the hallowed goals of peace, order, and good government, a haven of sanity and tolerance in a disturbed world, a country that is less aggressive and more humane than its American neighbour."[20] Again, this is a cultural stereotype, but one that is readily exploited by Ciccoritti. In *Victor* the chivalry and benevolence uncovered under the determinedly Canadian Davis's gruff exterior are revealed via the film's representations, while in *Shania*, the Canadian girl, Eileen, who is hard-working and willing to give up her dreams for her family, underpins the glamorous international idol Shania Twain. The other image identified by Rutherford is more negative, where "Canada appears as a victim, a vassal state, a perpetual colony, an imaginary nation or a non-nation."[21] In their articulation of a clear-cut Canadian identity, Ciccoritti's films stand in opposition to such an image. By being so overtly Canadian they counter the threat of colonization. Shania may be lost, in some ways, to global consumerism, living in Switzerland, maintaining close ties to Nashville, but Ciccoritti's film biography, in its focus on Eileen, reasserts the more familiarly Canadian aspect of her story while at the same time refusing to structure it in a manner that replicates more generic, non-Canadian, codes.

The Changing Landscape of Canadian Television

The issues raised in Ciccoritti's films point to broader issues facing Canadian television. The changing nature of television, and its relation to and competition with other media, particularly the Internet and other digital formats such as DVD box sets of popular shows, means that the impact that a network such as the CBC can have is becoming increasingly diminished. It is an era that John Ellis refers to as a third era for television: "The industry is rushing towards an emerging era of plenty whilst the majority of viewers are still coming to terms with the era of availability. Television is full of new technologies, new challenges and new uncertainties."[22] The impact of such changes in Canada have been pointed out by David Taras: "Since the 1980s, the CBC has faced at least three critical challenges: it has been shaken by severe budget cuts; it has had to cope with the suspicions and the wrath of its political masters in Ottawa;

and it has been jolted by the explosion of new TV channels and services and new information technologies."[23] Since Taras offered these observations in 1997, these issues have become more pronounced. The growth in digital cable and satellite television in Canada means that where once the CBC was one stop on a limited dial, it is now one of many options available. At the same time, cuts have continued, advertising revenue has been undermined as advertising dollars are spread over a wider range of "content providers," and successive governments have continued to look upon the CBC with disdain.

Such bleak prospects led to a revising of the CBC's mandate, with being competitive with Canada's private broadcasters now mandatory. Reality shows, which, as Derek Foster points out elsewhere in this volume, were held in disdain by former CBC president Robert Rabinovitch, are now a frequent part of the network's lineup. When Hubert Lacroix was appointed the new president of the CBC in November 2007, the corporation's change in direction was identified in the *Globe and Mail*: "'If it's a public broadcaster and it's paid for by all the taxpayers, then it has got to make an offer that is the broadest possible offer,' Richard Stursberg, vice-president of CBC-TV, said in a recent interview reviewing the current television season and defending the network's still unproven scheme, under Lacroix's direction, to boost ratings with populist formulas. 'It's not a service built for elites.'"[24] Yet the fear is that by reaching for the widest possible audience, and relying on imported formulas to shape its broadcasting, the CBC could aid a further erosion of any sense of Canadian identity. Taras has noted that many observers feared "that in order to compete for audiences and advertising, CBC programming, including news programming, has or will gradually become less distinctive."[25]

A made-for-television film such as *Shania: A Life in Eight Albums* would seem to strike an appropriate balance by offering material that will appeal to the broader audience that the CBC needs to reach, while not being overly reliant on formulaic structures that would erode any sense of Canadian cultural identity. Instead, as noted, the film is structured so as to draw out the more stereotypically Canadian aspects of the story. Elements that might be described as "Canadian" are used for thematic and narrative effect. Such use counters one of the primary concerns pointed to by Taras in relation to the impact of new technologies on television: "Others are concerned that as technologies break down barriers previously imposed by time and distance, the local, the particular—in other words, the special and precious flavours and dialects of community and national life—will be lost."[26] The elements employed by Ciccoritti draw on "the special and precious flavours and dialects of community and national life" in order to tell the story.

Again the use of locations is important here, particularly the ties to landscape and nature. A comparison of two homes employed as settings in the film reveals how this functions. Homes offer a sense of the domestic in two ways. They are of course the domestic space of the home, an important and frequent recourse of television settings since television is most frequently viewed in the home. They are also domestic in the sense of "domestic culture'—that of the national as opposed to the foreign. The Canadian-ness of Canadian homes thus has a dual impact. Mary Bailey's house represents a space of discovery for Eileen, though initially it serves as a space of potential entrapment. Knowing the owners of the house chosen by location scouts as Mary Bailey's adds some additional insight to my observations. The home is in Naughton, Ontario, just outside of Sudbury and is located at the end of a suburban street, with full municipal service; but the wood-sided home sits on the shore of McCharles Lake, with an unobstructed view of forests and water in three directions. This view is significant to the location, as it permits shots that capture broader natural vistas, and Ciccoritti's framing emphasizes these aspects as opposed to the municipal connections. This is particularly evident when Eileen is given her first opportunity to go to Nashville, performing under the name of Sophia Twain. In the scene where Mary (Lynne Cormack) gives her the news, Eileen is sitting on a bench, playing an acoustic guitar, surrounded by nature.

Her initial audition for Mary takes place in the home's living room. While a large picture window is present, it remains out of focus, as Ciccoritti instead favours tight close-up shots of Eileen, Mary, and Sharon (Eileen's mother). The effect here is not one of freedom or success, as even though Mary is clearly intrigued by Eileen's ability, she suggests that she is unable to help the younger singer with her career. As the two Twain women walk to their pickup truck in the driveway, the shot opens up in accordance with the hopefulness expressed by Sharon that something will come of the meeting. The image of the pickup pulling away fades into the previously mentioned "nature" shot where Mary and Eileen, silhouetted by the sun, are small figures within the idealized northern Ontario landscape. This scene is then contrasted with a tight close-up of Eileen/Sophia in a recording studio in Nashville. All sense of freedom is visually removed in this tight shot, with Eileen quite literally boxed in by the soundproof booth's walls. That her career is stalled at this point is clearly visually evident. As Eileen's career fails to progress and the relationship deteriorates, the outdoors shots are replaced by smoky interiors, with tighter shots and a far less orderly and idealized *mise en scène*.

The upshot of this analysis is that Ciccoritti is able to use a quintessentially northern Ontario lakeside home and its surrounding environment and incorporate them as a significant part of his storytelling structure. Setting and landscape are not incidental, but instead they function as emblematic of Canada, as well as serving a vital role in giving overt meaning to events as part of the "special and precious flavours of community and national life."

The second home is the Toronto home of Eileen's boyfriend, John Kim Bell (Darrell Dennis). Its inclusion in the film feels almost anachronistic. While the setting is the 1980s, the home more closely resembles an early twenty-first-century "reno" project. This seems purposeful, as it is better able to communicate the "new money" represented by John, as well as providing the necessary sterile environment for unfolding events. A home decorated in typical 1980s style would not have had the same impact. Key to the *mise en scène* of this home is the large assortment of cultural artifacts. There is a mix of European and Native art in the home. Yet all of the pieces feel less like organic items, and more like sterile, iconographic items that are for sale and show. Despite his being Native, Paul's relationship to Native culture is clearly mediated through artworks and through "traditional" performance. This is made abundantly clear when Eileen is made to perform as part of John's fundraiser. Her singing of "Amazing Grace" while dressed in beaded buckskin and a feathered headdress reduces her to the status of a commodity—an image of Native culture, not lived Native culture itself as we had seen the younger Eileen take part in. Ciccoritti's use of these traditions is evident in his emphasis on Twain's ties to Ojibwa culture throughout the film.

The morning following her benefit performance, Eileen retreats to the backyard of the house to cook moose meat, a gift from her parents, over an open fire. The cold sterility of the house is made obvious in its darkness and cold, the grey and black colours, and the absence of any natural sound. As the camera passes through the back door and joins Eileen in the yard, the sounds of nature become part of the soundtrack. The sound combined with a close-up of Eileen roasting moose meat suggest a negating of the effects of the city and a return to nature and her roots. By extension, the film then seems to suggest that these roots are an important part of who Shania is, despite her more global lifestyle. Again setting, and the "special and precious flavours and dialects of community and national life," come to the fore. In this case the false, commodified "flavours" of John and Toronto are in contrast to what the film offers as the genuine, natural, more authentic flavours of Native culture appreciated by Eileen as part of her Native (and Canadian) heritage. Once more, Ciccoritti employs televisual shorthand to communicate this message, eschewing the complexities surrounding indigenous Canadian culture in favour of an immediacy linking Twain to Ojibwa culture and nature as a means of reinforcing her Canadianness.

It is not just through content and setting that Ciccoritti addresses issues relating to Canadian identity. It is also through television style and structure. Jim Leach has noted: "The implications of the flow effect have rarely been discussed in relation to Canadian television because of the urgent need to identify specifically Canadian qualities in programs or to challenge the dominance of U.S. programming."[27] Ciccoritti's work, however, makes significant use of flow. Given the fragmented chronology of much of his work, flow is important in relation to meaning via the manner in which various story fragments come together. Leach addresses the differing approaches to flow offered by Raymond Williams and John Fiske. Williams, Leach states, "argued that the semiotic effect of the flow is far from democratic in that it is dependent on 'the production habits of a majority of professionals' that set 'limits to actual insights and perceptions' while ensuring 'a certain confidence of address.'"[28] In contrast, Leach notes Fiske's contention "that since commercial television programs must attract the largest possible audience, they must be open not only to readings in line with the dominant ideology but also to other readings that meet the needs of those groups whose cultural backgrounds place them outside the mainstream."[29] In the case of Ciccoritti, his approach to flow appears to incorporate aspects of both Williams's and Fiske's theories. In keeping with Williams, Ciccoritti's work does have a "certain confidence of address" as underscored by the consistencies found among his films in the analysis offered here. At the same time, the address employed is one that is outside the mainstream, placing the likely majority of viewers in the sorts of positions described by Fiske. This may, in part, explain some of the negative criticism aimed at *Shania: A Life in Eight Albums*, particularly online after the film had first aired. Mainstream audiences—and it is notable that Shania Twain is a mainstream artist—may have felt outsiders to the film's mode of address even if the Canadian stereotypes on offer were so familiar. Ciccoritti's stylistic flourishes and his often blatant use of television's modes of representation may have served to alienate audiences, and may even have reinforced perceptions, such as those Richard Stursberg hoped to alter, that CBC programming was "a service built for elites."

In challenging the normal expectations surrounding flow, that is by refusing the more common production habits and mode of address, Ciccoritti ruptures the expectations that viewers might have coming into a docudrama on the life of Shania Twain. By doing this while including so much popular iconography of Canada, Ciccoritti is able to call attention to structure, clearly marking out his approach as different, as coming from a different narrative tradition and thus allowing for greater viewer awareness. The films are recognizably "Canadian" in terms of offering up many common stereotypes, but they stray from the more familiar modes of address most commonly associated with American television, which is, of course, so dominant within Canada. Therefore both structurally as well as in terms of content, his films are able to provide what can be described as a more Canadian perspective or subjectivity. There is still room for Fiske's resistant readings, but they must acknowledge the confidence of address offered by the text, an address that differs from the US-influenced norm, but one that also risks alienating viewers comfortable with those norms. It is clearly a delicate balancing act, and the critical and commercial response to *Shania* suggests that in this case it may have been less successful.

In light of the challenges facing the CBC and Canadian television more generally, it is possible to see what Ciccoritti's approach to biopics is attempting to accomplish. With increased competition, both from other networks and from other forms of media, the CBC needs audiences. The use of familiar Canadian figures as subjects of docudrama biographical treatments has a clear appeal. An artist with broad appeal and huge popularity such as Shania Twain, provides potential for a ready-made audience, one that appeals to advertisers. At the same time, there would be a long-term risk for Canadian cultural producers, such as Jerry Ciccoritti, in encouraging formulaic productions that are not somehow distinct from other options offered up by mass culture. It is difficult to argue for the validity of an industry, and request funding for it, if the products it creates are readily available elsewhere and at lower cost.

The model provided by a film like *Shania: A Life in Eight Albums* allows for a Canadian story, told in a recognizably, if overtly stereotypical, Canadian manner. The revised mandate of the CBC is ostensibly fulfilled while the more idealistic appeal of cultural nationalism through unique style is retained. *Shania*'s uncovering of the Canadian in Eileen allows the film to twist genre, and narrative expectations, such as those anticipated by Horton's review, in order to locate the story of the international pop superstar that is Shania Twain as fundamentally Canadian. In offering subject matter that could be anticipated to attract a sizable Canadian audience, the film is able to fulfill our expectations of the CBC to show us to ourselves. Ultimately *Shania* demonstrates how television's current structures, both textual as well as industrial and cultural, can be harnessed to provide content that reaches Canadians with texts that address their concerns and help to forge a collective sense of nation.

Notes

1 Horton, "Shania Biopic a Twain Wreck," B1.
2 Quill, "What A Difference a Decade Makes," E8.
3 Nicks, "*Straight Up* and Youth Television," 147.
4 Ibid., 144.
5 It is conceivable to suggest that the verisimilitude forged by Ciccoritti is enhanced by the casting of Lutz as Davis. Lutz, also the writer of the screenplay, had been a former competitive swimmer and holder of Canadian records whose career was cut short by a shoulder injury.
6 Feldman, "Footnote to Fact," 348.
7 Ibid., 349.
8 Ibid., 354.
9 Ellis, *Visible Fictions*, 112.
10 Longfellow, "Globalization and National Identity," 4.
11 Ibid.
12 Gasher, "Decolonizing the Imagination," 104.
13 Gittings, *Canadian National Cinema*, 104.
14 Ibid.
15 Beaty and Sullivan, *Canadian Television Today*, 43.
16 Ibid., 12.
17 Ibid.
18 Rutherford, "Made in America," 278.
19 Harcourt, "The Canadian Nation," 9.
20 Rutherford, "Made in America," 278.
21 Ibid., 279.
22 Ellis, *Seeing Things*, 162.
23 Taras, "The CBC and Canadian Television," 268.
24 Taylor, "CBC's No. 2," R1.
25 Taras, "The CBC and Canadian Television," 269.
26 Ibid., 273.
27 Leach, "Reading Canadian 'Popular' Television," 114.
28 Ibid.
29 Ibid., 112.

Bibliography

Aboriginal Peoples Television Network (APTN). 2006 Annual Report. http://www.aptn.ca/content/view/27/197/.

———. *Aboriginal Peoples Television Network Request for Proposals*. Winnipeg: APTN, 2003.

———. APTN Factsheet. http://www.aptn.ca/content/view/124/188/.

———. *APTN Milestones*. http://www.aptn.ca/content/view/20/196/.

———. *Hank William's First Nation—The Series*. http://www.aptn.ca.

———. Our Audience. http://www.aptn.ca/sales/our_audience.php.

———. Producing for APTN, What We're Looking For. http://www.aptn.ca/content/view/174/111/.

———. Reply to Intervention of Independent Aboriginal Screen Producers Association, CRTC Licence Renewal Application. http://support.crtc.gc.ca/applicant/docs.aspx?pn_ph_no=2005-4&call_id=22610&lang=E&defaultName=Independent%20Aboriginal%20Screen%20Producers%20Association%20#24&replyonly=&addtInfo=&addtCmmt=&fnlSub=.

———. Supplementary Brief, CRTC Licence Renewal Application. http://www.crtc.gc.ca/archive/ENG/hearings/2005/n2005-4.htm#8.

———. *Towards a Truer Mirror ... Submission to the House of Commons Standing Committee on Canadian Heritage*. Winnipeg: APTN, 2001.

———. What's New (2004). http://www.aptn.ca/Whats_New/whatsnew_html.

Acland, Charles. "The Last Days of Videotape." Flowtv.org, November 12, 2009. http://flowtv.org/?p=4555 (accessed May 9, 2010).

———. "Screen Space, Screen Time, and Canadian Film Exhibition." In *North of Everything: English-Canadian Cinema since 1980*, edited by William Beard and Jerry White, 2–18. Edmonton: University of Alberta Press, 2002.

———. *Screen Time: Movies, Multiplexes and Global Culture*. Durham, NC: Duke University Press, 2003.

Akass, Kim, and Janet McCabe. *Reading Sex and the City*. London and New York: I.B. Tauris, 2004.

Akin, David. "CBC Axes Exec despite Ratings Success." *Toronto Sun*, August 9, 2010. http://www.torontosun.com/news/canada/2010/08/08/14962161.html.

Alia, Valerie. *Un/Covering the North: News, Media, and Aboriginal People*. Vancouver: University of British Columbia Press, 1999.

Allan, Blaine. Directory of Television Series 1952–1982. Queen's University. http://www.film.queensu.ca/CBC/Index.html.

Anderson, Jason. "Black Eyed Dog." *Globe and Mail*, October 27, 2006.

Ang, Ien. *Watching Dallas: Soap Opera and the Melodramatic Imagination*. London: Methuen, 1985.

Apparudai, Arjun. "Disjuncture and Difference in the Global Cultural Economy." *Theory, Culture and Society* 7 (1990): 295–310.

Appiah, Kwame Anthony. *Cosmopolitanism: Ethics in a World of Strangers*. London: Penguin, 2006.

Asen, Robert. "A Discourse Theory of Citizenship." *Quarterly Journal of Speech* 90, no. 2 (2004): 189–211.

Ash, Melanie C.T. "But Where Are You REALLY From? Reflections on Immigration, Multiculturalism, and Canadian Identity." In *Racism Eh? A Critical Inter-Disciplinary Anthology of Race and Racism in Canada*, edited by Camille Nelson and Charmaine Nelson, 398–409. Toronto: Captus Press, 2004.

Attallah, Paul. "Reading Television." *Canadian Journal of Communication Studies* 34, no. 1 (2009): 163–70.

———. "Richard Collins: The Debate on Culture and Polity." *Canadian Journal of Communications* 17, no. 2 (1992): 221–36.

Attallah, Paul, and Derek Foster. "Television in Canada." In *Mediascapes: New Patterns in Canadian Communication*, 2nd ed., edited by Paul Attallah and Leslie Regan Shade, 179–95. Toronto: Nelson Canada, 2006.

Audio-Visual Preservation Trust of Canada. Conservation, Preservation and Public Access. http://www.avtrust.ca/en_index.htm (accessed April 20, 2008).

———. Fading Away: Strategic Options to Ensure the Protection of and Access to Our Audio-Visual Memory. http://www.avtrust.ca/docs/fading_away.pdf (accessed April 20, 2008).

———. Mandate. http://avtrust.ca/en_mandate.htm (accessed April 20, 2008).

Audley, Paul. *Canada's Cultural Industries: Broadcasting, Publishing, Records and Film*. Ottawa: Canadian Institute for Economic Policy, 1983.

Austin, Guy. *Stars in Modern French Film*. London: Arnold, 2003.

Babe, Robert. "Regulation and Incentives, Two Sides of Any Policy." In *Canadian Broadcasting: The Challenge of Change*, edited by Colin Hoskins and Stuart McFadyen, 23–26. Edmonton: University of Alberta and ACCESS, 1985.

Babington, Bruce, ed. *British Stars and Stardom*. Manchester: Manchester University Press, 2001.

Banet-Weiser, Sarah. *Kids Rule! Nickelodeon and Consumer Citizenship*. Durham, NC: Duke University Press, 2007.

Bannerji, Himani. *The Dark Side of Nation: Essays on Multiculturalism, Nationalism and Gender*. Toronto: Canadian Scholars' Press, 2000.

Banting, Keith, Thomas J. Courchene, and F. Leslie Seidle. "Conclusion: Diversity, Belonging and Shared Citizenship." In *Belonging? Diversity, Recognition and Shared Citizenship in Canada*, edited by Keith Banting, Thomas J. Courchene, and F. Leslie Seidle, 647–86. Ottawa: Institute for Research on Public Policy, 2007.

Bear, Jeff, and Telefilm Canada. At the Crossroads. http://support.crtc.gc.ca/applicant/docs.aspx?pn_ph_no=2005-4&call_id=22610&lang=E&defaultName=Independent%20Aboriginal%20Screen%20Producers%20Association%20#24&replyonly=&addtInfo=&addtCmmt=&fnlSub=.

Beaty, Bart, and Rebecca Sullivan. *Canadian Television Today*. Calgary: University of Calgary Press, 2006.

Bell, Andrew. "Boob Tube." *Toronto Life*, May 2008. http://www.torontolife.com/features/boob-tube/.

Bennett, James. "The Television Personality System: Televisual Stardom Revisited after Film Theory." *Screen* 49, no. 1 (2008): 32–50.

Blakesley, David, ed. *The Terministic Screen: Rhetorical Perspectives on Film*. Carbondale: Southern Illinois University Press, 2003.

Blumler, Jay G. "The New Television Marketplace: Imperatives, Implications, Issues." In *Mass Media and Society*, edited by James Curran and Michael Gurevitch, 194–215. London: Edward Arnold, 1991.

Bociurkiw, Marusya. *Feeling Canadian: Television, Nationalism, and Affect*. Waterloo, ON: Wilfrid Laurier University Press, 2011.

Boddy, William. "Interactive Television and Advertising Form in Contemporary U.S. Television." In *Television after TV: Essays on a Medium in Transition*, edited by Lynn Spigel and Jan Olsson, 113–32. Durham, NC: Duke University Press, 2004.

Bodroghkozy, Aniko. "As Canadian as Possible ...: Anglo-Canadian Popular Culture and the American Other." *In Hop on Pop: The Politics and Pleasures of Popular Culture*, edited by Henry Jenkins, Tara McPherson, and Jane Shattue, 566–89. Durham, NC: Duke University Press, 2003.

Bredin, Marian. "APTN and Its Audience." In *Indigenous Screen Cultures in Canada*, edited by Marian Bredin and Sigurjon Baldur Hafsteinsson, 69–86. Winnipeg: University of Manitoba Press, 2008.

Brioux, Bill. "CBC Kerfuffle No National Emergency." *Toronto Sun* June 22, 2006. http://jam.canoe.ca/Television/TV_Shows/C/CBC/2006/06/22/1646660.html.

Broadcasting Act (1991). www.crtc.gc.ca/eng/LEGAL/BROAD.htm.

Brown, Wendy. *Regulating Aversion: Tolerance in the Age of Identity and Empire*. Princeton, NJ: Princeton University Press, 2008.

Brummett, Barry. "Rhetorical Theory as Heuristic and Moral: A Pedagogical Justification." *Communication Education* 33, no. 1 (1984): 97–107.

Buckingham, David. *After the Death of Childhood: Growing up in the Age of Electronic Media*. Cambridge: Polity Press, 2000.

Budd, Mike, Steve Craig, and Clay Steinman. *Consuming Environments: Television and Commercial Culture*. New Brunswick, NJ: Rutgers University Press, 1999.

Burton, Graeme. *Talking Television*. London: Arnold, 2000.

Butler, Judith. *Excitable Speech: A Politics of the Performative*. New York and London: Routledge, 1997.

Byers, Michele. "The Empty Archive: Canadian Television and the Erasure of History." Flowtv.org, March 6, 2007. http://flowtv.org/?p=520 (accessed May 10, 2010).

———, ed. *Growing Up Degrassi: Television, Identity and Youth Cultures*. Toronto: Sumach Press, 2005.

———. "*Little Mosque on the Prairie*: The Life and Times of the CBC." Flowtv.org, February 23, 2007. http://flowtv.org/?p=61.

Byers, Michele, and Rebecca Haines. "The White Girl from *That Show*." In *Growing Up Degrassi: Television, Identity and Youth Cultures*, edited by Michele Byers, 167–90. Toronto: Sumach Press, 2005.

Byers, Michele, and Jennifer VanderBurgh. "Trafficking (in) the Archive: Canada, Copyright, and the Study of Television." *English Studies in Canada* 36, no. 1 (2010): 109–26.

———. "What Was Canada? Locating the Language of an Empty National Archive." *Critical Studies in Television* 5, no. 2 (Fall 2010): 105–17.

Caldwell, John. "Convergence Television: Aggregating Form and Repurposing Content in the Future of Conglomeration." In *Television after TV: Essays on a Medium in Transition*, edited by Lynn Spigel and Jan Olsson, 41–74. Durham, NC: Duke University Press, 2004.

Canada. Department of Canadian Heritage. *Northern Native Broadcast Access Program (NNBAP) and Northern Distribution Program (NDP) Evaluation*. Ottawa, 2003.

Canada. Parliament. House of Commons. Standing Committee on Canadian Heritage, and Clifford Lincoln. *Our Cultural Sovereignty: The Second Century of Canadian Broadcasting.* Ottawa: Standing Committee on Canadian Heritage, 2003.

Canada. Royal Commission on Aboriginal Peoples (RCAP). *Gathering Strength, Final Report, Vol. 3*. 1996.

Canadian Broadcasting Corporation. Digital Archives Project. http://archives.cbc.ca/.

———. "Heritage Committee Grills CBC Bosses on Reality TV Hockey" (2006). http://www.cbc.ca/arts/story/2006/09/28/cbc-heritage-committee.html.

———. "Nash Slams CBC While Accepting Award." Canadian Broadcasting Corporation (2006). http://www.cbc.ca/story/arts/national/2006/06/23/nash-award.html.

Canadian Radio-television Telecommunications Commission (CRTC). *Broadcasting Decision CRTC 2005-445*. Ottawa: Canadian Radio-television Telecommunications Commission, 2005.

———. *Broadcasting Decision, CRTC 2007-246*. Ottawa: Canadian Radio-television Telecommunications Commission, 2007.

Canadian Television Fund (CTF). 2006–2007 Annual Report. http://www.ctf-fct.ca/assets/AR0607/index.html.

———. Aboriginal-Language Projects Funding Results 2007–2008. http://www.ctf-fct.ca/ctf_home_en.html.

———. Aboriginal-Language Projects Guidelines 2008–2009. http://www.ctf-fct.ca/ctf_home_en.html.

———. Approved Broadcaster Performance Envelope English-Language Applications. http://www.ctf-fct.ca/assets/funding/BPE-English-0708.pdf.

———. Broadcaster Performance Envelope Stream. http://www.ctf-fct.ca/ctf_home_en.html.

———. CTF 2008–2009 Broadcaster Performance Envelopes (BPE) Factor Weights—General Overview. http://www.ctf-fct.ca/assets/factor-weight0809.pdf.

CanWest News Service. "Little Mosque Earns Big Honour." *Saskatoon Star-Phoenix*, 10 October 2007.

Caughie, John. *Television Drama: Realism, Modernism, and British Culture*. Oxford: Oxford University Press, 2000.

Cavu Pictures. *Trailer Park Boys: A Visitor's Guide to the Sunnyvale Trailer Park*. New York: Cavu Pictures, n.d. http://www.screenmediafilms.net/.../Trailer%20Park%20Boys/trailerParkPK.doc.

Chicken Wing Picture Ltd. *Press Kit, Hank William's First Nation—The Series*. http://www.hwfn.com/files/HWFN_The_Series_Press_Kit.pdf.

Cho, Lily. "Citizenship and the Materiality of Affect." Paper presented at the Canadian Association of Cultural Studies Conference in Edmonton, AB (October 27, 2007).

Collins, Richard. *Culture, Communication and National Identity: The Case of Canadian Television*. Toronto: University of Toronto Press, 1990.

Content Media Corp. http://www.contentmediacorp.com/ (accessed May 4, 2011).

"Croooooozing across Canada with YTV's Weird on Wheels." YTV News Release (2003). http://www.corusent.com/corporate/press_room/press_kids_tv/pressReleaseDetail.asp?id=430.

"Cruisin' across Canada with YTV's Weird on Wheels." YTV News Release (2005). http://www.corusent.com/corporate/press_room/press_kids_tv/pressReleaseDetail.asp?id=855.

"Curling Gets Glitzy." *Toronto Star* (Editorial), February 12, 2008. http://www.thestar.com/article/302564.

Dale, Ann, and Ted Naylor. "Dialogue and Public Space: An Exploration of Radio and Information Communications Technologies." *Canadian Journal of Political Science* 38, no. 1 (2005): 203–25.

Davidson, Sean. "CBC Enters the *Dragon's Den*." *Playback* (2006). http://www.playbackonline.ca/articles/magazine/20060904/dragonsden.html.

Davis, Glyn, and Kay Dickinson. "Introduction." In *Teen TV: Genre, Consumption, Identity*, edited by Glyn Davis and Kay Dickinson, 1–16. London: BFI Publishing, 2004.

Day, Richard J.F. *Multiculturalism and the History of Canadian Diversity*. Toronto: University of Toronto Press, 2000.

DeDekker, Jeff. "Mercy! 'Little Mosque' Breaking New Ground." *Leader Post* (Regina), January 8, 2007.

De Kerckhove, Derrick, and Christopher Dewdney. *The Skin of Culture: Investigating the New Electronic Reality*. Toronto: Somerville House, 1995

de la Garde, Roger, and Veronique Nguyên-Duy. "TVTV: The Television Revolution—A Commentary." *Canadian Journal of Communication* 21, no. 1 (1996). http://www.cjc-online.ca/index.php/journal/article/view/911/817.

DeLuca, Kevin Michael, and Jennifer Peeples. "From Public Sphere to Public Screen: Democracy, Activism and the 'Violence' of Seattle." *Critical Studies in Media Communication* 19, no. 2 (2002): 125–51.

Derrida, Jacques. *Archive Fever: A Freudian Impression*. Chicago: University of Chicago Press, 1995.

Dick, Ernest J. *The Future of CBC's Past: A Review of Archives, Presentation for Senior Management*. CBC, August 1990.

Dickinson, Peter. "Being at Home with Roy Dupuis and Pascale Bussières or, Star-Gazing In and Out of Québec." *Cineaction* 73–74 (Summer 2007): 38–43.

Dillon, Mark. "CBC in Ratings Tailspin." *Playback* (2006). http://www. playbackonline.ca/articles/magaizine/20061030/comment.html.

Dixon, Guy. "Little Mosque Hits the Middle East." *Globe and Mail*. September 26, 2007.

Dodds, Gordon. "Provenance Must Remain the Archival Bottom Line." *Archivaria* 18 (Summer 1984): 4–7.

Doherty, Thomas. "The Sincerest Form of Flattery: A Brief History of the Mockumentary." *Cineaste* (Fall 2003): 24.

Doty, Alexander. "The Cabinet of Lucy Ricardo: Lucille Ball's Star Image." *Cinema Journal* 29, no. 4 (1990): 3–20.

Doyle, John. *A Great Feast of Light: Growing Up Irish in the Television Age*. Toronto: Anchor Canada, Random House, 2006.

———. "Little Mosque Is Gloriously Canadian." *Globe and Mail*, September 9, 2007.

———. "The Post-Stursberg CBC: Tilt Goes the Tightrope." *Globe and Mail*, August 14, 2010. http://www.theglobeandmail.com/news/arts/television/john-doyle/the-post-stursberg-cbc-tilt-goes-the-tightrope/article1671986.

Druick, Zoë, and Aspa Kotsopoulos. *Programming Reality: Perspectives on English-Canadian Television*. Waterloo, ON: Wilfrid Laurier University Press, 2008.

Dube, Rebecca Cook. "Muslim Comedy Debuts in Canada." *USA Today*, January 11, 2007.

Duff-Brown, Beth. "Sitcom Tackles Sensitive Religious Divide in Post-9/11 Era." *Ottawa Citizen*, January 6, 2007.

Dvorkin, Jeffrey. "Why Is Managing the CBC So Damn Difficult?" Now the Details: An Examination of What Works and What Doesn't in Media, Ethics and Journalism. And Why. August 10, 2010. http://nowthedetails.blogspot.com/2010/08/why-is-managing-cbc-so-damn-difficult.html.

Dyer, Richard. *Stars*. London: BFI, 1998.

Edwards, Leigh H. "Chasing the Real: Reality Television and Documentary Forms." In *Docufictions: Essays on the Intersection of Documentary and Fictional Filmmaking*, edited by Gary D. Rhodes and John Parris Spring, 253–69. Jefferson, NC: McFarland, 2006.

Ellis, John. *Seeing Things: Television in the Age of Uncertainty*. London: I.B.Tauris, 2000.

———. "Stars as Cinematic Phenomenon." In *Star Texts*, edited by Jeremy G. Butler, 300–15. Detroit: Wayne State University Press, 1991.

———. "Television as Working-Through." In *Television and Common Knowledge*, edited by Jostein Gripsrud, 55–70. London and New York: Routledge, 1999.

———. *Visible Fictions: Cinema: Television: Video*. London: Routledge, 1982.

Evans, Michael. *Isuma: Inuit Video Art*. Montreal: McGill-Queen's University Press, 2008.

Feldman, Seth. "Footnote to Fact: The Docudrama." In *Film Genre Reader*, edited by Barry Keith Grant, 344–56. Austin: University of Texas Press, 1986.

Feuer, Jane. "Situation Comedy, Part 2." In *The Television Genre Book*, edited by Glen Creeber, 67–70. London: British Film Institute, 2001.

Fisher, Donald. *75 Years of Congress: Celebrating the Learneds*. Ottawa: Canadian Federation for the Humanities and Social Sciences, 2006.

Fiske, John. *Television Culture: Popular Pleasures and Politics*. London and New York: Methuen, 1987.

Flaherty, David H., and Frank E. Manning, eds. *The Beaver Bites Back? American Popular Culture in Canada*. Montreal: McGill-Queen's University Press, 1993.

Fleras, Augie. "Racialising Culture/Culturalising Race: Multicultural Racism in a Multicultural Canada." In *Racism Eh? A Critical Inter-Disciplinary Anthology of Race and Racism in Canada*, edited by Camille Nelson and Charmaine Nelson, 429–43. Toronto: Captus Press, 2004.

Fleras, Augie, and Jean Leonard Elliott. *Unequal Relations: An Introduction to Race, Ethnic and Aboriginal Dynamics in Canada*, 5th ed. Toronto: Pearson, 2007.

Flint, Joe, and Brian Steinberg. "Ad Icon P&G Cuts Commitment to TV Commercials: Top US Advertiser Explores New Ways to Reach Viewers." *Wall Street Journal*, June 13, 2005, A1.

Friends of Canadian Broadcasting. About Us: Overview (Undated). http://www.friends.ca/About_Us/.

Gandhy, Behroze, and Rosie Thomas. "Three Indian Film Stars." In *Stardom: Industry of Desire*, edited by Christine Gledhill, 107–31. New York and London: Routledge, 1991.

Gasher, Mike. "Decolonizing the Imagination: Cultural Expressions as Vehicle of Self-Discovery." *Canadian Journal of Film Studies* 2, no. 2–3 (1993): 95–106.

Gittings, Christopher E. *Canadian National Cinema*. London: Routledge, 2002.

Gittins, Susan. *CTV: The Television Wars*. Toronto: Stoddart, 1999.

Goodman, Lee-Anne. "Can *Little Mosque*'s Message of Tolerance Help Heal Racially Divided France?" *Edmonton Journal*, May 9, 2007, D3.

Grant, Peter S., and Chris Wood. *Blockbusters and Trade Wars: Popular Culture in a Globalized World*. Vancouver and Toronto: Douglas and McIntyre, 2004.

Gray, Herman. "The Politics of Representation in Network Television." In *Media and Cultural Studies Key Works*, edited by Meenakshi Gigi Durham and Douglas M. Kellner, 439–61. Malden, MA: Blackwell, 2001.

———. *Watching Race*. Minneapolis: University of Minnesota Press, 1995.

Greene, Richard, and Peter Vernezze, eds. *The Sopranos and Philosophy: I Kill Therefore I Am*. Peru, IL: Open Court, 2004.

Gronbeck, Bruce E. "Rhetoric, Ethics, and Telespectacles in the Post-Everything Age." In *Postmodern Representations: Truth, Power, and Mimesis in the Human Sciences and Public Culture*, edited by Richard H. Brown, 216–38. Chicago: University of Illinois Press, 1995.

Gross, Larry. "Out of the Mainstream: Sexual Minorities and the Mass Media." In *Media and Cultural Studies Key Works*, edited by Meenakshi Gigi Durham and Douglas M. Kellner, 405–23. Malden, MA: Blackwell, 2001.

Hall, Stuart. "The Spectacle of the Other." In *Representation: Cultural Representation and Signfiying Practices*, edited by Stuart Hall, 223–90. London: Sage, 1997.

Hanhardt, John G. "Case Studies: Nam June Paik, TV Garden, 1974." Variable Media Network (undated). http://variablemedia.net/pdf/TV_Garden.pdf.

Haralovich, Mary Beth. "Sitcoms and Suburbs: Positioning the 1950s Homemaker." In *Private Screenings: Television and the Female Consumer*, edited by Lynn Spigel and Denise Mann, 111–41. Minneapolis: University of Minnesota Press, 1992.

Harcourt, Peter. "The Canadian Nation: An Unfinished Text?" *Canadian Journal of Film Studies* 2, no. 2–3 (1993): 5–26.

Hartley, John. "From Republic of Letters to Television Republic? Citizen Readers in the Era of Broadcast Television." In *Television after TV: Essays on a Medium in Transition*, edited by Lynn Spigel and Jan Olsson, 386–417. Durham, NC: Duke University Press, 2004.

———. *Uses of Television*. London: Routledge, 1999.

"Hasbro Partners with YTV and Teletoon in Summer Promos." *Media in Canada* (2006). http://www.mediaincanada.com/articles/mic/20060530/corus.html.

Hauser, Gerard A. *Vernacular Voices: The Rhetoric of Publics and Public Spheres*. Columbia: University of South Carolina Press, 1999.

Havens, Timothy, Amanda D. Lotz, and Serra Tinic. "Critical Media Industry Studies: A Research Approach." *Communication, Culture and Critique* 2 (2009): 234–53.

Hilderbrand, Lucas. *Inherent Vice: Bootleg Histories of Videotape and Copyright*. Durham, NC: Duke University Press, 2009.

Hill, Annette. *Reality TV: Audiences and Popular Factual Television*. London: Routledge, 2005.

Hills, Matt. "*Dawson's Creek*: 'Quality Teen TV' and 'Mainstream Cult'?" In *Teen TV: Genre, Consumption, Identity*, edited by Glyn Davis and Kay Dickinson, 54–67. London: BFI, 2004.

Himpele, Jeff. *Circuits of Culture: Media, Politics and Indigenous Identity in the Andes*. Minneapolis: University of Minnesota Press, 2008.

Hirsh, Jesse. Interview with Zarqa Nawaz. *3D Dialogue*. Rogers and OMNI media (June 19, 2007). http://youtube.com/watch?v=u2doozcRzCI (accessed May 10, 2011).

Hogarth, David. *Documentary Television in Canada: From National Public Service to Global Marketplace*. Montreal: McGill-Queen's University Press, 2002.

Holmes, Su. "When Will I Be Famous? Reappraising the Debate about Fame in Reality TV." In *How Real Is Reality TV? Essays on Representation and Truth*, edited by David S. Escoffery, 7–25. Jefferson, NC: McFarland, 2006.

Holmes, Su, and Deborah Jermyn. "Introduction: Understanding Reality TV." In *Understanding Reality Television*, edited by Sue Holmes and Deborah Jermyn, 1–32. New York: Routledge, 2004.

Horton, Marc. "Shania Biopic a Twain Wreck: Performances Deserve a Much Better Script." *Edmonton Journal*, November 7, 2005, B1.

Independent Aboriginal Screen Producers Association, and Jeff Bear. "Intervention, APTN CRTC Licence Renewal Application." http://support.crtc.gc.ca/applicant/docs.aspx?pn_ph_no=2005-4&call_id=22610&lang=E&defaultName=Independent%20Aboriginal%20Screen%20Producers%20Association%20#24&replyonly=&addtInfo=&addtCmmt=&fnlSub=.

IndieNewsQuebec. "Appointments" (2006). http://interact.cbc.ca/pipermail/indienewsquebec/2006-June/000026.html.

Innis, Harold Adams. *The Bias of Communication*. Toronto: University of Toronto Press, 1964.

International Federation of Television Archives. "Television Studies Commission." http://www.fiatifta.org/cont/tsc.aspx.

Intini, John. "It's a Good Hijab if You Can Get It." *Maclean's*, December 11, 2006, 67.

Irwin, William, ed. *Seinfeld and Philosophy: A Book about Everything and Nothing*. Peru, IL: Open Court, 1999.

———, ed. *The Simpsons and Philosophy: The D'oh of Homer*. Peru, IL: Open Court, 2001.

Jeffery, Bill. "The Supreme Court of Canada's Appraisal of the 1980 Ban on Advertising to Children in Quebec: Implications for 'Misleading' Advertising Elsewhere." *Loyola of Los Angeles Law Review* 39, no. 1 (2006): 237–76.

Jenkins, Henry. *Textual Poachers: Television Fans and Participatory Culture*. New York: Routledge, 1992.

Jermyn, Deborah. "'Bringing Out the Star in You': SJP, Carrie Bradshaw and the Evolution of Television Stardom." In *Framing Celebrity: New Directions in Celebrity Culture*, edited by Su Holmes and Sean Redmond, 67–85. London: Routledge, 2006.

Jiwani, Yasmin. *Discourses of Denial: Mediations of Race, Gender and Violence*. Vancouver: UBC Press, 2006.

John, Deborah Roedder. "Consumer Socialization of Children: A Retrospective Look at Twenty-Five Years of Research." *Journal of Consumer Research* 26, no. 3 (1999): 183–213.

Kaveney, Roz, ed. *Reading the Vampire Slayer*. London and New York: Tauris Parke, 2002.

Kay, Barbara. "The Joke's on Us." *National Post*, 11 January 2007.

Kirkland, Bruce. "Stardom Slips Off Screen into Real Life." Jam! Showbiz Movies (2000). http://jam.canoe.ca/Movies/Artists/A/Arcand_Denys/2000/10/25/756415.html.

Kline, Stephen. *Out of the Garden: Toys, TV, and Children's Culture in the Age of Marketing*. Toronto: Garamond, 1994.

Kline, Stephen, Nick Dyer-Witheford, and Greig de Peuter. *Digital Play: The Interaction of Technology, Culture and Marketing.* Montreal: McGill-Queen's University Press, 2003.

Kohl, Jesse. "Corus Gets Viewers Engaged with Sunlight." *Media in Canada* (2007). http://www.mediaincanada.com/articles/mic/20070309/sunlight.html.

———. "Corus Targets Tweens with Thebigrip.Com MMOG." *Media in Canada* (2007). http://www.mediaincanada.com/articles/mic/20070219/bigrip.html.

———. "YTV Gives Hasbro Star Turn on Saturday Morning Block." *Media in Canada* (2007). http://www.mediaincanada.com/articles/mic/20061107/ytv.html.

Köhler, Nicholas. "In Conversation: Brett Wilson" *Maclean's*, March 21, 2011, 14–15.

Kroker, Arthur. *Technology and the Canadian Mind: Innis/Mcluhan/Grant* (New World Perspectives). Montreal: New World Perspectives, 1984.

Lacroix, Hubert T. "CBC President Sets the Record Straight Following Stursberg's Departure." Inside the CBC.com, the Official Blog of the Canadian Broadcasting Corporation, August 10, 2010. http://www.insidethecbc.com/cbc-president-sets-the-record-straight-following-stursbergs-departure/.

Landy, Marcia. *Stardom Italian Style: Screen Performance and Personality in Italian Cinema.* Bloomington: Indiana University Press, 2008.

Langer, John. "Television's 'Personality System.'" In *The Celebrity Culture Reader*, edited by P. David Marshall, 181–95. New York and London: Routledge, 2006.

Lavery, David, ed. *This Thing of Ours: Investigating the Sopranos*. New York: Columbia University Press, 2002.

Lavery, David, Angela Hague, and Marla Cartwright, eds. *Deny All Knowledge: Reading the X-Files.* Syracuse, NY: Syracuse University Press, 1996.

Leach, Jim. "Reading Canadian 'Popular' Television: The Case of E.N.G." In *Slippery Pastimes: Reading the Popular in Canadian Culture*, edited by Joan Nicks and Jeanette Sloniowski, 111–26. Waterloo, ON: Wilfrid Laurier University Press, 2002.

Leiss, William, Stephen Kline, and Sut Jhally. *Social Communication in Advertising: Persons, Products and Images of Well-Being.* Scarborough, ON: Nelson Canada, 1990.

Leong, Melissa. "W. Brett Wilson Leaves *Dragons' Den* with a Challenge." *National Post*, February 28, 2011. http://arts.nationalpost.com/2011/02/28/w-brett-wilson-leaves-dragons-den-with-a-challenge.

Library and Archives Canada. "Activities and Projects: Semi-Annual Report, Part VI Transformation." http://www.collectionscanada.gc.ca/about-us/006/012006-219-e.html#h.

Lofaro, Tony. "A Short, Not-So-Sweet Run for CBC and *The One*." *Ottawa Citizen*, July 29, 2006. http://www.friends.ca/News/Friends_News/archives/articles07290604.asp.

Loiselle, André. "The Radically Moderate Canadian: Don McKellar's Cinematic Persona." In *North of Everything: English-Canadian Cinema since 1980*, edited by William Beard and Jerry White, 256–69. Edmonton: University of Alberta Press 2002.

Longfellow, Brenda. "Globalization and National Identity in Canadian Film." *Canadian Journal of Film Studies* 5, no. 2 (1996): 3–16.

MacDonald, Gayle. "Allah in the Family." *Globe and Mail*, January 6, 2007.

———. "Movie Night Scores for CBC." *Globe and Mail*, November 10, 2004. http://www.publicairwaves.ca/index.php?page=838.

MacFarquhar, Neil. "A Sitcom's Perilous Premise: The Funny Side of Being Muslim in North America." *Edmonton Journal*, December 13, 2006.

Mackenzie, Scott. *Screening Quebec: Québécois Moving Images, National Identity and the Public Sphere*. Manchester: Manchester University Press, 2004.

Mackey, Eva. *House of Difference: Cultural Politics and National Identity in Canada*. London and New York: Routledge, 1999.

Manning, Erin. *Ephemeral Territories: Representing Nation, Home, and Identity in Canada*. Minneapolis: University of Minnesota Press, 2003.

Manning, Frank E. "Reversible Resistance: Canadian Popular Culture and the American Other." In *The Beaver Bites Back? American Popular Culture in Canada*, edited by David Flaherty and Frank Manning, 3–32. Montreal: McGill-Queen's University Press, 1993.

Marchand, Philip. "Quebec Fans' Loyalty Pays Off at the Box Office." thestar.com (2008). http://www.thestar.com/entertainment/Movies/article/308751.

Martin, Des. The Classic TV Archive. http://www.angelfire.com/retro/cta/Can/_Canada.htm.

Matheson, Sarah. "Ruling the Inner City: Television, Citizenship and King of Kensington." *Canadian Journal of Film Studies* 15, no. 1 (2006): 46–62.

McAllister, Matthew P. "From Flick to Flack: The Increased Emphasis on Marketing by Media Entertainment Corporations." In *Critical Studies in Media Commercialism*, edited by Robin Andersen and Lance Strate, 101–22. New York: Oxford University Press, 2000.

McAllister, Matthew P., and Matt Giglio. "The Commodity Flow of U.S. Children's Television." *Critical Studies in Media Communication* 22, no. 1 (2005): 26–44.

McCarthy, Anna. *Ambient Television: Visual Culture and Public Space*. Durham, NC: Duke University Press, 2001.

McCauley, Michael P. "The Contested Meaning of Public Service in American Television." *The Communication Review* 5 (2002): 207–37.

McChesney, Robert. *The Problem of the Media: U.S. Communication Politics in the Twenty-First Century*. New York: Monthly Review Press, 2004.

———. *Rich Media, Poor Democracy: Communication Politics in Dubious Times*. Urbana: University of Illinois Press, 1999.

McChesney, Robert, and John Bellamy Foster. "The Commercial Tidal Wave." *Monthly Review*, March 2003, 1–16.

McGinn, Dave. "We're Not Looking for a Purely Muslim Viewership." *National Post*, January 9, 2007.

McKinley, E. Graham. Beverly Hills, 90210: *Television, Gender, and Identity*. Philadelphia: University of Pennsylvania Press, 1997.

McLuhan, Marshall. *Understanding Media: The Extensions of Man*. London: Sphere Books, 1967.

McLuhan, Marshall, and Bruce R. Powers. *The Global Village: Transformations in World Life and Media in the 21st Century*. Oxford: Oxford University Press, 1989.

Menon, Vinay. "Little Mirth on the Prairie: Under the Veil Is an Old-Style Sitcom." *Toronto Star*, January 9, 2007.

———. "These Dragons Light My Fire." *Toronto Star*, October 22, 2007. http://www.thestar.com/entertainment/article/269035.

Meyersohn, Rolf B. "Social Research in Television." In *Mass Culture: The Popular Arts in America*, edited by Bernard Rosenberg and David Manning White, 345–57. New York: Free Press, 1957.

Miller, Mary Jane. "Blind Faith and Pray TV—Canadian and American TV Look at the Same Issue." *Journal of Popular Culture* 20, no. 1 (1986): 127–40.

———. "Inflecting the Formula: The First Seasons of *Street Legal* and *L.A. Law*." In *The Beaver Bites Back? American Popular Culture in Canada*, edited by David Flaherty and Frank Manning, 104–22. Montreal: McGill-Queen's University Press, 1993.

———. *Outside Looking In: Viewing First Nations Peoples in Canadian Dramatic Television Series*. Montreal: McGill-Queen's University Press, 2008.

———. *Rewind and Search: Conversations with the Makers and Decision-Makers of CBC Television Drama*. Montreal: McGill-Queen's University Press, 1996.

———. *Turn Up the Contrast: CBC Television Drama since 1952*. Vancouver: University of British Columbia Press, 1987.

Moore, Paul. "Wrong Turn at the CBC." *Globe and Mail*, May 29, 2008. http://www.friends.ca/News/Friends_News/archives/articles05290804.asp.

Morin, Edgar. *The Stars*. Minneapolis: University of Minnesota Press, 2005.

Mosco, Vincent. *The Political Economy of Communication: Rethinking and Renewal*. London: Thousand Oaks, CA: Sage, 1996.

Moseley, Rachel. "The Teen Series." In *The Television Genre Book*, edited by Glen Creeber, 41–43. London: BFI, 2002.

Murray, Michael. "Little Mirth on the Prairie." *Ottawa Citizen*, January 20, 2007.

Mushkeg Media. About Mushkeg Media Inc. http://www.mushkeg.ca/about.html.

Negra, Diane. "'Queen of the Indies' Parker Posey's Niche Stardom and the Cultures of Independent Film." *Contemporary American Independent Film: From the Margins to the Mainstream*, edited by Chris Holmlund and Justin Wyatt, 71–88. New York: Routledge, 2005.

Nelson, Joyce. *The Perfect Machine: TV in the Nuclear Age*. Toronto: Between the Lines, 1987.

Newcomb, Horace, ed. *Encyclopedia of Television*. London: Fitzroy Dearborn, 2004.

Nichols, Bill. "Reality TV and Social Perversion." In *Media Studies: A Reader*, edited by Paul Marris and Sue Thornham, 393–403. New York: New York University Press, 2000.

Nicks, Joan. "*Straight Up* and Youth Television: Navigating Dreams without Nationhood." In *Slippery Pastimes: Reading the Popular in Canadian Culture*, edited by Joan Nicks and Jeanette Sloniowski, 141–57. Waterloo, ON: Wilfrid Laurier University Press, 2002.

Nicks, Joan, and Jeanette Sloniowski, eds. *Slippery Pastimes: Reading the Popular in Canadian Culture*. Waterloo, ON: Wilfrid Laurier University Press, 2002.

"*The One* Not the One." *Stratford Beacon Herald* (Editorial), August 2, 2006. http://www.publicairwaves.ca/index.php?page=1730&PHPSESSID=94e09c9.

Ouellette, Laurie, and James Hay. *Better Living through Reality TV: Television and Post-Welfare Citizenship*. Malden, MA: Blackwell, 2008.

Patriquin, Martin. "Canada: A Nation of Bigots." *Maclean's*, October 22, 2007, 16–22.

Peers, Frank. "Broadcasting and National Unity." In *Communications in Canadian Society*, edited by Benjamin D. Singer, 215–28. Toronto: Copp Clark, 1975.

________. *The Public Eye: Television and the Politics of Canadian Broadcasting, 1952–1968*. Toronto: University of Toronto Press, 1979.

Pellerin, Brigitte. "Equal Opportunity Humour." *Ottawa Citizen*, January 9, 2007.

Pevere, Geoff, and Greig Dymond, eds. *Mondo Canuck: A Canadian Pop Culture Odyssey*. Scarborough, ON: Prentice-Hall, 1996.

Poulton, Terry. "Online Advertising in Canada Tops $1 Billion." http://www.mediaincanada.com/articles/mic/20070430/onlineads.html.

Quill, Greg. "What a Difference a Decade Makes to Terror Tale: Docu-Thriller Reminds Us of Pre-9/11 Bomb Plot." *Toronto Star*, June 15, 2008, E8.

Raboy, Marc. "Canada: The Hybridization of Public Broadcasting." In *Public Broadcasting for the 21st Century*, edited by Marc Raboy, 103–19. Luton: University of Luton Press, 1995.

———. *Missed Opportunities: The Story of Canada's Broadcasting Policy*. Montreal: McGill-Queen's University Press, 1990.

Rainsberry, F.B. *A History of Children's Television in English Canada*, 1952–1986. Metuchen: Scarecrow Press, 1988.

Rasporich, Beverly. "Canadian Humour in the Media." In *Seeing Ourselves: Media Power and Policy in Canada*, edited by Helen Holmes and David Taras, 84–97. Toronto: Harcourt Brace Canada, 1990.

Realitytvmagazine.com. Responses to "The One—Who Will Go Home First?" (2006). http://www.realitytvmagazine.com/blog/2006/07/19/the-one-who-will-go-home-first/.

Reveler, Norma. "Drabinsky Looks to Elevate Reality TV." *Playback* (2007). http://www.playbackmag.com/articles/magazine/20070917/drabinsky.html.

Rezolution Pictures. Company Profile. http:// www. rezolutionpictures.com.

"Rick Campanelli." *Hello! Canada,* September 2006, 78.

Roth, Lorna. *Something New in the Air: The Story of First Peoples Television Broadcasting in Canada*. Montreal: McGill-Queen's University Press, 2005.

Rubinoff, Joel. "Muslims Take Their Satirical Turn." *The Record*, January 9, 2007.

Rutherford, Paul. "Made in America: The Problem of Mass Culture in Canada." In *The Beaver Bites Back? American Popular Culture in Canada*, edited by David Flaherty and Frank Manning, 260–80. Montreal and Kingston: McGill-Queen's University Press, 1993.

———. *When Television Was Young: Primetime Canada 1952–1967*. Toronto: University of Toronto Press, 1990.

Schutten, Julie Kalil. "Invoking Practical Magic: New Social Movements, Hidden Populations, and the Public Screen." *Western Journal of Communication* 70, no. 4 (2006): 331–54.

Seiter, Ellen. "A Place at the Table: *Aliens in America* and US Policy in the 'Islamic World.'" Flowtv.org, 27 February 2008. http://flowtv.org/?p=1200.

Shohat, Ella, and Robert Stam. *Unthinking Eurocentrism: Multiculturalism and the Media*. New York and London: Routledge, 1994.

Showcase. *Sometimes Culture Is All You Have. Showcase Launches Moccasin Flats*. Toronto: Alliance Atlantis Communications, 2004.

Simon, Ron. "The Changing Definition of Reality Television." In *Thinking Outside the Box: A Contemporary Television Genre Reader*, edited by Gary R. Edgerton and Brian G. Rose, 179–200. Lexington: University Press of Kentucky, 2005.

Simons, Paula. "Little Mosque on the Prairie Not Such a Stretch, Even for CBC." *Edmonton Journal*, January 9, 2007.

Smith, Matthew J., and Andrew F. Wood. "Introduction: Culture, Communication, and Community Revealed in and through Reality Television." In *Survivor Lessons: Essays on Communication and Reality Television*, edited by Matthew J. Smith and Andrew F. Wood. Jefferson, NC: McFarland, 2003.

Smyth, Carmel. "Richard Stursberg: Early Thoughts about a Demonized Man and His Impossible Job." *–30– from the Front Lines of Canada's Media*. August 6, 2010. http://newsshift.blogspot.com/2010/08/richard-stursberg-early-thoughts-about.html.

Smythe, Dallas. *Dependency Road: Communications, Capitalism, Consciousness, and Canada*. Norwood, NJ: Ablex, 1981.

Social Sciences and Humanities Research Council of Canada. "Policy Focus." http://www.sshrc.ca/web/about/policy_focus/index_e.asp.

Soroka, Stuart N., Richard Johnston, and Keith Banting. "Ties That Bind? Social Cohesion and Diversity in Canada." In *Belonging? Diversity, Recognition and Shared Citizenship in Canada*, edited by Keith Banting, Thomas J. Courchene, and F. Leslie Seidle, 1–40. Ottawa: Institute for Research on Public Policy, 2006.

South, James B., ed. *Buffy the Vampire Slayer and Philosophy: Fear and Trembling in Sunnydale*. Peru, IL: Open Court, 2003.

"Starcom Unleashes Interactive, Online Lego Campaign." *Media in Canada* (2006). http://www.mediaincanada.com/articles/mic/20060418/lego.html.

Statistics Canada. "Television Viewing." *The Daily* (2006). http://www.statcan.ca/Daily/English/060331/d060331b.htm (accessed 20 April 2008.

Stewart, Sandy, and CBC Enterprises. *Here's Looking at Us: A Personal History of Television in Canada*. Montreal: CBC Enterprises, 1986.

Storey, John. *Cultural Theory and Popular Culture: An Introduction*. 3rd ed. Harlow, UK: Pearson Education, 2001.

Strachan, Alex. "CBC's Fall Announcement: A Private Conversation with Kirstine Layfield." Canada.com (2008). http://communities.canada.com/shareit/blogs/tvguy/archive/2008/05/26/cbc-s-fall-announcement-a-conversation-with-kirstine-lay field.aspx.

Strategic Inc. *APTN: Brand Equity Measure, Programming and Promotional Test*. Winnipeg: APTN, 2002.

Straw, Will. "Dilemmas of Definition." In *Slippery Pastimes: Reading the Popular in Canadian Culture*, edited by Joan Nicks and Jeanette Sloniowski, 95–108. Waterloo, ON: Wilfrid Laurier University Press, 2002.

Sutherland, Anne, and Beth Thompson. *Kidfluence: The Market's Guide to Understanding and Reaching Generation Y—Kids, Tweens, and Teens*. New York: McGraw-Hill, 2003.

Szklarski, Cassandra. "CBC-TV to Reduce Reliance on Foreign Programs, Be 'More Canadian.'" *Maclean's*, March 30, 2011. http://www.macleans.ca/article.jsp?content=e6412146.

Taras, David. "The CBC and Canadian Television in the New Media Age." In *A Passion for Identity*, 3rd ed., edited by David Taras and Beverly Rasporich, 265–79. Scarborough: ITP Nelson, 1997.

Task Force on the Preservation and Enhanced Use of Canada's Audio-Visual Heritage. "Fading Away: Strategic Options to Ensure the Protection of and Access to Our Audio-Visual Memory." http://www.avtrust.ca/docs/fading_away.pdf (accessed April 20, 2008).

Taylor, Kate. "CBC's No. 2: Stursberg Sees a Kindred Spirit in the New Boss." *Globe and Mail*, November 7, 2007, R1.

———. "The Little Mosque That Could." *Globe and Mail*, 6 August 2007.

———. "Playwright Shoots from the Gut: George F. Walker Is All for Method." *Globe and Mail*, 3 February 2000, R4.

Tinic, Serra A. *On Location: Canada's Television Industry in a Global Market*. Toronto: University of Toronto Press, 2005.

Turner, John. "CBC-TV's Nemesis." http://parkdalepictures.blogspot.com /2006/10/cbc-tvs-nemesis.html.

Turow, Joseph. *Breaking Up America: Advertisers and the New Media World*. Chicago: University of Chicago Press, 1997.

tvarchive.ca. Home. http://www.tvarchive.ca/.

Urquhart, Peter, and Ira Wagman. "Considering Canadian Television: Intersections, Missed Directions, Prospects for Textual Expansion." *Canadian Journal of Film Studies* 15, no. 1 (2006): 2–7.

Varga, Darrell. "The Social Production of Place in Four Atlantic Canadian Fiction Films about Artists." In *Rain/Drizzle/Fog: Essays on Film and Television in Atlantic Canada*, edited by Darrell Varga, 235–58. Calgary: University of Calgary Press, 2008.

Vincendeau, Ginette. *Stars and Stardom in French Cinema*. London and New York: Continuum, 2000.

Wagman, Ira. "Wheat, Barley, Hops, Citizenship: Molson's 'I Am [Canadian]' Campaign and the Defense of Canadian National Identity through Advertising." *Velvet Light Trap* 50 (Fall 2002): 77–89.

Walcott, Rinaldo. *Black Like Who*? 2nd rev. ed. Toronto: Insomnia Press, 2003.

———. "'Keep On Moving': Rap, Black Atlantic Identities and the Problem of Nation." In *Popcan: Popular Culture in Canada*, edited by Lynne Van Luven and Priscilla Walton, 27–41. Scarborough: Prentice-Hall Canada, 1999.

Walton, Priscilla, and Lynne Van Luven. *Pop Can: Popular Culture in Canada*. Scarborough, ON: Prentice Hall Allyn and Bacon Canada, 1999.

Wente, Margaret. "Little Mosque: Way Too Cute." *Globe and Mail*, January 9, 2007.

Wernick, Andrew. *Promotional Culture: Advertising, Ideology and Symbolic Expression*. London: Sage, 1991.

Whyte, Murray. "CBC Taps American to Craft New Shows." *Toronto Star* (2006). http://www.friends.ca/News/Friends_News/archives/articles03300601.asp.

Wilcox, Rhonda V., and David Lavery, eds. *Fighting the Forces: What's at Stake in Buffy the Vampire Slayer*. Oxford: Rowman and Littlefield, 2002.

Williams, Raymond. *Television, Technology and Cultural Form*. London: Fontana, 1974.

"Winner Announced in 2006 Go Active! Film Festival." YTV News Release (2006). http://www.corusent.com/corporate/press_room/press_kids_tv/pressRelease Detail.asp?id=1094.

Winter, Patty. "North of 60." http://www.wintertime.com/OH/nof60.html.

Wittebols, James H. "Reality TV: This Is Just Like a Soap." In *The Soap Opera Paradigm: Television Programming and Corporate Priorities*. Lanham, MD: Rowman and Littlefield, 2004.

Wolfe, Morris. *Jolts: The TV Wasteland and the Canadian Oasis*. Toronto: Lorimer, 1985.

Wood, Chris. *Live to Air: The Craig Broadcast Story*. Vancouver: Douglas and McIntyre, 2000.

Worboy, Martha. "Little Mosque Lands Big New Deal." *Calgary Herald*, May 9, 2007.

Wright, Robert A. *Virtual Sovereignty: Nationalism, Culture and the Canadian Question*. Toronto: Canadian Scholars' Press, 2004.

YTV. "Client Marketing." http://www.corusmedia.com/ytv/opportunities.aspx.

"YTV Forks up Integrated Ad Opps." *Media in Canada* (2006). http://www.mediaincanada.com/articles/mic/20060831/ytv.html.

"YTV Takes Weird on the Road." *Media in Canada* (2006). http://www.mediaincanada.com/articles/mic/20050607/ytv.html.

Zahn, Paula. "Out in the Open" (2007). www.youtube.com/watch?v=-uT-StoCB7k.

Zerbisias, Antonia. "TV Misguide." *Toronto Star*, November 17, 2005. http://thestar.blogs.com/azerb/2005/11/there_was_a_lot.html.

Contributors

Kyle Asquith is a lecturer and PhD candidate in the Media Studies program at the University of Western Ontario. His research and teaching interests broadly encompass the complementary fields of advertising and consumer culture, media history, and the political economy of communication.

Marian Bredin is Associate Professor in the Department of Communication, Popular Culture and Film, and former director of the Centre for Canadian Studies at Brock University. Along with her participation in the Popular Culture Niagara Research Group, her main research interests include Aboriginal media, communications policy, and Canadian television. Most recently she co-edited *Indigenous Screen Cultures in Canada* for the University of Manitoba Press in 2010.

Michele Byers is Associate Professor in the Department of Sociology and Criminology at Saint Mary's University. She is editor or co-editor of four books on television, and her work on television text, identity, and the archive has appeared in a broad range of journals and edited collections. She has held several SSHRC grants for the study of Canadian television, the most recent of which focuses on Canadian television and ethnicity.

Liz Czach is Assistant Professor in the Department of English and Film Studies at the University of Alberta. Her research interests include home movies, film festivals, and Canadian film. Her articles and reviews have appeared in numerous journals including *The Moving Image*, *Cinema Journal*, and *Journal of Canadian Studies*. She has contributed to the books *La Casa Abierta: El cine domestico y sus reciclajes contemporaneos* (2010) and *Challenge for Change: Activist Documentary at the National Film Board of Canada* (2010). She was a film programmer at the Toronto International Film Festival from 1995 to 2005 and currently organizes Edmonton's Home Movie Day.

John Doyle has been television critic at *The Globe and Mail* since 2000 and was the critic for *Broadcast Week*, the *Globe*'s television magazine, from 1995 to 2000. His book *A Great Feast of Light: Growing Up Irish in the Television Age* was published to acclaim in Canada, the United States, Britain, Ireland, and Australia in 2005. His second book, *The World Is a Ball: The Joy, Madness and Meaning of Soccer* (2010), was also a national bestseller in Canada and has been published in the United States, Britain, Ireland, and Croatia.

Derek S. Foster is an Associate Professor in the Department of Communication, Popular Culture and Film at Brock University. His research consistently focuses on visual rhetoric in the public sphere and "mining the gap" between mass communication and speech communication. To this end, he has written numerous publications studying discourses of reality television and the rhetoric surrounding other forms of visual and material culture. His current research combines these foci in examining television-based memorials and commemorative exercises.

Scott Henderson is an Associate Professor in the Department of Communication, Popular Culture and Film at Brock University. He received his MA and PhD in Film Studies from the University of East Anglia. His research focuses on issues of identity and representation in popular culture. He has published on diverse subject matter, including YouTube and youth identity, gay and lesbian film, British cinema, Canadian cinema and popular culture, and Canadian radio policy.

Sarah A. Matheson is Associate Professor in the Department of Communication, Popular Culture and Film and the M.A. in Popular Culture at Brock University. Her main areas of research and teaching are film and popular culture with a special focus on Canadian television studies. Her recent work has appeared in the *Canadian Journal of Film Studies* and *Film and History* and in the anthologies *Programming Reality: Perspectives on English-Canadian Television* and *The Tube Has Spoken: Reality TV and History*.

Mary Jane Miller is retired professor (Emerita) of the Department of Dramatic Arts, Brock University. She has taught television and Canadian television drama and Canadian dramatic literature, publishing articles on both topics. Her books include: *Turn Up the Contrast: Canadian Television Drama since 1952* (UBC Press/CBC, 1987); *Rewind and Search: Conversations with Makers and Decision Makers of CBC Television Drama* (McGill-Queen's University Press, 1996); and *Outside Looking In: Viewing First Nations People in Canadian Dramatic Television Series* (McGill-Queen's University Press, 2008).

Jennifer VanderBurgh is Assistant Professor (Film and Media Studies) in the Department of English at Saint Mary's University in Nova Scotia. Her writing on a diverse range of texts—from *Videodrome* to *Don Messer's Jubilee*—has appeared in various journals and edited collections. She is currently writing a book on archives and footprints of television in Toronto and recently co-edited an issue of *PUBLIC: Art/Culture/Ideas on Screens*.

Index

Books in the Film+Media Studies Series
Published by Wilfrid Laurier University Press

Image and Territory: Essays on Atom Egoyan / Monique Tschofen and Jennifer Burwell, editors / 2006 / viii + 418 pp / photos / ISBN 978-0-88920-487-4

The Young, the Restless, and the Dead: Interviews with Canadian Filmmakers / George Melnyk, editor / 2008 / xiv + 134 pp. / photos / ISBN 978-1-55458-036-1

Programming Reality: Perspectives on English-Canadian Television / Zoë Druick and Aspa Kotsopoulos, editors / 2008 / x + 344 pp. / photos / ISBN 978-1-55458-010-1

Harmony and Dissent: Film and Avant-garde Art Movements in the Early Twentieth Century / R. Bruce Elder / 2008 / xxxiv + 482 pp. / ISBN 978-1-55458-028-6

He Was Some Kind of a Man: Masculinities in the B Western / Roderick McGillis / 2009 / xii + 210 pp. / photos / ISBN 978-1-55458-059-0

The Radio Eye: Cinema in the North Atlantic, 1958–1988 / Jerry White / 2009 / xvi + 284 pp. / photos / ISBN 978-1-55458-178-8

The Gendered Screen: Canadian Women Filmmakers / Brenda Austin-Smith and George Melnyk, editors / 2010 / x + 272 pp. / ISBN 978-1-55458-179-5

Feeling Canadian: Nationalism, Affect, and Television / Marusya Bociurkiw / 2011 / viii + 184 pp. / ISBN 978-1-55458-268-6

Beyond Bylines: Media Workers and Women's Rights in Canada / Barbara M. Freeman / 2011 / xii + 328 pp. / photos / ISBN 978-1-55458-269-3

Canadian Television: Text and Context / Marian Bredin, Scott Henderson, and Sarah A. Matheson, editors / xvi + 238 pp. / ISBN 978-1-55458-361-4